The Allotment Book

The Allotment Book

A practical guide
to creating and enjoying
your own perfect plot

Andi Clevely

Collins

This book is dedicated with love to Ruth Prentice, who devised the idea. Nice one!

This paperback edition published in 2008

First published in 2006 by Collins
an imprint of HarperCollins Publishers
77–85 Fulham Palace Road
London W6 8JB

www.harpercollins.co.uk

Collins is a registered trademark of HarperCollins Publishers Ltd

15 14 13
8 7

Created and produced by Airedale Publishing Ltd

Photographs, text and design © 2006 HarperCollins Publishers Ltd except those photographs indicated © on page 224

A catalogue record for this book is available from the British Library

For Airedale Publishing
Art Director: Ruth Prentice
PA to Art Director: Amanda Jensen
Designer: Elly King
Project Editor: Helen Ridge
Colour and DTP: Max Newton
Index: Hilary Bird
All main photography by Sarah Cuttle, David Murphy and Mike Newton

For Collins
Commissioning editors: Angela Newton and Jenny Heller

978-0-00-727077-4

Pre-Press by F. E. Burman, London
Printed and bound by Printing Express, Hong Kong

contents

foreword by jekka mcvicar

I vividly remember as a child helping my mother to dig up the new potatoes in our garden and being amazed that the one potato we had planted had produced so many baby potatoes. I also remember the delight of helping to pick the strawberries, which included eating as many as I put in the punnet.

The many bonuses of being brought up with a productive garden was not only the abundance of fruit and vegetables but also the fact that, because my mother was a fantastic cook, the house was often filled with the aroma of wonderful food. This was most prevalent at harvest time when she made jellies, jams and chutneys, which we used throughout the winter months and which she also gave as Christmas presents to friends and family.

I have been lucky enough to re-create these fond memories for my own children with a vegetable plot for which they have sown the seeds and harvested the crop. Growing your own vegetables and fruit not only gives you control of what you and your children eat but also the goodness of delicious fresh produce and the added bonus of fresh air, good fun and great exercise.

In this beautiful book, Andi Clevely captures the essence of the allotment, showing how it is a relaxing and sociable way to garden, and a great opportunity to meet fellow gardeners, young and old. You are guaranteed the sharing of fresh food, expertise, gossip, fun and friendship, which goes to prove that the allotment is a microcosm of today's society without walls. More importantly, this book is teeming with valuable information based on the experience that Andi has gained over the years in his garden and on his allotment; this includes seed germination times, average yields and his recommended varieties of fruit and vegetables. He also demystifies gardening terminology and gives good basic down-to-earth information on dealing with pests and diseases, making this book relevant for both the novice and the connoisseur.

With this book I defy anyone not to enjoy the wonderful world of the allotment, from the soil to the table.

Crowned the 'queen of herbs' by Jamie Oliver and one of Rick Stein's food heroes, Jekka McVicar is the UK's leading organic herb grower. Her family-run organic herb farm now grows over 500 varieties and holds the largest collection of culinary and medicinal herbs in the country. In addition to managing the farm business, Jekka is a regular TV and radio presenter and has published several successful books on growing herbs, raising plants from seed and cooking with flowers. This picture shows Jekka at work on the farm with her dog Hampton (also known as Mutty). Visit her website at: www.jekkasherbfarm.com.

introduction

Pause for a while as you walk around your allotment, and reflect. All land has a hidden history and, unless the site is very new, you will be treading in the footsteps of previous tenants, possibly going back for generations.

Other hands turned the same soil before you, sowing seeds, tending rows of plants and harvesting produce from the piece of earth that is now yours. The biography of any allotment plot is an intimate tale of dreams and necessities, success and failure that, in most cases, is sadly unrecorded but cherished privately as part of everyday personal or family memories. The background to allotment gardening as a unique and important social movement is more clearly charted. Its origins can vary widely from one community or country to another, but common to all is the need for access to other people's land by those with none of their own. The word 'allotment' means portion, in this context a rented allocation of ground, together with conditions of tenure and use that will vary depending on the owner or the culture.

The right to dig

The earliest allocations were often acts of charity or benevolence, aimed at addressing poverty and hunger and the costs of relieving these misfortunes. The situation was gravest wherever ancient local traditions and conventions allowing people to cultivate common land and to pasture animals had been eroded by the rich and powerful. In Britain for example, almost from the Norman Conquest onwards, landowners had steadily enclosed land, evicting its inhabitants and dismantling well-established local subsistence economies and their elaborate heritage of safeguards, and in the process producing a whole class of rural dispossessed.

Outrage boiled over into action in 1649 when the Diggers, a group of hungry victims of recession, took over waste land in a mass trespass and began to sow it with beans, carrots, parsnips and wheat. One of their leaders, Gerrard Winstanley, called passionately on 'the common people to manure and work upon the common lands' and insisted all should have the 'right to dig', a sentiment still heard wherever urban radicals invade unused land with the intention of growing food.

Although quickly dispersed by the Government of the time, the Diggers gave direction and powerful moral impetus to the general claim to land. They turned a fundamental urgent need to fill empty bellies into political principles of social rights and economic equality that gathered support as discontent grew. Their protest gradually provoked a response, at first local and individual – a few far-sighted landlords supplied their labourers with plots for cultivation – and then more generally as crucial legislation was passed. This culminated in 1845 with the General Inclosure Act, which made the provision of allotments for the working poor mandatory throughout Britain.

A woodcut depicting Gerrard Winstanley, one of the leaders of the Digger movement, and his followers, who in 1649 proclaimed *'England is not a free people, till the poor that have no land have a free allowance to dig and labour the commons...'*

Elsewhere in the world similar sequences of necessity and challenge or confrontation can be traced, often leading to land seizure or allocation, events that are usually driven by the same tensions of inequality between landowners and landless. By contrast, the outcome can be a model of equity: on an allotment site all pay equal rent for the same size portion of land and rights of use, whatever their wealth, ability or social standing. It might be seen as a glimpse of Winstanley's dream of the day when 'the whole earth shall be a common treasury for every man'.

Winstanley was just one key activist, probably the earliest, among many in the chequered history of the international allotment movement, and every country has its own heroes – Anna and Carl Lindhagen in Sweden, Abbé Lemire in France, Bolton Hall in the USA with his vision of 'little plots well tilled'. When tilling your own plot it might take a leap of imagination to link your efforts with these prime movers and their supporting thinkers, such as Peter Kropotkin with his anarchist philosophy of self help and mutual aid, the libertarian Proudhon who famously asserted 'Property is theft', or the New Englander Henry Thoreau, hoeing beans beside Walden Pond.

Every allotment gardener is a participant in this great evolving story

The author digging on his allotment.

Changing fortunes For many people, however, desperate hunger or economic need was the chief, often sole reason for growing their own, a drive that was reinforced early last century by the equally imperative national demands of world war and inter-war depression. In many parts of Europe and the USA both a sense of patriotism and enforced self-sufficiency caused a boom in allotment gardening, urged on by slogans such as 'Hoe for Liberty', 'Soldiers of the Soil' and 'Dig for Victory'. Numbers of plots and active tenancies reached a peak that has rarely been equalled since, even during the brief and idealized back-to-the-land fashion of the 1960s.

From the 1950s onwards, enthusiasm for allotments began to wane in the UK as a result of greater affluence, higher employment and the wider availability of food supplies, and many plots, even whole sites, were under-used, neglected or abandoned. This decline, interpreted by pessimists as the imminent end of the allotment movement, was not reflected worldwide, where material necessity often remained (and still remains) an urgent motivation. The decline was in any case short-lived, for a couple of decades later allotment gardening in many industrialized countries experienced a major revival as a new breed of plot-holders began to emerge.

The priorities of these fresh recruits were often focused more on the quality of life, rather than survival itself. Concern about chemical residues in fresh food and its limited choice, excessive packaging and transport costs all made growing your own organically an appealing and reasonable proposition. The proven physical and mental health benefits gave gardening a central role in therapy and rehabilitation programmes, as well as making it an effective way to escape from the stress and highly organized structure of modern society – for many, working on their plot became a kind of declaration of independence, an emancipation from uniformity. The old utilitarian image of allotment sites began to change as the plots were seen to be important recreational facilities for the whole family as well as vital habitats in the process of 'greening' our cities.

Many parks and open spaces in England were turned into allotments during the Second World War, and everyone, young and old, was encouraged to 'Dig for Victory'. Here, schoolboys from the Drury Halls Council School in Hornchurch, Essex, arrive at their allotment ready for work. The boys also ran a shop where they sold the produce that they cultivated.

The global garden

Although still firmly rooted in its tradition of individual land access and cultivation, the modern allotment now thrives in a more diverse and stimulating cultural context. There is no neat pattern of social stratification: increasing numbers of women, families, young professionals and gardeners from all ethnic cultures are bringing both variety and vitality to plots that, until quite recently, were tended mainly by older men striving to make ends meet. Kurdish strains of coriander, South American arugula, Ethiopian teff and dengi for Bangladeshi curries have joined the carrots and cabbages in narrow, neatly edged organic or no-dig beds as well as in the contoured meanders of permaculture plots (see *page 31*).

These days, urban allotments are just as likely to sport barbecue sites, wildlife sanctuaries, heritage seed collections, forest gardens, sculpture, beehives and ponds as once-derided rows of yellowing Brussels sprouts. Schools use sites for wildlife projects, environmental groups turn them into tree nurseries for urban regeneration and disabled gardeners have found new challenges and satisfactions on allotment sites.

Wherever you look, allotments continue to grow in social and economic importance as well as lively diversity. In New York, the City Farms project revived the Victory Garden zeal of the 1940s, organizing the production, marketing and distribution of fresh food among disadvantaged neighbourhoods from over 30 community gardens. Brazilian street children grow radishes for sale, St Petersburg prisoners raise black trifele tomatoes in their prison rooftop allotment, and German *Kleingartens* help refugee women to settle in their new home as they grow their traditional crops. Community gardening is as much about greening cities and healing wounds as simply ensuring food security.

ABOVE A Bangladeshi plot-holder picks mustard leaves growing in her inner city allotment.

LEFT Tomatoes and chilli peppers – traditional and more exotic allotment produce.

RIGHT Growing your own crops can be hugely rewarding – giant parsnips may be among the many benefits you reap.

Community gardening is as much about greening cities and healing wounds as simply ensuring food security

This Danish allotment is a 'daytime garden', open only in the summer from 8am to 6pm. Cultivation is in accordance with organic principles, and there is an overall plan to ensure the rotation of crops.

The future

The unique value of allotment plots is set to grow both internationally and on a personal level. In urban areas land use is becoming increasingly competitive, and many plot-holders are having to make a political stand to prevent their sites and rights being eroded to make way for roads and new buildings. In 2001, Denmark set an enlightened example to other countries by making all community gardens permanent and secure in law, but elsewhere their status is more precarious. Winstanley and the Diggers would probably recognize the modern threats to land rights and our 'common treasury', and his crusading spirit might be welcome back in many site offices.

Agenda 21 of the 1997 Kyoto Agreement imposes a moral obligation on governments to commit themselves to support sustainable development, fight poverty and avoid destroying the resources of future generations. Allotments are an environmental asset, both for wildlife and for the health and well-being of plot-holders, and they add texture to lives and communities, while soil is possibly mankind's most precious resource. So protecting and regenerating these community plots should be a key part of local strategies in the changing environmental context.

For many tenants, however, the main value of their plot of ground will always be intensely personal. On an allotment you might have responsibilities, but you also have freedom: the freedom to enjoy the company of like-minded, supportive and often highly experienced gardeners or simply to relax in the fresh air, away from modern pressures. You are free to grow your food by your own chosen methods, indulging whim, tradition and individuality to your own satisfaction, and to harvest it close to home in peak condition.

Ideas and attitudes might change – modern tenants may be quite different from their predecessors of two or three generations back, and allotments continue to evolve socially, from 'plots for the poor' to 'gardens for a greener world'. But some aspects of allotment gardening are reassuringly constant, and from a down-to-earth perspective nothing has fundamentally changed: the soil is almost the same as it was (slightly improved in the best cases), the weather remains a seasonal challenge (but a little more so with the advent of climate change), and the basic gardening techniques are those familiar to the Diggers of more than three centuries ago.

Getting involved

Allotments do not exist in a vacuum, and sooner or later you are sure to encounter politics. Local authorities vary in their commitment to the sites in their care, from fiercely supportive to indifferent or hostile, and the land itself is often a valuable asset coveted by developers. Committees and associations have sometimes had to respond to threatened erosion of rights by assuming self-management, mobilizing defence campaigns or filing legal challenges.

Elsewhere stable, thriving sites are regenerated by introducing projects that involve other local residents or improve interaction with the wider community. Advertising, special events, training courses, mentoring schemes and shared work days on tenants' plots have all helped to revive flagging enthusiasm. Unused areas or merged plots have been transformed into wildlife sites or communal gardens where schools or special interest organizations can have their own facilities.

A growing awareness of environmental issues, social inequalities, sustainability and funding has led to a host of constructive and exciting developments that reinvent the nature of allotment gardening. How much you participate is for you to decide: growing good food remains the main purpose of an allotment plot, and this can bring you both peace and productivity, but you may be surprised just how beneficial it can be to feel part of the wider allotment community.

Growing good food remains the main purpose of an allotment plot

ABOVE The Number One Allotment Project in London is for people with learning difficulties and physical disabilities who wish to develop their horticultural skills. With the help of gardeners in the local allotment society, they have planted and harvested a variety of organic vegetables, fruit and flowers.

LEFT Many plot-holders have ambitious plans for their allotments, including growing their own grapes for making wine.

the perfect allotment

From first contemplating and acquiring an allotment to choosing gardening methods and tools, there are many opportunities and options to consider before you set out to sow or plant your first crops.

making a start

Why have an allotment?

There are numerous compelling reasons to have an allotment. For some people, it is an instinctive and traditional activity, and even in industrialized countries no one is more than a few generations away from working the land. Others feel that manufacturers and processors have systematically destroyed their food culture, and that the only way to ensure a reliable (often affordable) source of favourite fruit and vegetables without chemical intervention is to grow them oneself. And growing crops close to home reduces the environmental cost of 'food miles' associated with long-distance transport.

Fresh, good-quality food is not the only essential ingredient of a healthy lifestyle, however. Regular exercise is just as vital, and working in the open air on your own piece of ground can be a more agreeable and productive way of keeping fit than going to the gym. In urban areas, allotments are vital oases of open recreational space, healing places that soothe the spirit and subdue mental stress.

Many welcome the strong, supportive sense of community (although you are equally free to be peacefully alone, if you prefer). Tending a plot can be a shared activity for families, while the wider community of plotholders, uniting gardeners of varied ages, abilities and backgrounds around a shared interest, offers the kind of support, co-operation and tolerance often lacking beyond the site boundary. You can find sanity and sanctuary as well as opportunity on an allotment.

FINDING AN ALLOTMENT

How you go about finding an allotment depends to a great extent on where you live, but in the UK you should first contact your local authority because most allotments are council-owned. These allotments may be statutory, in which case they are protected by law, or temporary sites on leased or rented land, where long-term tenancy is not guaranteed. Some sites are privately owned – by churches or public utilities, for example – and the best way to find out how to rent one of these is to ask an existing tenant.

A standard full-size allotment is about 250 sq.m (300 sq.yd), but half, quarter, even one-tenth plots are sometimes offered. You may find a vacant plot to take over straight away, or have to join a waiting list if demand is high and the site full. A tenancy agreement, which usually lasts for a year and is renewable, is signed by you and the owner or owner's agent (such as a site association) and you will pay rent, which the law says must be reasonable, in advance.

In return you can usually expect safe access to your plot, an easily accessible water supply (its cost often included in the rent), and adequate site security. The site will usually have at least toilet facilities and a communal hut for storage, meetings and the sale of materials. Your plot may also be equipped with a shed, sometimes for extra rent, and permanent paths.

The agreement will explain your rights – to grow vegetables and fruit for personal use, and also possibly to keep hens or rabbits and sometimes other livestock such as pigeons or bees, depending on local bye-laws – and your responsibilities. Chief among these is the duty to maintain the plot in good cultivation, with respect to your neighbours and other plot-holders. There may also be restrictions on using hosepipes, lighting bonfires, creating ponds, planting trees or fencing the plot (especially with dangerous materials like barbed wire). You are normally not permitted to sublet or use the plot as a business.

ALLOTMENT ASSOCIATIONS

Well-managed allotment associations welcome new tenants in different ways. You may be given a starter pack that includes all the benefits and opportunities open to you (like sharing in a bulk purchase of materials or manure), a full description of the site as a whole and possibly details of your own plot, and even the offer of assistance from volunteer members to help you clear an overgrown plot and get started.

A key common reason for taking on a plot, whatever the private social or therapeutic motivation might be, is the deep sense of achievement when you harvest your own food. Daily work is often far removed from the basic satisfaction of making or producing something, while increasing pressure on the use of land results in gardens becoming ever smaller. An allotment can be a wonderful place to rediscover a sense of fulfilment.

Assessing yourself

Whatever your motivation for acquiring an allotment, it is a good idea to assess your aims and capabilities. Be realistic about what you can achieve – it is easy for idealism to cloud judgement. However, owning an allotment may be less demanding than you imagine.

TIME It is possible to manage a plot well with a single weekly visit, although you will probably want to visit more often, especially when regular watering and harvesting are necessary. Add in your journey time if you live far from the site. If you don't have your own vehicle, check out public transport links and consider whether you will be able to call upon friends to give you a lift with heavy items. Techniques like mulching can postpone the need for urgent attention, and neighbours will often share the care if you are away.

COMMITMENT Regular care is essential, even required in some tenancy agreements. As the sun doesn't always shine, this will sometimes mean working in cold or wet weather. Low-maintenance methods, however, reduce the amount of routine tasks. You ultimately decide how much or how little you do, and even sitting out a rain shower in the shed can be therapeutic.

STAMINA Basic physical abilities are an advantage. Cultivating some soils can be strenuous work, and you might prefer to get someone to rotavate the plot for you. Routine skill and dexterity come with experience, and techniques are easily adapted for elderly and disabled plot-holders. And, with the goodwill

EXPLORING YOUR PLOT

Before contemplating crops and how you intend to grow them, assess the plot as a place where you would enjoy working and possibly spending a lot of leisure time. Note all its apparent deficiencies as well as its merits and, if necessary, its scope for change. Although you will probably alter or adjust things as you go on, discoveries and decisions that are made now can affect future plans. Don't rush into anything because time, weather and inclination are all unpredictable.

▶ The condition of the plot may be immediately obvious if it is overgrown, still partly planted up, or empty and cleared. Find some exposed soil and examine its character (see *page 115*) – plans that ignore the nature of the soil are unlikely to succeed.

▶ Note the lie of the land – whether it slopes and in which direction (this can affect temperature and the amount of sunshine it receives); low ground could be a frost-pocket or it may be waterlogged. Find out about prevailing winds. (See also *pages 116* and *169*.)

▶ Light and shade are important influences, so notice if existing tree canopies cast deep shadow, which might interfere with growth, or merely light shade, which is a valuable asset for sensitive crops in midsummer.

▶ Identify convenient places for essential accessories like compost bins, a shed, cold frame or manure stack. Try to find a draught-free position for sitting or eating.

▶ Access is vital: evaluate existing paths, their condition and durability, whether they are wide enough to take a wheelbarrow, and if they provide a direct, clear route to important places such as the shed, compost bin and main access road.

▶ Explore your surroundings. Locate the nearest water source, and assess any boundaries, hedges and fences for security, shelter or perhaps wild crops to harvest later. Study other plots for ideas and encouragement. Introduce yourself to neighbours, who can usually add information to your important first impressions.

of most allotment-holders, help with a particular task is often only a plot away.

AMBITION You need an aim in mind, confidence in yourself and sufficient common sense to temper your dreams with an awareness of your limitations, particularly at those times of year when a plot can seem both huge and unmanageable. Remember, though, that every year is a fresh beginning, when you can revise or simplify your plans. A plot that is too large can be shared with others or you can usually rent a part-allotment, and persistence always pays in the end.

COST If you have to buy tools, starting up can be expensive, especially if you add refinements, such as edging beds with boards and a greenhouse, shed or fruit cage. Don't forget to include rent and travel expenses in your costs. However, you don't have to renovate or plant up a whole allotment in the first season. You can start on the most neglected plot with just a mattock or spade and a few packets of seeds.

SEE ALSO ▶ **Tools** *pages 54–5* Mulching *page 119* **The allotment year** *pages 166–215* Resources *pages 216–18*

devising a plan

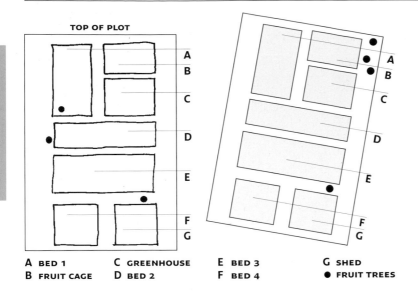

TOP OF PLOT

A
B
C
D
E
F
G

A
B
C
D
E
F
G

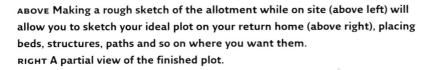

A	BED 1	C	GREENHOUSE	E	BED 3	G	SHED
B	FRUIT CAGE	D	BED 2	F	BED 4	●	FRUIT TREES

ABOVE Making a rough sketch of the allotment while on site (above left) will allow you to sketch your ideal plot on your return home (above right), placing beds, structures, paths and so on where you want them.
RIGHT A partial view of the finished plot.

Making sketches

During your first visit to the allotment, make a rough sketch plan of the plot with the position of all the important features like paths and any buildings, existing beds and perennial plants or remaining crops. Annotate the plan with any information you might gather about soil, aspect, exposure or neighbouring plots. Note any sloping ground because you will tend to take loads of manure or water in one direction more than others, and this might influence your layout.

When you are back home, make another plan, this time of your ideal plot. Allocate space for all your favourite crops and anything else you would like to grow, bearing in mind which need sun, shade or plenty of water and attention, as this could affect their siting. Consider the extra facilities you might like now or in the future – a family gathering place, cold frames or a fruit cage – but remember that you can always change your mind and adapt the plan later.

All this preliminary thought can help you to visualize life on the plot and so translate your dream into reality.

BOUNDARIES & PATHS

These are important, and establish the plot's shape and means of access.

The edges of your plot could simply be paths or lines on the ground, or a previous tenant may have arranged something more elaborate. However, comprehensive fencing of any kind is inappropriate and a waste of ground; it may also possibly contravene site rules.

A useful way to define boundaries is to make natural boundaries, such as training fruit on posts and horizontal wires (see *page 147*), which can be very productive while occupying little space. Free-standing fruit bushes or seasonal hedges of runner beans, Jerusalem artichokes, sunflowers or herbs like angelica can confer privacy and relief from wind, perhaps screening an area for a sheltered seat.

There may only be one or two existing paths, dividing your plot from those next door. As these will probably be shared, any changes, improvement or maintenance should be negotiated with neighbours.

Paths within the plot are your exclusive responsibility. For practical purposes, main paths usually need to be straight, weather-proof, wide enough for comfort, and run directly between important points. Subsidiary paths (between beds, for example)

can be narrower, even temporary arrangements, planned to allow access to cultivate and tend the various areas.

The material used will vary from plot to plot, although some sites are laid out with a grid of permanent paved paths. They will often be made of grass, which needs mowing or trimming periodically, while trampled earth is sufficient to allow simple maintenance between beds – protect those on wet ground with sacking, bark or waste timber slats. Paving slabs are the best long-term solution, or you could use gravel spread about 5cm (2in) deep on top of a weed-suppressant membrane (but beware: deep or smooth gravel can impede laden wheelbarrows).

A narrow gravel path edged with bricks separates two beds.

how to garden

Methods of cultivation

Plot-holders quickly become very attached to their allotments. If growing your own produce is a new experience, you will probably find that your initial attention is focused on the routine of starting and tending plants, culminating in the anticipation and triumph of harvesting fresh food that you have produced yourself, an experience that never palls.

BIODIVERSITY

News reports document the alarming worldwide decline in biodiversity, the variety and numbers of plants and creatures on earth. How you manage your plot can have an equally critical impact on wildlife at a much more local level, and is more within your power to control. Using sustainable gardening methods and minimizing disturbance to natural life cycles can help safeguard the future for other species that use the plot. An allotment is often teeming with life, whether it is soil-based and out of sight, or more obvious, like the birds, insects, amphibians and reptiles that may be found on any sensitively managed site.

A ladybird feasting on blackfly.

Before long, however, you will become aware of a wider context: life in the soil and surroundings, the influence of local geography and climate, and even the old-fashioned concept of stewardship – your responsibility for the continuing welfare of the land in your care. This could lead you into asking more fundamental questions about the way you are growing your crops, and the implications of simply imposing a basic plan on the plot for short-term results.

Alternative methods

Gardeners have explored and tested alternative methods of cultivation, particularly since a spreading ecological awareness has meant that chemical-based gardening seems increasingly untenable and is no longer the norm. Attempts to treat nature as an ally and work in harmony with the environment have resulted in a variety of sympathetic approaches.

The most familiar of these is organic gardening, but other approaches have gone further: biodynamic gardening harnesses the subtle influence of the moon's phases on growth, for example, while forest gardening imitates the natural structure of woodland habitats to pack a lot of plants amicably into a small space.

None of these methods has a monopoly on success, nor are they mutually exclusive, and the basic mechanics of sowing, planting, tending and harvesting remain broadly the same whichever you choose. In the end your own inclination and personal conviction through good

results will help you decide which and how many of these methods feels right for managing your allotment.

ORGANIC GARDENING Many plot-holders first choose to grow their own because they want top-quality fresh food produced in a way they

Feeding the soil, rather than the plant, with organic materials such as garden compost is one of the basic principles of organic gardening.

if you prefer, and concentrate instead on garden compost, leafmould (see *page 208*), plant-based fertilizers and green manures (see *page 119*) as sources of fertility.

Controlling problems involves a range of precautions and treatments (often termed 'integrated pest management') rather than simply reaching for a specific spray. Efficient crop rotation (see *pages 32–5*) is one sound method. This can be combined with using resistant plants sown at times when pests are less prevalent, encouraging natural predators and companion plants (see *page 35*), and keeping the plot tidy and well maintained.

> ### GIVING UP CHEMICALS
> A plot that has been maintained with inorganic fertilizers and chemical treatments can often show signs of an impoverished soil structure and a dependence on supplementary feeding. Improving and feeding the soil will have long-term benefits, whether you choose to grow organically or continue to use chemical inputs. Growing fully organic crops on it immediately may, at first, lead to depressed yields, especially while it is difficult to produce or acquire enough compost and manure. Also, pest and disease problems can escalate when plants are not sufficiently vigorous to withstand attacks. If you decide to garden organically, you may prefer to adopt a gradualist approach and compromise, using chemical treatments at least for the first two to three seasons while the new routine is established.

approve, which often means organically. But there is more to organic gardening than simply giving up artificial fertilizers and chemical pesticides. Replacing these inorganic inputs involves following a different cultural routine more in harmony with natural cycles and environmental susceptibilities.

Possibly the most fundamental principle is to feed the soil rather than the plant, using organic materials, such as compost and manure (see *pages 116–19*), that encourage soil organisms to flourish and make nutrients available to plants. It is even possible to abandon animal manures

You can respond to particular pests and diseases with treatments of low toxicity or short persistence, or try to avoid them with traps, barriers and deterrents. Instead of using herbicides, you can manage weeds by mulching, hoeing, hand-weeding, spacing the crops in such a way that denies weeds light, and minimal cultivation to avoid germinating weed seeds.

The result is produce that may taste better – but this is also affected by other cultural factors such as variety, season or the amount of watering – and that will certainly be free from any chemical residues. The soil will be nurtured rather than exploited, abused or simply taken for granted; wildlife is respected and encouraged; and you will have avoided waste by recycling compostable materials and returning them to the soil.

BIODYNAMIC GARDENING

Some find biodynamics slightly esoteric or metaphysical, but this gardening philosophy has had a strong following ever since the 1920s, when Rudolf Steiner, the Austrian philosopher and agricultural expert, first outlined his rules for rescuing soil fertility from over-intensive cropping and chemicals.

The approach is essentially holistic as well as organic, acknowledging the effects of natural rhythms and cycles on growth and following principles that restore the vitality as well as fertility lost when ground is cultivated and crops harvested. Biodynamics embraces organic and ecologically sound gardening methods, but it goes further than that: feeding the soil is not considered sufficient because the earth itself needs healing from past abuses.

Remedies for this include treating the land with special herbal tonics, and gardening in tune with all the

Pulling out weeds by hand and not using weedkillers plays an important role in organic gardening.

influences that can possibly affect plant growth – these range from street lighting and water quality to planetary aspects and phases of the moon. Followers accept that some of these beliefs defy current scientific knowledge, but suggest that proof lies in the pudding – pragmatic trials seem to work, even if the reasons for the results are unknown.

Key elements when exploring this approach include making compost the biodynamic way, with special therapeutic preparations and a planting calendar, which uses the positions of

Beneficial plants like trefoil, which supply minerals and nutrients to other plants, are an essential part of forest gardening.

Under this is a shrub layer of shade-tolerant soft fruit bushes, such as gooseberries or redcurrants, surrounded by perennial herbs and vegetables at ground level; climbers filter through from the ground to the top tier.

Total productivity from the plot is high because plants of different habit and height can fit around each other to make the most of available resources. And the diversity of crops shares fertility efficiently by feeding at different levels; it also discourages specific pests and diseases from taking hold. Beneficial plants such as legumes and comfrey are included to supply minerals and nutrients to their neighbours; others are planted to attract both insect predators and pollinating insects.

The majority of plants are either perennial or self-seeding annuals, which makes digging almost unnecessary, although some cultivated patches can be integrated for growing extra crops like annual roots or runner beans to climb into the tree layer. A few open areas can be left for sun-loving vegetables and herbs. The whole garden is kept heavily mulched to control water loss and most weeds, so maintenance consists chiefly of clipping or pulling up invasive species or the odd weed.

PERMACULTURE This is an ethical design system that attempts to minimize our environmental impact by planning a sustainable and ecologically sound lifestyle, including the way in which we grow our food. Permaculture gardening draws together many ideas from other philosophies, such as no-dig practices (see *page 36*), the edible perennials of forest gardening, most of the established organic principles, and the ornamental aims of the French potager and the North American 'edible landscape' movement.

PERENNIAL CROPS

Forest gardening depends heavily on perennial crops, but even under conventional methods of management there are some popular perennial vegetables that can be fitted into the allotment's layout where they can grow undisturbed for five years or more. Asparagus is best allocated a bed to itself, although the attractive fern will blend with perennial flowers in an integrated border; globe artichokes, rhubarb and Welsh onions could be included, too. Perennial cauliflowers, good king henry and salad dandelions are less appealing and would be better in a separate corner. Clean the ground well before planting, feed or mulch annually to sustain growth, and replant the crops on fresh ground when they need renewal. Check regularly for pests and diseases that might be passed to seasonal crops.

With this design system, the garden or allotment is divided into zones, with plants that require the most attention closer to hand. A typical border will include 'keyholes', which are short paths branching to the side of a main pathway. These paths are surrounded by zones of plants, the closest (salads or spinach, for example) requiring frequent care or harvest, while the furthest, such as cabbages or squashes, need tending only once in a while. The overall aim is to combine beauty and bounty with easy maintenance.

SEE ALSO ▶ **Improving your soil** *pages 116-21* Green manures *page 119* **The case for weeding pages 152-3** Keeping your plants healthy *pages 154-7*

the planets to find the ideal times for sowing or harvesting. It also involves becoming aware of the unique character of your plot, so that you gradually develop a full understanding of the land and an intuitive sense of what it needs to boost the vitality and abundance of its produce.

FOREST GARDENING A natural forest or wood has a layered structure that allows all kinds of plants to grow together and share resources such as light, water and fertility. Forest gardening imitates this by arranging edible plants in a series of tiers. The highest is a canopy of fruit trees like plums and apples, which are pruned to admit plenty of light to plants below.

crop rotation

What is crop rotation? This is the custom of moving annual and biennial vegetables year by year around a number of different beds. A key technique in traditional husbandry, and equally important as part of efficient organic gardening, crop rotation ensures the same type of plant is not grown in successive years in the same piece of ground. Crops with similar needs and susceptibilities are grouped together, each group moving on to the next bed in the rotation the following year. Thus a crop literally rotates around the arrangement of beds until it returns to the first bed in the sequence a number of years later (see *pages 32–5*).

Rotation helps to avoid disorders by interrupting the life cycles of pests and diseases. It can also prevent the gradual depletion of certain soil nutrients. The principle is a sound insurance against inviting unnecessary problems, even in its simplest form of growing crops wherever you like but making sure no group or individual vegetable occupies the same spot in two consecutive years (with the exception of perennials, see *page 31*). Just moving a crop a few metres is a worthwhile precaution, but this minimalist approach requires a good memory and efficient organization. Following a full crop rotation scheme is usually more dependable.

A simple, efficient way to organize crops is to divide them into the three main traditional groups of root crops, brassicas and legumes, and base the rotation on these. The advantage of this approach is that members of each group need similar soil preparation, so the whole bed can be cultivated accordingly. Vegetables like salad greens, tomatoes and squashes, which do not obviously belong in any of these categories, are fitted in wherever there is space; perennial crops are, of course, not rotated.

VARIATIONS With three vegetable groups and three beds to rotate them in annually, each group will get back to where it started in the fourth year, so this standard system is called a four-year ('course' or 'stage') rotation. It is not inflexible: you can extend the number of years before a group returns to its original position by adding extra courses; some gardeners give maincrop onions a bed to themselves, grow potatoes as a separate course from other roots, or allow one or more fallow years for green manure crops.

Nor is the system infallible. Some vegetables, especially winter crops, overlap inconveniently with others. Some pathogens survive in the soil for many years, so you still need to be alert for symptoms of disorders. Opinions differ about whether it is better to isolate crops with common serious disorders – separating potatoes and tomatoes to prevent the spread of blight – or grow them together to keep the problem in one place, where it is more manageable. Experience will determine your own preferred approach.

Different crops are more easily managed if given separate beds to themselves, as here where two beds of brassicas are safely netted against birds, and squashes (foreground) sprawl freely in another.

SAMPLE ROTATION PLAN

This example of a rotation plan shows how three different allotment beds are planted up with the three main plant groups of legumes, brassicas and root crops over a four-year period.

LEGUMES Podded crops like garden peas, French beans, runner beans and broad beans.
▶ Grow the onion family (bulbing onions, leeks, shallots, salad onions and garlic) here, as they like the same soil preparation.

BRASSICAS Cabbages, cauliflowers, Chinese cabbages, oriental greens, Brussels sprouts, calabrese, sprouting broccoli and kale. If brassica diseases are a problem, include turnips and swedes in the brassica group; otherwise treat them as root crops.
▶ Interplant fully spaced brassicas with salad and leaf crops such as lettuce, chicory, endive, corn salad, land cress, claytonia and spinach.

ROOT CROPS Potatoes, carrots, beetroot, radishes, parsnips, swedes, turnips.
▶ Salad and leaf crops may also be grown with this group. Add sweetcorn, celery and celeriac.

OTHER PLANT GROUPS Members of the pumpkin family (squashes, courgettes, marrows, outdoor cucumbers and melons), as well as summer-fruiting vegetables like tomatoes, peppers and aubergines, may be grown with any of the above plant groups, wherever there is space.

BED A

YEAR 1: LEGUMES

CROPS TO GROW Podded vegetables and onion family.
CULTIVATION Dig in plenty of manure or compost. After harvest plant onions to overwinter and overlap with **Brassicas** in Year 2.

YEAR 2: BRASSICAS

CROPS TO GROW Cabbage family interplanted with salads.
CULTIVATION Add leafmould or more compost, forked in or as a mulch, and lime the soil if it is acid. In autumn mulch with more compost, to raise fertility for **Root crops** in Year 3.

YEAR 3: ROOT CROPS

CROPS TO GROW Root crops, leaf crops and extras like sweetcorn.
CULTIVATION Add more compost. After harvest sow green manure to dig in before **Legumes** in Year 4.

YEAR 4: LEGUMES

BED B

YEAR 1: BRASSICAS

CROPS TO GROW Cabbage family interplanted with salads.
CULTIVATION Dig in leafmould or compost, and lime the soil if it is acid. In autumn mulch with more compost, to raise fertility for **Root crops** in Year 2.

YEAR 2: ROOT CROPS

CROPS TO GROW Root crops, leaf crops and extras like sweetcorn.
CULTIVATION Add more compost. After harvest sow green manure to dig in before **Legumes** in Year 3.

YEAR 3: LEGUMES

CROPS TO GROW Podded vegetables and the onion family.
CULTIVATION Dig in plenty of manure or compost. After harvest plant onions to overwinter and overlap with **Brassicas** in Year 4.

YEAR 4: BRASSICAS

BED C

YEAR 1: ROOT CROPS

CROPS TO GROW Grow root crops, leaf crops and extras like sweetcorn.
CULTIVATION Dig in plenty of compost. After harvest sow green manure to dig in before **Legumes** in Year 2.

YEAR 2: LEGUMES

CROPS TO GROW Podded vegetables and the onion family.
CULTIVATION Add plenty of manure or compost. After harvest plant onions to overwinter and overlap with **Brassicas** in Year 3.

YEAR 3: BRASSICAS

CROPS TO GROW Cabbage family interplanted with salads.
CULTIVATION Add leafmould or more compost, forked in or as a mulch, and lime the soil if it is acid. In autumn mulch with more compost, to raise fertility for **Root crops** in Year 4.

YEAR 4: ROOT CROPS

COMPANION PLANTING

Few plants grow in isolation, and an allotment is as much a community of interactive plants as any natural ecosystem. Plants can influence the welfare of their neighbours for good (symbiosis) or bad (allelopathy). beans do not grow well next to onions, rue suppresses growth and very little thrives under a walnut tree; on the other hand, legumes help root crops to grow well, chives can ward off carrot root flies, and elderberries will encourage soil organisms to decompose organic material.

Crop rotation is one obvious form of companion planting, grouping plants with similar needs together. Another example is growing flowers attractive to pollinators or pest predators close to a vulnerable crop: poached egg plant (*Limnanthes*) flowers early and attracts hoverflies that can control aphids on

Marigolds (*Tagetes*) planted alongside carrots help prevent carrot root fly.

broad beans, or you could grow a sacrificial alternative host like nasturtiums to lure aphids away from the beans.

It is worth experimenting with various different combinations, and observing the results, which can vary from one season or variety to the next. Marigolds (*Tagetes*), for example, help prevent carrot root fly, and in the greenhouse they are used to discourage whitefly, but you need to choose a strong-smelling variety. Other combinations to explore might include planting tomatoes near asparagus, whose roots exude a substance toxic to tomato eelworms, while French beans interplanted among the brassicas can deter some cabbage root and leaf pests.

choosing the bed system

The benefits Dividing your growing area into separate beds is the simplest way to organize crop rotation on the ground (see *pages 32–5*). It makes the routine of tending the whole plot more manageable than when crops are arranged in long rows right across the allotment. The beds are attractive, which is also psychologically satisfying because they are easy to maintain and keep tidy. They also maximize yields because plants can be grown at closer spacings than when access is needed between rows. They are particularly appropriate for organic and biodynamic gardeners, since cultivation concentrates on maintaining very high levels of organic material and fertility in the soil.

The beds can be permanent, defined with fixed edging and separated by maintained paths, or marked out with string and pegs, with intervening paths trodden in. Most paths are straight, but elegant curves are equally practical and can introduce a welcome aesthetic element into a functional landscape. You will find that managing the beds from the paths rather than by walking between rows of vegetables eliminates compaction of the soil and so reduces the need to dig the beds regularly.

The critical size for a bed is its width – it must allow you to reach the middle without walking on the soil. Most people find 90–120cm (3–4ft) is a comfortable width. Narrow beds may

be as long as you like, although much more than 3m (10ft) means a long walk round to the other side. Plants are usually arranged in short rows from side to side for easy cultivation. Square beds, 90–120cm (3–4ft) each way and accessible from all sides, are good for gradually colonizing new ground, with each square devoted to a single crop.

Both styles can be transformed into raised beds by building timber edges or walls to a convenient height, usually 10–20cm (4–8in) or as much as 60cm (2ft) if you have difficulty with bending or mobility. A raised bed of this kind is also an effective remedy for serious drainage problems. Paths should be at least 30cm (12in) wide.

No-dig beds Annual digging can destroy soil structure, dry out light soils and bring more weed seeds to the surface to germinate. If you adopt a minimal cultivation or 'no-dig' policy, remember that it is worth deeply digging over the plot or individual beds initially, to open up heavy or compacted ground, improve aeration and work in manure or compost. Thereafter it should be enough to cultivate the top 10–20cm (4–8in) of soil, where root growth tends to be concentrated, loosening the surface and turning in annual dressings or 8cm- (3in-) deep mulches of organic material. Decreasing yields or poor drainage will indicate if deep digging and manuring will need to be repeated in the future.

A layer of compost is added to these 'no-dig' raised beds each year to improve the soil.

INCREASING YOUR SPACE

Although your plot might seem adequate, even enormous at first, it can quickly fill up with conventionally spaced crops unless you adopt measures to stretch the available space. Gardening in beds might appear to increase the area devoted to paths, but the more intensive plant spacings used can actually raise total yields; forest gardening (see *page 31*) exploits the vertical dimension by adding extra tiers of productive plant growth above normal ground-level vegetables.

Many plants can be grown for height rather than spread to save space. Fruits like apples, plums, gooseberries and redcurrants adapt readily to restricted forms such as cordons, espaliers and fans on posts and wires, or as short (often decorative) standards with branches spreading above ground level plants. Tall varieties of peas

or beans and trailing forms of cucumbers or squashes can all be trained on upright structures to limit spread, releasing soil at their base for other shade-tolerant plants.

If your plot lies on a slope, consider contouring this in a series of level terraces supported by low walls or banks that can be used for trailing and scrambling plants. Raised beds provide the same growing space as at ground level, but are more comfortable to manage and offer vertical support for extra crops grown round their sides. Fencing or dividing parts of the plot with screens provides sites for extra climbing plants, as do the sides of a fruit cage. And don't forget shed walls, which can be clothed with seasonal or permanent climbers, together with shorter plants in window boxes and ground-level containers or on shelves (see *page 42*).

allotment story
ON THE WATERFRONT

Many allotment sites have a long history, sometimes stretching back centuries, and even millennia in the case of the floating gardens of Amiens, in the French region of Picardie.

Not far from the cathedral the River Somme flows through the city, across a low marshy floodplain that was first drained by the Romans when France was part of Gaul. They cultivated the reclaimed ground to produce vegetables to feed the troops, a practice that has continued to this day. The land is liable to flood, which replenished its fertility and often allowed three main crops a year to be raised by the market gardeners who developed the area and maintained its 55 kilometres (34 miles) of irrigation and drainage channels, or *rieux*. By the end of the 19th century there were more than a thousand growers, who sold their produce at the water market in Amiens every Saturday.

Today only a few commercial growers are left on 25 hectares (62 acres) of *Les Hortillonages*, as the floating gardens are known. The rest of the 300 hectares (741 acres) is divided into about 1,300 allotment plots and leisure gardens, often with a weekend cabin, and accessible mainly by shallow-bottomed boat through the intricate network of channels. It is possible to visit the gardens, as well as the surviving Saturday water market, throughout the year, and every June there is a medieval market and festival.

structures & equipment

The shed The allotment shed stands at the heart of the plot-holder's domain, a private sanctuary that has often inspired creativity and latent building skills (see *pages 42–3*). Whether flatpack or makeshift in style, it is a key structure that dominates the plot and provides refuge from bad weather, a store for tools and materials, and very often a simple retreat in which to relax, brew tea and potter.

On some allotment sites, inspired DIY and frugal recycling of old doors, pallets, plastic sheeting, household paint and roofing felt is permissible. The result is an enchanted huddle of shacks and shanties that tap into childhood memories of dens and seem to be in a constant state of renovation or repair. Elsewhere, strict regulations insist that all plot-holders use the standard issue of a basic weatherboarded and unpainted tool store.

Whatever its design, your shed is an essential part of the allotment's working environment, and so needs some thought if it is to be weatherproof, secure and well equipped for your various activities on site.

IDEAL SPECIFICATION If you are considering buying or building your own shed, you should take into account the following important features.
Size Many allotment associations set a maximum base size of 2.1 x 1.5m (7 x 5ft). A smaller area might seem sufficient, but you should decide first if you need room for working or for sitting and resting as well as for storing your tools and tackle. Make sure that there is enough headroom to stand

comfortably, allowing for any structural cross-braces in the roof.
Floor The floor should be sound, firm and durable. Pressure-treated boards are standard, laid on treated bearers that sit on a bed of gravel for good drainage. A permanent concrete foundation may not be allowed, but concrete blocks will keep the floor bearers off the ground.
Roof The roof must be strong, ideally made of tongue-and-groove boards rather than plywood, and waterproofed with felt that covers overhanging eaves. A flat roof must have sufficient fall to shed rainwater. A covering of turf or plants would provide a 'green' solution. Add guttering to collect rainwater (into water butts) and protect the shed walls.
Door The door should be wide enough for comfortable access by you and your largest equipment, such as a wheelbarrow, and soundly constructed with strong ledges and braces. Furniture

such as hinges and latches should be rust-resistant – galvanized or stainless steel, for example – and you must have a strong lock (see also *page 43*).

MATERIALS If allowed by your allotment association, a serviceable shed can be built from a host of discarded materials. Traditional materials include doors, window frames, wooden pallets

A 'green' roof of sedum or other plants is an environmental asset but the roof needs to be sturdy, with a well-made substrate, to support the plants.

and corrugated iron. On some sites, redundant structures such as railway wagons, upturned boats, sectional concrete garages, even seaside chalets and refreshment kiosks have been used.

Most new sheds are made of pressure-treated or resinous softwood, clad with shiplap, feather-edged or tongue-and-groove weatherboarding, and with a ridged or nearly flat roof protected with felt. Hot-dipped galvanized steel sheds are durable and secure, but unattractive.

FOUNDATIONS Any shed will need a sound, dry foundation. All but the cheapest will be supplied with a floor and instructions for constructing a firm, damp-proof foundation. Site rules often specify how this should be constructed, or give alternative ways to stabilize the structure – for example, sitting the shed on a damp-proof membrane and anchoring it by sinking metal or wooden piles to which it may be fastened.

One reliable method is to remove enough soil over the base area to accommodate a shingle, sand and slab floor. Consolidate the exposed soil firmly, spread a 5cm (2in) deep layer of shingle and firm this in turn. Top with a 2.5cm (1in) layer of sharp sand, then lay paving slabs to finish. Extending this arrangement beyond the floor area would provide a surface for seating and for standing containers or equipment.

An alternative (and also simpler) arrangement is to dig out trenches one-spit deep where the floor bearers rest, fill these with gravel and position the bearers on these: make sure the bearers and the floor are made of treated timber, and that the floor itself sits clear of the ground.

The shed plays a crucial role in the allotment, as a private sanctuary as well as secure storage for equipment.

FITTING OUT YOUR SHED

You can adapt or equip the outside of your shed for a number of working purposes or use it to extend your growing space in various ways. Furnishing the shed depends on its proposed use and the amount of room inside. You could simply stack and store materials in a small building, but tools and equipment soon accumulate and it will be much easier to find what you want with a little organization.

◄ Walls can be used to extend the potential storage space if you construct shelves for small tools, gloves, seeds and tins. Attach these to the main framework (not the boarding) with brackets. Screw an old bookcase or wooden frame to the wall for storing pots and seed trays out of the way. You might also find a small cupboard, tool box or old chest of drawers useful, but make sure it is securely fastened to the shed frame or floor to prevent easy removal by thieves.

► Suspend gardening tools from hooks or clips on the wall or roof braces to free floor space for larger items like rolls of netting, a wheelbarrow, boxes of stored root crops. Hang up empty paint tins or small buckets to hold string, cloths, gloves, plant labels and hand tools, and have a large hook or bracket for coiled hoses. A rack or simple timber hangers attached to roof members will keep canes and poles tidy and off the floor.

◄ A bulldog clip on the back of the door gives instant access to gloves. A nail keeps keys in a safe place.

► Old mats, a chair, tea-making facilities, even a small camp stove can help transform a functional shed into a welcoming haven where you can rest, admire or plan your work or shelter from the rain. (Make sure you check with your site manager what the regulations are concerning the use of flammable equipment.)

▲ Window boxes (whether your shed has windows or not) can accommodate flowering plants and crops like herbs, trailing tomatoes or leaf salads at a convenient height. Attach trellis to the walls for growing sweet peas, climbing annual crops or fruit such as trained figs, grapes, cordon apples and pears, or thornless brambles.

▶ Use overhanging eaves to support strings for climbing crops like runner beans and outdoor cucumbers, growing in the ground or in troughs of compost.

▶ Build a bench for sitting in the sun, with useful storage space beneath it.

▶ Attach a collapsible table-top or work surface to the outside for potting and sowing activities, especially if space is restricted inside the shed. You might want an old table or home made work surface within for various jobs and as extra storage. If you make your own, consider a drop-down top hinged to the inside wall, supported by folding brackets.

SECURITY

The risks of forcible entry and theft from an unattended shed are high, and exempt from many association insurance schemes, but guidelines have been issued by police forces and site committees to help prevent loss.

▶ Provide a strong door and a large lock or padlock.
▶ Cover any windows with rigid wire mesh or grilles.
▶ Conceal screw fittings with metal plates.
▶ Use clutch head or 'one-way' screws because they are hard to remove.
▶ Fit a battery-operated alarm.
▶ Mark tools with barcodes or postcodes.
▶ Anchor the shed to piles so it is hard to topple over.
▶ Cover walls with trellis and plants for disguise and stability.

The greenhouse

Adding a greenhouse to the site can enhance your growing options by offering a protected environment for tender crops and those at sensitive stages of growth, especially early and late in the season. Some gardeners consider a cold frame more essential and versatile (see *pages 48–9*), but the two structures can work hand in hand, and it is always an advantage to have an all-weather place with enough headroom for working comfortably. A greenhouse can accommodate larger plants, though, including permanent fruiting climbers such as a grapevine or trained apricots.

The minimum useful size is considered to be 2.4m (8ft) long by 1.8m (6ft) wide, or 1.2m (4ft) for a lean-to model, but even the smallest house can be an asset in a limited area, especially if you arrange the internal layout to exclude a permanent central pathway. Although a great variety of shapes is possible, the most serviceable is the traditional span design, with sides that are upright or gently inclining inwards, and glazed to ground level. Some kinds need a foundation similar to that used for sheds (see *page 41*), while many aluminium models can be pegged down into level ground.

MATERIALS Greenhouse frames usually come in softwood or aluminium, while the glazing is either glass or plastic.

Softwood is cheap, but the construction needs to be strong and this can reduce the total glazed area. Regular maintenance, even of comparatively durable cedar models, is essential for long life.

Aluminium-framed greenhouses are virtually indestructible and maintenance-free, and have thin glazing bars that maximize light transmission. They are more expensive than timber models, though, and need a very firm base to ensure rigidity.

Glass is the best glazing material because of its good light transmission and heat retention. It is, however, expensive, heavy and easily broken

CHECK POINTS
▶ Check if a base is included with your chosen model, and whether this creates a step or barrier in the doorway.
▶ The door should fit tightly and include a kick panel at the bottom for safety; sliding doors make it easier to adjust the ventilation.
▶ Make sure the height at the ridge provides adequate headroom.
▶ Most greenhouses come with a single ventilator, which provides insufficient ventilation: add another on the opposite side of the roof, and at least one (possibly a louvred type) in the side for a free flow of air.

a possible risk on allotments where vandalism is a problem, but if treated with care, it will last indefinitely.

Plastic is lighter and cheaper than glass, but has a limited life according to its type. Flat and corrugated polyester rigid panels are the most expensive. They are almost as clear as glass, but difficult to keep clean. Polycarbonate, especially if double or triple-walled, is more serviceable and affordable. Cheapest of all is flexible plastic sheeting, with a useful life of five years or more, after which it turns yellow and brittle.

FITTING & EQUIPPING Careful organization of a greenhouse is vital, especially in spring and autumn when the house can be full of plants waiting to go out or plants just brought in for frost protection.

Plan the floor space first. You might prefer a solid floor with fixed staging round the sides, or ground-level growing space, perhaps in raised beds and with removable staging that can be moved outside in summer or collapsed

ABOVE A home-made greenhouse, using plastic sheeting and bubble wrap.
OPPOSITE A traditional, aluminium-framed greenhouse.

POLYTUNNEL ALTERNATIVE

Cheaper and easier to erect than a greenhouse, a polytunnel can offer most of the advantages of a greenhouse, although the cladding of heavy-duty plastic sheeting is less heat-retentive and condensation can be a problem. Depending on its quality, the plastic sheet will need replacing every 3–5 years. Make sure there is a door at each end of the tunnel for efficient ventilation.

for storing. Growing bags can be arranged on the soil or solid floors and on staging to house plants temporarily. Shelves on the sides and in the roof can extend the growing and display space, while brackets will support hanging baskets and strings or wires for training climbing plants.

Fitting automatic vent openers that can be adjusted to open at a certain temperature can relieve you from worry and prevent injury to plants. An overhead reservoir can be used to supply water to capillary matting on the staging or to drip tubes positioned in containers to alleviate watering chores. Blinds are expensive, but shade netting is available for installing in summer as an alternative to applying shade paint.

Cold frames

Although they are sometimes regarded as simple greenhouse accessories, cold frames are versatile, sometimes portable, infinitely adjustable and often efficient substitutes for a greenhouse. They are also less expensive than a greenhouse, and provide more space and greater adjustability than cloches. Easily constructed at home, they can be adapted to span a narrow bed or to fit on top of a compost heap to make a hot bed (see *page 53*).

At its simplest the standard frame is a four-sided box structure with a lid that slopes to shed water and opens to admit air. It is accessed from the top, via a lid that is glazed with plastic or glass, and that can be lifted or removed to adjust ventilation. The sides may be glazed or solid. Fixed frames can have a soil floor for planting, or a solid base of slabs or gravel spread over a weed-proof membrane, which is useful for housing pots and trays. A portable frame can be moved directly over a growing crop for protection until established, after which it is moved elsewhere in the same way as cloches.

SITING A COLD FRAME

You usually have little choice over the position of a greenhouse on your allotment – it may be decided for you by accessibility or site rules – but a permanent frame can go almost anywhere. The traditional position is against one side of the greenhouse to avoid carrying plants far and to share some of the stored warmth (some sophisticated frames have adjustable rear panels to allow heat transfer from the greenhouse). Installing a frame on each side of the greenhouse should provide all the space you will need for protection and hardening off.

There will probably be a lot of plant movement to and from the frame, so site a freestanding version in a convenient position: placing it at the end of a nursery bed would keep all plant-raising activities together, or you might prefer a corner of a main vegetable bed to save time when planting out. Make sure the frame is easily accessible all round, and ideally not too far from your water supply. If possible, provide shelter from prevailing winds and avoid shade from overhanging trees. A frame is normally aligned so that its sloping lid receives maximum sunlight and heat, but a lightly shaded frame can be equally useful in summer to avoid scorching sensitive plants.

TEMPORARY FRAMES

You may be reluctant to sacrifice good growing space to a structure that might be needed for only part of the year, perhaps for spring frost protection. Lightweight collapsible frames are available that can be dismantled when they are not needed. Alternatively, you could make your own from a variety of materials. For example, a large bottomless box with its top replaced by a sheet of clear plastic can cover several seed trays (on very cold nights simply spread an old blanket or sheets of bubble polythene over the top). An enclosure of straw bales covered with old car windscreens or double glazing panels makes a snug frame, and the straw can be used afterwards for mulching or as a carbon ingredient in a compost heap (see *pages 116–17*). Professional growers often arrange empty crates and boxes to make the frame walls, draping black polythene over the walls and floor like a pond liner, and then sheeting over the top with thick polythene (polytunnel grade).

A continuous mini-tunnel and plastic cloches are used to warm the soil prior to planting out seedlings.

Covers Protective sheets such as transparent plastic film and woven horticultural fleece can be used to cover crops and exclude a couple of degrees of frost. Horticultural fleece is light and permeable, and may be left in place over the lifetime of a crop for warmth or protection from pests or diseases, floating higher as the plants grow.

Cloches Glass sheets (discarded window panes, for example) are joined with special clips (see *page 146*) or a home-made arrangement of clothes pegs, string or wire to make tents for covering rows or individual plants. Traditional lantern and commercial barn or tent cloches are also available. Plastic cloches and continuous mini-tunnels of film supported by wire hoops can cover a large area. Use cloches early and late in the year to add several weeks to the growing season.

SEE ALSO ▸ The greenhouse year *pages 170-4* The cold frame year *page 175*

USING A COLD FRAME

▸ Spread a layer of gravel over a weed-proof membrane if you intend to use the frame for containers or for trays and plugs of seedlings (below).

▸ Fit a hinged lid with casement stays or notch a strip of wood to make a support for adjusting ventilation. Hinge the lid and prop it open to ventilate the cold frame during the day (bottom), then close it at night to keep in the heat.

▸ When not in use, prevent wooden frames from rotting by lifting them clear of the ground with a block at each corner.

▸ Stand pots and trays on a layer of gravel over a woven plastic membrane to suppress weeds and deter slugs and snails.

▸ Treat a soil-based frame like an extra vegetable bed: water, manure, mulch and rotate crops as you would in the open ground.

49

Fruit cages If you can disperse fruit around the plot, it is possible to harvest good crops from unprotected plants without significant losses to birds or squirrels. But smaller plantings, especially of attractive fruit such as redcurrants, raspberries, strawberries and blueberries, may be stripped before they even show colour, and some kind of protection could be vital.

An individual bush can be enclosed with netting draped like a tent over 3–4 flexible canes arched to meet at the top, where they are tied. Protect a row of raspberries or cordon redcurrants by erecting a post at each end, with several timber cross-pieces, like a telegraph pole: attach wire to these, stretched from one end of the row to the other, and arrange curtains of netting over the wires and clear of the fruit.

Gathering vulnerable fruit together in a cage is a more permanent solution. Various ready-made cages are available to buy, or you can build your own from strong bamboo canes, coppiced hazel poles or metal pipes. Erect uprights 1.8–2.1m (6–7ft) high for clear headroom, space them about 1.8m (6ft) apart, and join their tops with cross bars to support the roof. Clad the sides with 1–2cm (½–¾in) mesh plastic or wire netting (but note that squirrels

A purpose-made fruit cage may seem a luxury but, if you have the space and grow a quantity of fruit, it will significantly increase your harvest.

easily chew through plastic), and the roof with 2cm (¾in) plastic netting.

Either fold back part of the side netting for access or add a hinged door, but make sure this fits tightly. The roof net can be removed after fruit crops are harvested to allow birds to clean up any pests, but leave it in place if finches tend to attack the fruit buds in winter.

However, the roof should always be taken off if snow is forecast. Open the door or (where this is possible) roll up the sides while the fruit is flowering, to admit pollinating insects.

Somewhere to sit As in any
other garden, an allotment plot should have a place for you to recover from hard work, entertain friends and other plot-holders, or just plan and dream. It doesn't matter whether you choose to sit on an upturned bucket or a cast-off chaise longue, although comfort is obviously important.

Collapsible furniture such as picnic tables or deck chairs can be stored safely in a locked shed. Permanent structures like benches or café tables need to be secured by bolting them to the shed wall or anchoring them with metal straps to pegs or piles driven firmly into the ground. Treat your furniture to an annual spring clean: treat or paint metal with rust-proofing, and paint or oil timber pieces to keep rot and woodworm at bay.

RECYCLING SCAFFOLDING

Discarded scaffolding poles and their unions are a valuable resource for a host of structures on the plot. Use them, for example, to build fruit cages and low frames round brassica beds for netting against birds in winter; use them as row supports for runner beans or sweet peas and trained fruit like raspberries or tree-fruit cordons and espaliers; also for arches over paths, planted with squash, climbing cucumbers and thornless brambles.

A cherry tree is draped with netting to protect the fruit from birds.

FAMILY AREAS

Looking after a plot is often a family activity that can be made more appealing to children by creating one or two areas especially for them. While you might feel that a small lawn and its attendant mowing is a waste of space and effort, other places for play will often fit in unobtrusively.

▶ Perhaps the most popular piece of equipment is a swing, easily made from a strong board, old tyre or special rubber safety seat suspended on lengths of rope from a tree branch. Ropes on their own or a rope ladder may be suitable, but check for wear once or twice a year.

▶ Younger children might prefer a sand pit, made from a sunken rigid pond liner filled with clean silver sand; when no longer used, the sand can be incorporated into potting compost, and the pit transformed into a pond.

▶ If fires are allowed on site, construct a simple fire pit for those end-of-day family gatherings. Excavate a circular hole a spit or so deep and line it with 3–4 courses of bricks to form a neat ring wall. A fire of wood offcuts and dry prunings will make a safe fire, where you can bake some of your own foil-wrapped potatoes.

Children are never too young to introduce to gardening. Allocate a small plot of good soil, equip them with a few greenhouse or miniature hand tools, and provide a selection of seeds or, for faster results, young plants. Popular kinds include courgettes, onion sets, sunflowers, calendulas, nasturtiums, pumpkins and alpine strawberries.

Sloping guttering fixed to an allotment shed directs rainwater into a water butt that has been fitted with a tight lid and a tap for easy access.

Watering equipment

Changing environmental conditions mean that conserving water is becoming a priority for many, and if you need to walk any distance with a full can of mains water, making the most of what is available can be imperative.

COLLECTING & STORING Rain is the obvious source of water, apart from the site tap, and you need to arrange ways to collect it for use during dry periods. Fit guttering and downpipes to all roofs and collect the water in a butt. If possible, attach an overflow to a second container, or direct surplus water to a nearby wildlife pond. To supplement the supply, run sloping lengths of guttering along fences and walls, and leave out buckets in rainy weather. Bring from home containers of 'grey' water (domestic waste from

washing and bathing) and keep in a separate tank for watering permanent crops. Feed a pond with water from gullies, drains and overflows from water butts, and make sure it is deep enough for submerging a watering can. If the ground lies wet or waterlogged, lay drains leading to a pond or buried tank.

Water butts are often available from local authorities or discounted from the allotment site office. Substitutes include plastic dustbins, fruit barrels, old baths, discarded water tanks and cisterns and oil drums. Make sure you cover them with lids in dry weather to reduce evaporation.

....

SEE ALSO ▶ Making your own compost *pages 116–17* Managing water *pages 148–9* **Fertilizers & feeding *pages 150–1***

COMPOST BINS

The tidiest and most efficient way to make compost (see *pages 116–17*) is to assemble all the ingredients in a bin. (Having two bins is preferable, though: after you have filled one bin, leave the contents to decompose while you fill the second.) There are various kinds, from simple folding corrugated plastic squares to sophisticated models with liquid reservoirs, insulating jackets and integral top blankets. Many local authorities offer discounted bins.

Building your own compost bin is an easy and inexpensive alternative, using a simple style and waste materials. Possibilities include:

▶ wire mesh arranged round four corner stakes to make a square container, lined with cardboard for insulation.

▶ a large sturdy cardboard box with holes cut in the base and sides; this rots down with the contents.

▶ complete builder's pallets set on edge and tied or wired together; pack the cavities with newspapers or straw.

▶ a clean oil drum or plastic barrel, perforated with 2.5cm (1in) holes in the base and about halfway up the sides of the drum.

▶ a plastic dustbin raised on concrete blocks: drill holes in the base and catch the liquid in a tin.

ABOVE Having more than one compost bin is a distinct advantage, as it allows the compost to rot down thoroughly in the first bin while a second is filled with garden and household waste.

Courgette plants growing in a hot bed.

MAKING A HOT BED

Fresh manure or green waste heats up as it decays. A hot bed can use this warmth to help raise early crops and provide extra growing space later in the season. If you can get a load of fresh farmyard manure or make a new compost heap in late winter, pack the material inside a timber container (old pallet boards are ideal). Adding moist tree leaves to the manure helps to moderate the initial surge of heat and the subsequent cooling. Cover and leave to warm up for two weeks.

Spread a 10–15cm (4–6in) layer of sieved soil over the heap and top with a portable cold frame. Sow this with early radishes and carrots or turnips in rows, interplanted with young lettuces started in early winter. Pull the radishes 3–4 weeks later, leaving the lettuces to finish bulking up. When these are cleared, replace with summer cauliflower plants, and finally thin the carrots or turnips. All should be harvested in time to plant courgettes, marrows or cucumbers for summer. In the autumn, clear the plants and empty the entire contents of the hot bed for digging in.

A wire mesh bin arranged around four corner stakes. A cardboard lining would help insulate the heap and speed up decomposition.

Tools Good tools help to make light work of the allotment routine. Buy the best, use them sensitively and maintain them well, and they could give a lifetime's service; regular use will condition them until they are comfortable and familiar, like an old gardening jacket or pair of boots.

CHOOSING TOOLS Buying cheap tools is a false economy, as they rarely perform well or last long, and the experience could disillusion you. Go for top quality, and be prepared to spend money; handle the tool before buying (never buy unseen), and ask advice if you are in doubt. Test it for size, weight and balance: you need to be confident about possibly using it for long periods without tiring. Consider the materials the tool is made from. An expensive stainless steel spade is easier to use and to clean when digging clay, for example, but might be unjustifiably costly if your soil is light and sandy; a round-tined rake is more durable in stony soil than one with flat pressed tines; a trowel with a brightly painted handle is easier to find in undergrowth.

TOOL CARE
- Clean your tools regularly and particularly thoroughly before storing them for any length of time.
- Pay special attention to soil on the blades and handles, where it can set hard and cause discomfort, and sap or resin deposits on pruning tools, which can be hard to clean once dry.
- Collect up all tools and equipment at the end of each day: rain does them no good, and overlooked tools are easily lost or stolen.
- Lock them safely in your shed, in their usual places to save time searching.
- Give them a thorough service at the end of the season: clean, sharpen and oil parts as appropriate (see *page 210*).

BASIC NECESSITIES

Although allotment tools often seem to multiply over the years, you need only a simple selection of essential tools for most cultivation jobs.

▶ **SPADE** This is the main digging tool, with a full size or smaller (border) steel blade attached to a shaft of varying length, topped with a plastic or wooden T- or D-shaped handle. Metal shafts are stronger, but less sympathetic in use and they cannot be replaced if they break. For comfort, make sure the blade has a tread on both shoulders, and its neck should be made from a single forged piece of metal.

▶ **FORK** Structurally similar in other respects to a spade, this has tines instead of a blade, and is used for loosening and breaking down soil after digging, and for lifting plants. The tines should be forged from a single piece of steel for maximum strength. Some forks and spades have cranked handles or very long, straight handles for extra leverage.

▶ **HOE** There are two important types of hoe, the main weeding tool. A Dutch, or push, hoe has a flat rectangular blade

that is scuffled through the soil as you walk backwards, whereas the draw, or swan-necked, hoe, with its blade at right angles to the handle, is used with a chopping action as you move forwards. Gardeners generally disagree about which kind is the more useful. Other variations are available.

▶ **RAKE** This is a valuable tool for levelling and refining the soil. The width of the heads and length of the shafts can vary, but the most important quality is the strength of the head and tines, which should be made from forged steel. Check carefully for weight and balance, as it is difficult to manoeuvre a too-heavy rake head.

▶ **TROWEL & HAND FORK** These key hand tools are used for planting and a host of other operations. The trowel blade and fork tines are of varying shapes and sizes, and are joined to their handles by a straight or cranked neck – test which is easier to wield, check that the handle fits your palm comfortably, and make sure the

blade/tines are secured in the handle with a separate ferrule, or metal ring.

▶ **GARDEN LINE** Convenient, but easily replaced by sticks and strong twine.

▶ **WATERING CAN** Essential on plots where hosepipes cannot be used. Metal is more durable than plastic, but it is heavier and may be less comfortable for frequent use. A large can holds about 9 litres (2 gals) and a filled can will weigh around 9 kilos (20lbs), so you may prefer to choose a smaller model. A fine rose (sprinkler head) for seedlings and a coarser one for general watering should cover all needs.

▶ **GARDENING GLOVES** These are invaluable for the messier jobs and for handling prickly and stinging plants. Leather is the strongest material; choose a supple kind for easier manipulation when pruning, for example, and a stronger rigger's quality for the heaviest tasks.

USEFUL EXTRAS

Other tools can be acquired as needed, and might include the following:

▶ **WHEELBARROW** An early addition to your equipment, for moving large amounts of soil or manure.

▶ **SECATEURS, SHEARS, KNIFE** For pruning fruit and hedges.

▶ **MATTOCK** Heavy chisel-bladed hoe, easier than a spade for hard ground.

▶ **CULTIVATOR** Hand tiller with bent tines and a long or short handle.

▶ **BUCKET** Always useful for holding both solid and liquid materials.

▶ **CARRYING SHEET OR BAG** Reduces trips to the compost heap with handfuls of weeds or trimmings.

▶ **SHARPENING STONE, FILE** Essential for keeping tool edges keen.

▶ **POWER TOOLS** A rotary cultivator and hedge trimmer are both useful but they can be hired.

A garden line, spade and fork, gardening gloves, hoes and rake, trowel and hand fork and watering cans are the basic allotment tools.

Wheelbarrow, mattock and bucket.

crops for your allotment

The allotment landscape is full of all kinds of vegetables, herbs, fruit and even flowers. Choosing, planning and organizing your own personal selection of varieties to grow is an important part of ensuring success and productivity on your plot.

selecting your crops

Making a wish list The initial stages in establishing your perfect allotment all involve a certain amount of inevitability: the size of your plot, the type of soil and so on. Deciding how you are going to manage the land and plants, however, depends more on personal criteria, as does choosing what to grow, which is the subject of this chapter. The following pages will help you compile a wish list of appropriate crops and varieties from the wealth that is available.

GREENHOUSE CROPS If you have a greenhouse or cold frame, explore the possibilities for growing extra plants to mature under glass, with all the advantages of extra warmth and shelter.

You can grow many of the principal outdoor vegetables like carrots and lettuces earlier and later than you would in the open air, as well as tender crops such as cucumbers, peppers, okra and lima (butter) beans. Make sure you choose appropriate varieties: some of those used outside are dual-purpose and crop equally well (or better) under glass, but varieties that are listed only for indoor use have often been developed specifically for that purpose. Check whether these crops require additional heat, which will add to your growing costs, or merely passive protection from the elements.

Although their basic needs differ, tomatoes and cucumbers are popular and successful partners for an unheated allotment greenhouse.

HELPING YOU CHOOSE

► Compile a list of essential crops: include your favourites and any that might be expensive or elusive in shops. Add flowers for cutting and extras such as green manure or companion plants.

► Make a reserve list of plants you would grow if there is room. This could include vegetables like swedes, cabbages and maincrop potatoes that might be readily available locally; those difficult to grow well – cauliflowers or celery, for example; or crops to try for the first time.

► Match the essential list to your resources, to check that you have the space to accommodate them all, as well as enough time and energy to see to their needs. Check how long they take to mature, in case you can double-crop the space or fit in a catch- or intercrop.

► Decide if you want a long, steady harvest of a wide variety of produce, or perhaps several main flushes for freezing and storing: this will often determine which variety you choose and how much to grow. Make sure not everything matures at once.

► Go through catalogues to choose varieties. Note their qualities, especially commendations such

as the RHS Award of Garden Merit. Compare with other plot-holders, who might already have discovered the ideal variety for the local soil and climate.

The easiest vegetables to grow
Beetroot, broad beans, carrots, dwarf French beans, courgettes, kale, loose leaf lettuce (left), marrows, New Zealand spinach, perpetual spinach, ridge cucumbers, Swiss chard

Crops with the greatest yield for the least effort
Beetroot, carrots, courgettes (above), dwarf French beans, gooseberries, lettuce, parsley, tomatoes

PLANNING YOUR PLOT You will find it useful to draw up a rough plan of the plot, together with any intended rotation scheme (see *pages 32–5*) and the positions of permanent plants such as fruit and perennial herbs or vegetables. Break down your list of crops into rotation groups (brassicas, root crops and so on), so you can allocate these to particular beds, and annotate each crop with the length of time it is in the ground – remember to deduct any time that the crop spends growing under glass or in a nursery bed before being planted out.

Now use this raw information to work out the growing sequences in each bed. For example, if you have chosen a fast-

growing variety of a particular crop, you might be able to fit two or more successional sowings in the same place before the end of the season. Overwintered crops like Brussels sprouts and autumn-planted onions overlap from one year to the next, but there is usually time before and after they occupy the ground to grow a crop of something else. Identify gaps and see if you can fit in a quick catch crop, or use the space to grow a green manure.

CHIEF CROPS The variety of vegetables, fruit and herbs you could grow is enormous, but practical considerations such as time, climate and limited space inevitably mean

that you have to be very selective, concentrating first on staples and favourites, and adding a few minor or speculative crops if you have the room or inclination.

This section of the book includes the most commonly grown allotment crops in their traditional garden groups: roots (potatoes, carrots, for example), legumes (peas, beans), brassicas (cabbages, calabrese), onion family, pumpkin family

SEE ALSO ► **Crop rotation** *pages 32–5* Green manures *page 119* **Combining crops** *page 142* Growing under glass *pages 170–5* **Sowing for succession** *page 185*

(squashes, courgettes), leaves and salads (lettuce, spinach), stem and perennial vegetables (celery, asparagus) and fruiting vegetables (sweetcorn, tomatoes), together with a selection of herbs and fruit. For rotation purposes, however, the botanical grouping for certain crops may need to override popular perception – for example, most gardeners regard turnips as a root crop, whereas botanically they are brassicas.

Don't ignore marginal or less familiar crops, though: the plot is yours for growing almost anything you choose. You might like to try Asian vegetables like karella or chick peas, grains such as wild rice or bread wheat, grapes for wine-making, or those crops that are generally unobtainable in shops, for example, whitecurrants, hyacinth beans, golden raspberries, skirret or fresh fenugreek.

GROWING FOR SHOW

Rivalry is traditional on allotments and there will often be an annual show for the best produce: you have every right to be proud of a good crop and might like to consider entering a particularly outstanding sample. Growing crops for competition, however, involves dedication, careful attention to detail and even esoteric growing methods (these are widely alleged but seldom revealed). Special seed varieties, an early start under glass to ensure the longest possible growing season and lavish preparation are usually essential, as well as a knowledge of class qualifying rules in the show schedule. Winning is immensely satisfying, but it is a good idea to wait until you are experienced at raising conventional crops before venturing into this challenging field, where the size, appearance and grooming of the entry often count for more than consumer delight.

DESIRABLE QUALITIES

Even the dourest gardener looks forward to the arrival of seed and plant lists in the winter – the annual opportunity to dream and experiment. Choices on offer may seem bewildering, especially varieties of popular crops like peas, peppers and tomatoes. The best catalogues give an honest appraisal of varieties, although you sometimes need to read between the lines, especially with new, highly praised introductions. Don't readily abandon a dependable, old variety for a new, untried one; always grow it alongside for comparison first. Characteristics you might want to consider include:

Eating quality This is probably the most important characteristic, and includes flavour and texture as well as nutritional value.

Tolerance Hardiness and resistance to pests, diseases or drought all reduce the need for intervention or treatment.

Appearance We eat with our eyes, so crop size, shape and colour may be important, as are height and spread.

Time to maturity This helps you allocate space and plan early or successional sowings.

Performance Includes quick germination and predictable growth under a range of conditions.

Ease of care Self-supporting or self-blanching, easy to harvest or quick to prepare.

Adaptability Flexible sowing times or growing methods, or perhaps ability to overwinter.

Keeping time Stays good when mature or stores well.

SEE ALSO ▶ Crop rotation *pages 32–5* Sowing & planting times *pages 132–3* Keeping your plants healthy *pages 154–7* Harvesting & storing *pages 160–3*

QUICK GUIDE TO CROP GROWING TIMES

Knowing roughly how long a particular vegetable occupies the ground can help you match crops to available space and avoid leaving areas unused. Planning an ambitious growing programme may seem complicated, but sorting the various vegetables into slower crops and those that sprint to maturity can often simplify the task. First decide where to grow staples like potatoes and long-term crops such as winter leeks or sprouting broccoli, and then fit the faster ones around or between them. This table of sprinter and long-distance vegetables gives the number of months you can expect each to be in the ground, but this is an approximate guide and times can be longer or shorter depending on variety, locality and season.

SPRINTER CROPS	MONTHS IN THE GROUND	LONG-DISTANCE CROPS	MONTHS IN THE GROUND
Beans, broad	4	Beans, broad (overwintered)	8
climbing	3	Broccoli, sprouting	10
dwarf French	2–3	Brussels sprouts	6–10
runner	3–4	Cabbage, autumn	6
Beetroot	3–4	winter	8–10
Cabbage, summer	4	spring	8
Calabrese	3–4	Cauliflowers	5–8
Endive	4	Celery	6–9
Kohlrabi	3	Kale	10
Lettuce	2–3	Leeks	8–10
Onions, salad	4	Onions, maincrop	7–8
Peas	2–3	Parsnips	8
Potatoes, first early	4	Potatoes, maincrop	6–8
Radish, summer	1		
Spinach	3		
Squashes	4		

allotment story
FROM ONE COB...

Many tenants on British allotments come from all over the world, bringing with them local crops that might seem unfamiliar to their neighbours. A generation ago, novelties that are now commonplace would have included peppers, aubergines, sweetcorn, squash, mizuna, even garlic, but they have been replaced by more recent introductions such as callaloo from the Caribbean, Far Eastern rat-tail radishes and bitter gourds from the Indian subcontinent.

Interest and curiosity spread fast on an allotment site, and other plot-holders are generally keen to try any uncommon fruit or vegetable. Seed suppliers, always alert to something new, soon follow suit, with results that can be seen in their expanding and diversified catalogues.

Raising from seed is the mainstay of vegetable growing on an allotment. Every packet is a promise in the hand, each seed the simple source of a new plant from which more seeds can be saved to perpetuate a new, superior or favourite strain. Saving your own seed is the traditional way in which crops and varieties have spread from one garden or continent to another.

Charlie came to England from Jamaica decades ago, and having an allotment meant that he could grow some of his favourites from home, especially callaloo and sweetcorn. He didn't always save the seeds, but one particular year he threw out a whole cob and its grains germinated. Soon he had the best corn on site, and now he never buys seed, just saves it in time-honoured style from one year to the next.

root crops

crops for your allotment

The main root crops profiled here belong to several families, so their specific needs differ in various ways. Radishes, swedes and turnips are brassicas, sharing vulnerability to family problems like clubroot as well as a dislike of acid or dry soils. Most other roots enjoy well-broken, slightly acid soil with good drainage and fairly high nutrient residues from a previous crop, and fit well in rotations after legumes and brassicas. To avoid root distortion during transplanting, they are generally sown direct, in a deep, finely tilthed seedbed free from stones, although some varieties can be multi-sown in modules. Potatoes like rich, well-manured ground and are often planted on their own as a separate rotation course. (See also alternative root crops, *page 180*.)

Potatoes 'Maxine'

Potatoes *Solanum tuberosum*

Easy to grow and highly productive in improved soils, potatoes are an important staple on most plots and can also be used as a pioneer crop on poor or reclaimed ground. Most gardeners grow early varieties for lifting in summer for 'new' potatoes, and the same kinds can be planted after midsummer for a late crop (see also *page 199*).

Plants are raised from small, selected, certified (disease-free) tubers, or 'sets', which are started into growth indoors. The plants are not hardy and their topgrowth needs protection from frost. There are hundreds of varieties, many of them classic kinds with distinctive colours and flavours; modern kinds are often bred for disease- and pest-resistance or drought-tolerance.

HOW TO GROW Buy sets early and chit them (see *page 135*) at least 6 weeks before planting – early varieties in early spring and late summer, second earlies and maincrop kinds in late spring. Choose an open, sunny position in well-drained soil that has not been recently limed; avoid ground where potatoes were grown in the past 3 years. (Potatoes can also be grown in containers and sacks, see *page 199*.)

Plant tubers with their shoots uppermost, 10–15cm (4–6in) deep (the greater depth on light soils), in straight drills or individual holes (see *page 184* for pogo planter), and cover with soil to leave a slight ridge. First earlies can be cloched to protect and advance growth; all varieties can be planted through black polythene or a sheet mulch (see *page 122*) to avoid earthing up later.

Protect the tops from frost with soil or newspaper, and earth up stems when 15–20cm (6–8in) high by drawing soil with a hoe or rake up to half their height in a uniform ridge – this stops tubers turning green in the light. Once is enough for first earlies, but repeat with other varieties every 2–3 weeks until their tops meet. Water earlies regularly throughout, main crops once or twice when flowering begins.

Start harvesting earlies when their flowers open fully and a trial scrape reveals useful tubers: lift with a fork and continue as needed. Lift maincrops when the foliage turns brown: cut this off and wait about 2 weeks before forking up the complete crop for storing (see *page 206*).

WHEN TO PLANT Early spring (earlies) to late spring

SPACING *Earlies*: between tubers 30cm (12in), between rows 45cm (18in); *others*: between tubers 38cm (15in), between rows 75cm (30in)

TIME TO MATURITY *Earlies*: 12–14 weeks; *2nd earlies*: 15–18 weeks; *maincrop*: 18–22 weeks

HEIGHT 45–90cm (18–36in)

AVERAGE YIELD Up to 1.3kg (3lb) per plant

VARIETIES *Extra early*: 'Rocket', 'Swift'; *1st early*: 'Arran Pilot', 'Concorde', 'Pentland Javelin'; *2nd early*: 'Estima', 'Kestrel', 'Wilja'; *maincrop*: 'Cara', 'Maxine', 'Picasso'

Carrots 'Carson'

Carrots *Daucus carota*

The numerous varieties – mainly orange or red but sometimes purple, yellow or white – are divided into two main groups. Small fast-maturing ('early' or 'bunching') varieties are used for early, late (see *page 200*) and successional sowings, while maincrop kinds are larger, take longer to grow and keep well in store.

HOW TO GROW Choose warm, sheltered sites for early sowings and open, sunny positions for other kinds. Soils should be light and friable, well drained and free from larger stones, and with plenty of organic matter from a previous crop.

Sow thinly in drills, 1–2cm (½–¾in) deep, in a finely prepared seedbed, earliest and last sowings in a frame or under cloches. If carrot fly is a problem, time sowings to miss attacks or take suitable precautions (see *page 190*). Keep the soil consistently moist during germination, and water every 2–3 weeks thereafter.

Thin in stages by pinching off surplus seedlings at surface level (destroy these to avoid luring pests); weed carefully at first, and then mulch when plants have 2–3 true leaves. Pull or fork up roots when large enough, and then

firm or water the disturbed soil; clear maincrops for storing (see *page 160*) from mid-autumn onwards.

Sowing in modules For the earliest crops, sow a round variety like 'Lisa' or 'Parmex' in pots, soil blocks or modules in late winter. Sow 5–6 seeds in each cell and leave unthinned. Plant strong clusters 23cm (9in) apart each way in a frame or used growing bags indoors, or outdoors after hardening off in mid-spring (see *page 139*).

WHEN TO SOW Early spring to early autumn
GERMINATION 2–3 weeks at 7°C (45°F) minimum
SPACING *Early*: 8–10cm (3–4in); *maincrop*: 5–8cm (2–3in); all in rows 15cm (6in) apart
TIME TO MATURITY *Early*: 7–10 weeks; *maincrop*: 10–16 weeks
HEIGHT 23–38cm (9–15in)
AVERAGE YIELD 225–450g (8–16oz) per 30cm (12in) row
VARIETIES *Early*: 'Amsterdam Forcing', 'Early Nantes', 'Flyaway', 'Sytan'; *maincrop*: 'Autumn King', 'Carson', 'Favourite'

Beetroot *Beta vulgaris*

An easy crop with round, flat or tapering roots that are usually red, but also yellow, white or bicoloured. With the exception of 'monogerm' varieties like 'Solo', seeds are capsules producing several seedlings that need thinning. Choose a bolt-resistant variety for earliest sowings. For 'baby beet' grow at half the normal distance apart, or use alternate roots from maincrops, leaving the rest to mature for storing. The white variety 'Albina Vereduna' has good-flavoured leaves for use as greens; those of 'Bull's Blood' are deepest red and ornamental.

HOW TO GROW Sow outdoors in full sun for good roots and less foliage, 2cm (¾in) deep at monthly intervals from about 4 weeks before the last frosts; earlier crops can be multi-sown indoors (see *page 135*). Sow maincrops at least 12–14 weeks before autumn frosts. Thin several times, keep weed-free until large enough to mulch, and water every 2–3 weeks in dry weather. Start pulling alternate roots when 5cm (2in) across, about 2 months after sowing. Lift and store maincrops like carrots after twisting, rather than cutting, off the foliage.

WHEN TO SOW Late spring to late summer; from late winter under glass
GERMINATION 2 weeks at 7°C (45°F) minimum
SPACING 10cm (4in) in rows 23–30cm (9–12in) apart; or 15cm (6in) square
TIME TO MATURITY 8–16 weeks
HEIGHT 15–30cm (6–12in)
AVERAGE YIELD 450g (1lb) per 30cm (12in) row
VARIETIES 'Alto', 'Boltardy', 'Burpees Golden', 'Chioggia', 'Cylindra', 'Forono'

Beetroot 'Alto'

root crops

67

Radishes 'Cherry Belle'

Radishes 'Mantanghong'

Radishes *Raphanus sativus*

One of the fastest crops from seed, radishes have red, white or bicoloured roots in a range of shapes and sizes. Summer varieties with small, mildly flavoured roots are successively sown over a long season, often as a catch- or intercrop (see *page 142*); low temperature kinds like 'Ribella' and 'Saxa' are good for early and late sowings under glass. Hardy winter radishes (see *page 190*) and Japanese mooli radishes are sown in summer and can produce very large roots. Radishes are brassicas: summer kinds are soon cleared and will grow anywhere, but larger varieties should be included with other cabbage family members.

HOW TO GROW Sow small quantities 1cm (½in) deep every 2 weeks for a steady supply. Thin seedlings as early as possible, and water regularly for fast, juicy growth. (Add any surplus radish seeds to salad leaf mixtures for cutting as a seedling crop.) Pull for use when roots are large enough, and always clear sowings before they become hollow or woody. Mooli varieties take about 10 weeks to mature. Use winter radishes as needed: leave in the ground over winter or lift and store like carrots. Unripe radish seedpods are crisp and pleasantly spicy: 'München Bier' is outstanding for this purpose, with prolific, large pods.

WHEN TO SOW Early spring to late summer; winter radishes mid- to late summer

GERMINATION 3–7 days at 5°C (41°F) minimum

SPACING 2.5cm (1in) in rows 15cm (6in) apart; *winter radishes* 20cm (8in) square

TIME TO MATURITY 3–4 weeks; winter 10–12 weeks

HEIGHT 10–15cm (4–6in); winter radishes 60cm (24in)

AVERAGE YIELD 225g (8oz) per 30cm (12in) row; *winter radishes* at least double

VARIETIES 'Cherry Belle', 'French Breakfast', '(Long) White Icicle', 'Sparkler'; *winter radishes*: 'China Rose', 'Mantanghong', 'München Bier'

Parsnips *Pastinaca sativa*

This reliable winter crop with sweetly flavoured roots can reach enormous sizes on well-broken ground free from stones, although shorter varieties are better for shallow or heavy soils. Canker can be a problem, especially after damage from hoeing or on stony ground, but resistant varieties are available. Early sowings may be slow to germinate. Sow at stations (see *page 130*) and mark rows with summer radishes as a fast intercrop (see *page 142*). Frost improves flavour.

HOW TO GROW Choose a still day for sowing the light papery seeds, and sow 2cm (¾in) deep continuously in drills or at spaced stations (see *page 130*) from early spring to early summer, or later for small, single-portion roots. Thin, weed and water as for carrots. Lift with a fork when large enough to use (about 4 months after sowing); remaining roots will overwinter safely in the ground, but mark the dormant rows with canes. Clear and heel in (see *page 141*) the last of the crop as winter ends. Surplus roots make a classic country wine.

WHEN TO SOW Early spring for large roots, up to early summer
GERMINATION 2–4 weeks at 7°C (45°F)
SPACING 10–15cm (4–6in) in rows 20–30cm (8–12in) apart; or 15–20cm (6–8in) square
TIME TO MATURITY 20–35 weeks
HEIGHT 38–45cm (15–18in)
AVERAGE YIELD 450g (1lb) per 30cm (12in) row, or more.
VARIETIES 'Avonresister', 'Cobham Marrow', 'Gladiator', 'Tender & True', 'White Gem'

Parsnips 'Gladiator'

Swedes

Brassica napus Napobrassica Group
Hardier and more productive than maincrop turnips, and with a milder flavour, swedes are a rewarding autumn and winter vegetable for moist, fertile soils that do not dry out in summer. Modern varieties tend to be more robust and resistant to drought and disease than older kinds. A slow-growing brassica to grow with other family relatives.
HOW TO GROW Sow before midsummer 2cm (¾in) deep, in drills with seedlings thinned in stages to final distances, or at stations (see *page 130*), singling the seedlings to leave the best. Keep moist, especially while small, to reduce flea beetle damage. Start pulling roots while still young and firm. Keep over winter in the ground under straw or tree leaves, or lift and store like carrots – twist, don't cut, off the tops.

WHEN TO SOW Late spring and early summer
GERMINATION 6–10 days at 5°C (41°F) minimum
SPACING 23cm (9in) in rows 38cm (15in) apart
TIME TO MATURITY 20–26 weeks
HEIGHT 25–30cm (10–12in)
AVERAGE YIELD 1.3kg (3lb) per 30cm (12in) run
VARIETIES 'Acme Purple Top', 'Lizzy', 'Marian'

Turnips

Brassica campestris Rapifera Group
Varieties range from small, fast 'Tokyo Cross', which is sometimes ready in 35 days, to large maincrops for winter use; they have various shapes and skin colours with white or yellow flesh.

Turnips 'Purple Top Milan'

Good roots need moist, fertile soil and warmth. A brassica to grow with others in the family.
HOW TO GROW Sow thinly 2cm (¾in) deep in drills, every 3–4 weeks from early spring to late summer; earlier and later sowings can be made under cover. Sow hardy kinds for turnip tops in early autumn. Thin seedlings in stages and keep plants evenly moist (irregular watering causes roots to split). Start harvesting young turnips while less than 5cm (2in) across. Maincrops are left in situ or, in cold or wet soils, lifted in late autumn for storing like carrots. Turnips and swedes left in over winter can be covered with a 15cm (6in) high ridge of soil in late winter to force and blanch an early harvest of leafy tops.

WHEN TO SOW Early spring to early autumn
GERMINATION 6–10 days at 5°C (41°F) minimum
SPACING 15–23cm (6–9in) square
TIME TO MATURITY 6–12 weeks
HEIGHT 30–45cm (12–18in)
AVERAGE YIELD 450g–1kg (1–2lbs) per 30cm (12in) run
VARIETIES 'Golden Ball', 'Purple Top Milan', 'Snowball', 'Tokyo Cross'

legumes

Leguminous vegetables like peas and beans are productive crops, extolled by nutritionists for their high protein value and by enlightened gardeners for their ability to transfer nitrogen from the atmosphere to the soil. The process is carried out by nitrifying bacteria that live in small swellings, or 'nodules', on the roots – for this reason exhausted plants are always cut off at ground level so the roots can decay and enrich the soil. For best results, the bacteria need slightly alkaline surroundings, and acid soils should be limed before growing pulses. They all prefer good drainage and deeply worked sites, with plenty of humus worked in to keep roots cool and prevent them from drying out.

Garden peas *Pisum sativum*

There are countless varieties of podding peas, with green or purple pods and a range of heights from very dwarf ('Meteor', 'Little Marvel') to very tall ('Alderman'). They are divided into two groups: round-seeded kinds, which are the hardiest and best for early sowings and for overwintering under cloches; and those with wrinkled seeds, which are sweeter and used for maincrop and successional sowings. All kinds support themselves with tendrils; leafless and semi-leafless types have many more tendrils replacing some of their foliage. They all benefit from support, dwarf kinds on netting or twiggy sticks, and tall varieties – which make the most productive use of space – on bean poles or tall canes covered with net or strings.

HOW TO GROW Plan varieties and sowing schedules according to your needs (see *page 179*); to help estimate quantities, 50g (2oz) will sow 3m (10ft) of a 23cm (9in) wide row. Choose a position in full sun, or slight shade for summer sowings. Sow round varieties in early spring, followed a month later by a wrinkled variety sown at 3–4 week intervals until midsummer, ending with a mildew-resistant variety like 'Kelvedon Wonder'. Sow a round variety again in late autumn to cloche over winter; in cold areas sow instead in late

Garden peas 'Twinkle'

winter indoors in degradable pots or lengths of guttering (see *page 179*).

Space seeds evenly in drills or wide bands, and protect from birds with wire netting. Provide support when the first tendrils appear, and mulch when plants are 15cm (6in) high. Water when dry, every week from the time flowers appear. Start harvesting when pods are well filled but before they lose their surface bloom, and pick regularly to ensure continued flowering. Crops for drying are left until all the pods mature (see *page 204*).

The grubs of the pea moth can sometimes spoil a whole crop. Prevent this by covering flowering plants with fleece during midsummer, when the moth is on the wing; earlier and later sowings usually escape trouble. To deter mice from excavating the seeds, cover the crops with holly leaves after sowing.

WHEN TO SOW Early spring to early summer, and late autumn
GERMINATION 2–3 weeks at 10°C (50°F) minimum
SPACING 8–10cm (3–4in) in rows 45–60cm (18–24in) apart
TIME TO MATURITY 12–16 weeks; autumn-sown 30–34 weeks
HEIGHT 30–150cm (1–5ft)
AVERAGE YIELD 450g–1kg (1–2lbs) per 30cm (12in) run
VARIETIES 'Douce Provence', 'Early Onward', 'Greenshaft', 'Kelvedon Wonder', 'Little Marvel', 'Twinkle'

OTHER PEA CROPS

MANGETOUT & SUGAR PEAS Varieties like flat-podded 'Carouby de Mausanne' and crisp, round-podded 'Sugar Snap' are grown for their edible, immature pods, although a few ('Delikata', for example) are still usable when their seeds are large enough to shell. Sow and grow in the same way as podding peas, but harvest mangetout pods while the seeds are barely visible, and sugar peas while their pods still snap cleanly. (The pods of 'Norli', pictured, are ready for picking.) Mangetout varieties are hardy enough to sow in autumn for overwintering.

ASPARAGUS PEA This prostrate annual has rich red flowers and small, fluted pods, which are picked while still immature and about 4cm (1½in) long for steaming whole. A minor crop for groundcover.

LENTILS & CHICK PEAS These pea crops need large areas to be worthwhile, but they are easy to grow if sown after the last frosts, and make excellent summer green manure crops.

DUN, GREY & MAPLE (PARTRIDGE) PEAS These field varieties of garden pea are occasionally grown for drying or for a green manure.

French beans *Phaseolus vulgaris*

Also known as kidney, snap, string or common bean, this is perhaps the most widely cultivated bean in the world. Varieties may have green, yellow, purple or mottled pods, which are flat or round ('pencil-podded'); some are grown for drying as haricot beans (see *page 204*), others for harvesting while small and slim (filet beans). Repeated sowings at 3–4 week intervals will ensure a succession of pods all season. The plants are tender with fragile foliage, so need sunny sheltered positions, and prefer light, rich soil; they tolerate drier, poorer conditions than runner beans.

HOW TO GROW Grow climbing kinds like runner beans (see *page 72*). Sow dwarf varieties 4–5cm (1½–2in) deep, indoors in pots 3–4 weeks before the last frosts, or direct from late spring (under cloches) until midsummer. Mulch plants after earthing up stems for stability, and support the topgrowth with twiggy sticks. Water regularly, especially when flowering starts. Pick beans while still young – they should snap cleanly; cropping continues for 6–8 weeks.

WHEN TO SOW Late spring to late summer; earlier under glass

GERMINATION 10–14 days at 12°C (54°F) minimum

SPACING 10cm (4in) in rows 45cm (18in) apart; *climbers*: as for runner beans

TIME TO MATURITY 8–12 weeks

HEIGHT Dwarf 30–45cm (12–18in); climbers 3m (10ft)

AVERAGE YIELD 112–225g (4–8oz) per plant; *climbers*: double

VARIETIES 'Blue Lake', 'Cobra', 'Delinel', 'Dutch Brown', 'Hunter' 'Montano', 'Purple Tepee'

French beans 'Delinel'

Runner beans

Phaseolus coccineus

A popular and decorative tender perennial, grown as an annual, with red, pink, white or bicoloured flowers and flattened pods up to 60cm (2ft) long; some varieties are stringless if they are picked young. Tall, climbing varieties are the most prolific, while dwarf kinds crop earlier. They are deep-rooting plants for well-cultivated, manured soil and warm, sheltered positions, and need sturdy support for their lush, heavy topgrowth. Climbing French beans are grown in the same way (see *page 71*).

HOW TO GROW Sow 5cm (2in) deep, indoors in pots a month before the last frost or in situ in late spring or early summer. Erect strong canes or poles as wigwams or pairs of parallel rows before sowing or planting. Mulch while plants are small and water regularly, especially after flower buds appear. Pinch out growing tips at the tops of canes. For a really lavish crop, allow twice as much space between canes and grow 2 plants at each; pinch out growing tips at 60cm (2ft) high and again at 1.2m (4ft) to stimulate a mass of productive sideshoots. Dwarf varieties are naturally bushy, but you can pinch out tall kinds when plants are 30cm (12in) high; pinch the tips of sideshoots every 7–10 days. Keep the pods off the soil by supporting growth with twiggy sticks. Harvest pods when 15–20cm (6–8in) long, and check for more every 2–3 days (pods left to ripen suppress flowering); surplus pods can be frozen, and the ripe beans dry well for soups. Early sowings may be reluctant to set their flowers (see *pages 198–9*) and do not crop as heavily as those sown to flower in late summer.

Runner beans 'Wisley Magic'

Runner beans 'Scarlet Emperor'

WHEN TO SOW Late spring and early summer

GERMINATION 7–10 days at 12°C (54°F) minimum

SPACING 15cm (6in) in double rows 60cm (24in) apart

TIME TO MATURITY 12–16 weeks

HEIGHT Up to 3m (10ft) or more

AVERAGE YIELD 1–1.3kg (2–3lbs) per plant

VARIETIES 'Desiree', 'Enorma', 'Pickwick', 'Scarlet Emperor', 'White Lady', 'Wisley Magic'

Broad beans *Vicia faba*

A prolific cool season crop, with long pods (edible while young) and highly nutritious seeds that vary in number according to type: slightly less hardy but tastier Windsor kinds have 2–5 beans per pod, while Longpods contain up to 11 smaller seeds. The leguminous roots are a good source of nitrogen after cropping, and surplus ripe seeds can be sown in autumn or spring for green manure. The flowers have an intense heady fragrance (drowsing in a bean field was once considered ill-advised).

HOW TO GROW Choose full sun for spring sowings, a sheltered spot with good drainage for autumn ones. Start sowing in late winter or early spring, and repeat twice at monthly intervals; a hardy variety like 'Aquadulce' can be sown in late autumn to overwinter for earliest pickings. Sow in situ 5cm (2in) deep, or in pots in a frame for the first sowings in cold areas. Cover with fleece or cloches in cold or late winters.

Earth up tall varieties and support individually with strong canes or enclose blocks of plants with stakes and string. Mulch after soils warm in spring and water whenever dry – plants dislike drought as much as heat. Pinch off tips when plants are flowering well and the first pods are set, to hasten maturity and help deter aphids. Pick 5–8cm (2–3in) pods to cook whole, or leave for shelling while seeds are plump but not yet leathery. Freeze any surplus or let seeds ripen for drying.

WHEN TO SOW Early and late spring (earlier under glass), and late autumn and early winter
GERMINATION 10–14 days, below 15°C (60°F)
SPACING 25cm (10in) square
TIME TO MATURITY 12–15 weeks; autumn-sown 26–30 weeks
HEIGHT 60–120cm (2–4ft)
AVERAGE YIELD 225–450g (8–16oz) per plant; higher if pods used
VARIETIES 'Aquadulce', 'Express', 'Jubilee Hysor', 'Red Epicure', 'The Sutton', 'Witkiem Manita'

Broad beans 'Express'

OTHER BEAN CROPS

LIMA (BUTTER) BEANS Heat-loving crop that needs at least 80 days' growth above 18°C (65°F). Dwarf and climbing varieties do well in polytunnels.

BLACKEYE BEANS (SOUTHERN PEA) Slightly faster crop for warm sites and light soils. Most varieties make upright bushes.

PEA BEANS Climbing bean with brown and white bicoloured seeds. Use whole pods like French beans; shell immature seeds as flageolets or dry like haricots.

YARD-LONG BEANS Climbing blackeye bean relative, with slim pods up to 1m (39in) long, but usually less. Sow early in pots and train on strings under glass.

LABLABS (HYACINTH BEAN) Vigorous twining perennial, grown as an annual under glass. Leaves, pods, immature and ripe seeds are all edible. Needs heat.

SOYA BEANS Need a large area for a useful seed harvest, but an early bush variety like 'Envy' will produce plenty of pods for using green.

BORLOTTO BEANS Beautiful Italian bean with mottled cream and red pods ripening mid- to late season. Fine flavour as fresh snap beans, or dry for storage.

Borlotto beans 'Rob Roy'

brassicas

The cabbage family includes a vast and diverse collection of staple crops, from the simple rape plant that often comprises the 'mustard' of mustard and cress to the complex cauliflower (the white head, or 'curd', is a mass of aborted flower buds), which is possibly the most challenging green vegetable to grow well. Just one species, *Brassica oleracea*, has mutated over thousands of years from the ancestral weedy kale into Brussels sprouts, kohlrabi, calabrese, cauliflowers and all the various modern kinds of cabbage.

Because they are closely related, brassicas all enjoy similar conditions and are grown together in the same bed or rotation step (see *pages 32–5*). They are cool weather crops, often bolting in hot dry weather, and like moist, rich, firm soils and alkaline conditions: pH7.2 or higher. Virtually indistinguishable as seeds and seedlings (label rows clearly!), most are sown in a nursery bed first; brassica root crops like turnips, swedes and radishes (see *pages 68–9*) are sown direct, however, as are summer batches of calabrese to avoid root disturbance and subsequent bolting. All respond to consistent watering every 7–10 days in dry weather, and are equally susceptible to problems such as clubroot disease (see *page 185*).

Several common pests target all brassicas. Surround the stems of transplants with felt or paper mats against cabbage root fly. Covering the crop with fleece protects plants from butterflies, or you can pick off the

Summer cabbage 'Hotspur'

caterpillars when seen. Slugs and snails relish seedlings and transplants, so take precautions (see *pages 154–5* and *178*). Aphids and white fly can be sprayed with insecticidal soap every 3–4 weeks after they are first seen. In some areas you might have to net crops in winter against pigeons.

Cabbage

Brassica oleracea Capitata Group

You can easily have cabbages all year round if you so wish, and they may be smooth-leaved or savoy, hearted or leafy, and green, red or white. The numerous varieties are grouped into different types according to their

season of use, although these often overlap. Where space is precious, it makes sense to choose compact varieties that stand well when mature. F1 hybrids are more uniform and predictable, often with built-in pest- and disease-resistance, while more variable older kinds are worth exploring for their flavour, hardiness or other outstanding quality.

HOW TO GROW Sow 2–2.5cm (¾–1in) deep in situ or, more usually, in a nursery bed, and thin or transplant to 8cm (3in) apart; plant out when 6–8 weeks old (see *page 190*), with 4–6 leaves. Early sowings can be made under glass for pricking out into pots or modules; harden off well before transplanting to final positions outside.

Choose an open sunny position sheltered from cold winds, and prepare the ground by digging in plenty of compost or well-rotted manure to bolster fertility and moisture retention. Leave for several weeks to settle, or firm by light treading just before planting. Lime individual positions at planting time or complete beds at least 6 weeks before or after manuring.

SPRING CABBAGES

These are popular and welcome varieties that grow over winter for use when little else is available, either as well-flavoured leafy greens from late winter onwards or as headed cabbages from around mid-spring. Choose varieties carefully: many produce only greens or heads, while others are dual-purpose; some can be sown in spring for summer crops, and others such as 'Duncan' are versatile all-year-round cabbages. Maincrops are sown in two batches a month apart for transplanting in early and mid-autumn. Plant dual-purpose kinds at the closest spacing and thin for greens, leaving every third plant to heart up. Net against birds in winter and early spring.

For a very late spring crop, sow in early autumn in a cold frame and plant out in early spring. Sow all-year kinds in early spring for summer cutting, early summer for autumn, and late summer for winter and spring use. For extra 'spring greens', see *page 214*.

WHEN TO SOW Mid- to late summer
GERMINATION 1–2 weeks at 5°C (41°F) minimum
SPACING 10–15cm (4–6in) for greens, 30cm (12in) for heads, in rows 30cm (12in) apart
TIME TO MATURITY 20–35 weeks
HEIGHT 25–38cm (10–15in)
AVERAGE YIELD 450g–1.5kg (1–4lb) per plant
VARIETIES 'Dorado', 'Duncan', 'Durham Early', 'Pixie', 'Spring Hero'; *greens only:* 'Wintergreen'

SUMMER CABBAGES
Fast, non-hardy plants with small juicy heads; earliest varieties are usually pointed and leafy, later kinds round and dense. Although they are the sweetest and mildest of the cabbages, all but the first sowings tend to be ready at the same time as peas, beans and other summer crops, so don't grow too many unless they are a favourite. Start pulling heads when they feel firm and hearty, or cut to leave 5–8cm (2–3in) stumps that resprout if you cut a cross 1cm (⅜in) deep on top.

WHEN TO SOW Early spring (late winter under glass)
GERMINATION 1–2 weeks at 5°C (41°F) minimum
SPACING 35–45cm (14–18in) square
TIME TO MATURITY 20 weeks
HEIGHT 25–38cm (10–15in)
AVERAGE YIELD 450g–1.5kg (1–4lb) per plant
VARIETIES 'Derby Day', 'Golden Acre', 'Greyhound', 'Hispi', 'Hotspur', 'Kingspi', 'Minicole'

AUTUMN CABBAGES
Cabbages for autumn use include slow-growing summer varieties like 'Stonehead' or earlier ones sown for succession, true autumn kinds like 'Winnigstadt', red and savoy cabbages, and the earliest hardy winter kinds such as 'Christmas Drumhead'. As a rough guide, autumn cabbages are sown and transplanted about 4 weeks later than summer types, and are grown in the same way. Pay special attention to watering during mid- and late summer. Harvest any remaining heads in late autumn and keep them cool and dry in boxes of straw for use in winter. Sow a hardy red variety in early autumn in a cold frame and plant out in early spring to cut in summer.

WHEN TO SOW Early to mid-spring
GERMINATION 1–2 weeks at 5°C (41°F) minimum
SPACING 45cm (18in) square
TIME TO MATURITY 26–30 weeks
HEIGHT 25–38cm (10–15in)
AVERAGE YIELD 450g–1.5kg (1–4lb) per plant
VARIETIES 'Minicole', 'Stonehead', 'Winnigstadt'; *savoy:* 'Clarissa'; *red:* 'Hardora', 'Marnier Early Red', 'Ruby Ball'

Autumn cabbage 'Marnier Early Red'

WINTER CABBAGES
These are large, solid hardy varieties that stand well for many weeks. They include savoy and savoy/white hybrids, maincrop red cabbages like 'Red Dutch' and 'Hardora', as well as hard white cabbages that store well on shelves or in nets in a shed. Plant very firmly to prevent disturbance from wind and frost, and in exposed areas earth up stems for extra stability. Pull as needed, and do not leave roots in the ground.

WHEN TO SOW Late spring
GERMINATION 1–2 weeks at 5°C (41°F) minimum.
SPACING 50–60cm (20–24in) square
TIME TO MATURITY 30–35 weeks
HEIGHT 25–38cm (10–15in)
AVERAGE YIELD 450g–1.5kg (1–4lb) per plant
VARIETIES 'Christmas Drumhead', 'Holland Winter White', 'January King', 'Tundra'; *savoy:* 'Celtic', 'Tarvoy'

ABOVE Cauliflower 'Violetta Italia'
RIGHT Cauliflower 'Romanesco'

Cauliflowers

Brassica oleracea Botrytis Group

This fussy, greedy crop can be a triumph on heavy ground if given lashings of manure, but it will break hearts where the soil is light or impoverished. Summer-heading varieties give the best return – especially if they are sown little and often, starting early indoors – whereas winter kinds (broccoli, or 'brocs') need wider spacing and a much longer growing period, and do well only in mild areas (elsewhere they hold back until spring before heading up). The solid curds are usually white, but may be purple, creamy yellow or green (romanesco types).

HOW TO GROW Start early summer varieties under glass in late winter, prick out into pots, and plant out in early spring. Sow main summer crops at 2-week intervals from early to late spring; sow winter varieties in late spring. Make these outdoor sowings in a nursery bed and plant out while the stems are still green and supple. Plant very firmly, water generously every 10–14 days, and mulch. As the heads form, break some of the outer leaves over the curds to shield them from the sun or frost. Batches often mature together, so start cutting heads while small and tight, and freeze any that break apart or deteriorate.

WHEN TO SOW Early spring to early summer; also autumn for early summer

GERMINATION 1–2 weeks at 5°C (41°F) minimum

SPACING 50–60cm (20–24in) square

TIME TO MATURITY *Summer*: 16–20 weeks; *winter*: 40–50 weeks

HEIGHT 30–45cm (12–18in)

AVERAGE YIELD 450g–1kg (1–2lb) per plant

VARIETIES *Summer*: 'Alpha Polaris', 'Snowball', 'Romanesco', 'Violetta Italia'; *winter*: 'Markanta', 'Purple Cape', 'Snowcap', 'Vilna'

ORIENTAL GREENS

There is a host of Asian greens to explore, most with a more delicate flavour than Western brassicas, which suits them to stir frying, steaming and eating raw. They mature fast, often when only 5–6 weeks old. The majority are sown after the longest day, in situ for thinning to about 15cm (6in) apart.

CHINESE BROCCOLI (OR KALE) Edible stems and flowers like sprouting broccoli 2 months after sowing. 'Green Lance' can be sown in late spring.

Mizuna

Mustard greens

KOMATSUNA A leafy cabbage or mustard spinach to grow as a seedling crop for repeated cutting, or 30cm (12in) apart to make large heads after 10 weeks.

MIZUNA Decorative leaves for salads and stir fries. Sow spring to autumn for year-round use; grow winter crops in frames.

MUSTARD GREENS Fringed loose-leaf plants to sow spring to autumn. Picked young, the leaves are pleasantly spicy; older ones are pungent.

PAK CHOI Loose-headed celery mustard with spoon-shaped leaves and pronounced midribs to use like chard (see *page 93*). 'Joy Choi' is outstanding.

Pak choi

Chinese cabbages

Brassica rapa var. *pekinensis*

These are mostly short-day crops that tend to bolt if sown much before the longest day of the year. They grow very fast to produce heavy, dense heads that may be cooked or eaten raw like a large cos lettuce.

HOW TO GROW As these plants resent root disturbance, sow them direct for thinning, or in modules and degradable pots. A late summer sowing in a cold frame will often stand all winter. Cut as needed and protect late crops from frost with cloches.

WHEN TO SOW Early and late summer

GERMINATION 1–2 weeks at 5°C (41°F) minimum

SPACING 30cm (12in) square

TIME TO MATURITY 6–10 weeks

HEIGHT 25–38cm (10–15in)

AVERAGE YIELD 450g–1.5kg (1–4lb) per plant

VARIETIES 'Green Rocket', 'Kasumi', 'Nagaoka', 'Tip Top', 'Wong Bok'

Chinese cabbage 'Wong Bok'

Brussels sprouts

Brassica oleracea Gemmifera Group

By choosing a range of varieties you can pick sprouts from early autumn (or earlier, see *page 200*) until mid-spring, and have the leafy tops for 'greens' as a bonus. Plants of a traditional open-pollinated variety mature unevenly, which can spread the harvest; F1 hybrids are more predictable and stand better on light soils. Red varieties such as 'Red Bull' and 'Rubine' are handsome, with a subtly different flavour and less appeal to pigeons, which select food by looks rather than taste. A hardy, robust crop that dislikes warmer climates, where winter varieties sown in early autumn tend to do best.

HOW TO GROW Sow in a nursery bed, spacing early, maincrop and late sowings about 2 weeks apart. Transplant very firmly into fertile ground (but not too rich, or loose leafy sprouts will result). Water occasionally in dry weather, and in autumn earth up or stake stems on windy sites. Remove yellow leaves and watch out for insect pests, which tend to target this crop. Start harvesting sprouts from the bottom when large enough, snapping them off cleanly and removing leaves as you pick.

WHEN TO SOW Early to late spring
GERMINATION 1–2 weeks at 5°C (41°F) minimum
SPACING 60cm (24in) square
TIME TO MATURITY 20–36 weeks
HEIGHT 45–120cm (18–48in)
AVERAGE YIELD 1–1.3kg (2–3lb) per plant
VARIETIES 'Brilliant', 'Cromwell', 'Early Half Tall', 'Montgomery', 'Seven Hills', 'Wellington'; *red*: 'Red Bull'

Brussels sprouts 'Montgomery'

Calabrese

Brassica oleracea Italica Group

A fast, non-hardy green broccoli that is grown for summer and early autumn use. For large heads, choose a selection or mixture of F1 hybrids to give an extended harvest; older kinds, especially 'Green Sprouting', produce a long succession of smaller secondary spears. As plants resent root disturbance, either sow direct and thin seedlings, or start indoors in pots or modules. Very early sowings usually escape caterpillars, but later crops are best covered with fleece for protection. 'Trixie' is naturally tolerant of club root.

HOW TO GROW Make early sowings 6–8 weeks before the last frost, prick out in pots and plant out in mid-spring under cloches or fleece. Sow later batches in situ up to early summer; sow an early kind in late summer or early autumn in a frame for early spring crops. Always sow pinches of seed at stations (see *page 130*) and then thin the seedlings to one survivor.

Water well every 2 weeks, and mulch. Cut central heads while still tight and unopened; then feed to encourage sideshoots for cutting when 10–13cm (4–5in) long.

WHEN TO SOW Early spring to early summer, also early autumn
GERMINATION 1–2 weeks at 5°C (41°F) minimum
SPACING 15–23cm (6–9in) in rows 30cm (12in) apart
TIME TO MATURITY 10–15 weeks
HEIGHT 38–60cm (15–24in)
AVERAGE YIELD 450g–1kg (1–2lb) per plant
VARIETIES 'Fiesta', '(Italian) Green Sprouting', 'Kabuki', 'Marathon', 'Monteray', 'Trixie'

Sprouting broccoli

Brassica oleracea Italica Group

This popular and hardy calabrese relative is sown one spring to crop the next, when the large plants produce masses of tasty white- or purple-flowering shoots at a time when other vegetables are scarce. Extend the season by growing two or more varieties, and try some newer kinds: 'Rudolph' and 'Garnet' crop from early winter, 'Claret' starts heading very late, and 'Bordeaux' will crop all summer and autumn from spring sowings. Make the best use of space by growing plants at full spacings with an intercrop of summer cabbages or cauliflowers.

HOW TO GROW Sow in batches in a nursery bed, starting with the earliest kinds, and transplant very firmly with lowest leaves at soil level. Water regularly, mulch, and earth up or stake stems in autumn in windy positions; net against birds in winter. Harvest the first shoots when 10–15cm (4–6in)

ABOVE Curly kale 'Redbor'
LEFT Broccoli 'Purple Sprouting'

long, and feed with general fertilizer: more shoots will appear for 6–8 weeks if plants are not allowed to flower.

WHEN TO SOW Mid- to late spring
GERMINATION 1–2 weeks at 5°C (41°F) minimum
SPACING 60–75cm (24–30in) square
TIME TO MATURITY 40 weeks
HEIGHT 90–120cm (3–4ft)
AVERAGE YIELD 450g–1kg (1–2lb) per plant
VARIETIES 'Bordeaux', 'Claret', 'Garnet', 'Purple Sprouting', 'Rudolph', 'White Sprouting'

Kale

Brassica oleracea Acephala Group
Sometimes called borecole, this is possibly the hardiest of winter greens, and certainly the best for poor soils.

Plain-leaved varieties such as 'Thousandhead' are grown for their young shoots, ready from late winter onwards, while the young leaves of curly kinds can be used from autumn onwards.

HOW TO GROW Sow, plant and grow like sprouting broccoli. Plants are rarely affected by pests or diseases.

WHEN TO SOW Late spring
GERMINATION 1–2 weeks at 5°C (41°F) minimum
SPACING 30–60cm (12–24in)
TIME TO MATURITY 26–40 weeks
HEIGHT 45–120cm (18–48in)
AVERAGE YIELD 1–1.3kg (2–3lb) per plant, or more
VARIETIES '(Dwarf) Green Curled', 'Nero di Toscana', 'Pentland Brig', 'Thousandhead', 'Winterbor'; *red*: 'Redbor'

OTHER FORMS OF KALE

KOHLRABI (*Brassica oleracea* Gongylodes Group) A curious form of kale, with a green or purple, turnip-like thickened stem that sprouts leaves on its upper surface. Grow quickly like turnips, sowing from early spring to late summer. Thin to 23cm (9in) square or 15cm (6in) apart in rows between taller brassicas. Harvest 8–10 weeks after sowing when stems are about the size of a tennis ball.

JERSEY WALKING STICK (*Brassica oleracea* Acephala Group) This giant kale variety grows 1.8m (6ft) in its first year, up to 3m (10ft) the following season. Sow in late spring like ordinary kale, harvest younger leaves throughout the season, and cut down in the second winter. Dry the stems to use as garden stakes, or trim and varnish them to make walking sticks.

onion family

Members of the onion family (Alliaceae) all have a distinctive, sometimes pungent flavour, and tall drumstick flower heads that attract bees and make long-lasting cut or dried flowers. They like well-drained, settled and fairly fertile ground, and prefer light or medium neutral soils to clay and acid conditions. Although they are often grown successfully in the same place each year, rotating them as a separate group or with legumes (see *pages 32–5*) is a sound precaution against fungal diseases. Choose sunny open sites, avoid lavish feeding, and keep well weeded because the slim foliage cannot shade out competing weeds.

Bulbing onions *Allium cepa*

These need a long growing season: the more leaves a plant has in the first half of its season, the larger its bulb will be. Maincrop varieties are started in spring (mid-winter for exhibition bulbs and where seasons are short) and ripen from midsummer for autumn harvest and storage until the next spring. Overwintered and Japanese kinds are sown or planted in late summer for use over 2–3 summer months the following year. Final spacings influence size, so grow at the widest distances for large bulbs.

HOW TO GROW Sow under glass and prick out into modules for planting out when they have two true leaves, or sow in situ and thin in 2–3 stages, using thinnings as salad onions. (It is best to prick out onion seedlings while they are still small and looped over – the 'hairpin' stage – because once the stems straighten up, the roots can be long and difficult to transplant undamaged.) Instead of sowing under glass, plant onion sets (miniature bulbs that have already made several weeks' growth), burying these so their tips barely show, which prevents birds uprooting them. Water and feed spring-sown crops regularly until midsummer, when the bulbs can be allowed to ripen naturally (overfeeding shortens storage life); feed overwintered bulbs once in early spring.

Onions 'Red Baron'

Onions 'Sturon'

I et the tops die down before lifting bulbs carefully with a fork to avoid causing any damage. Dry on the surface of the ground or under glass until the skins are papery (see *page 196*), and then store in cool but frost-free conditions on shelves, in nets or plaited in strings.

WHEN TO SOW/PLANT Early and late spring, and late summer
GERMINATION 2–3 weeks at 7°C (45°F)
SPACING 5–10cm (2–4in) in rows 30cm (12in) apart
TIME TO MATURITY *Spring-sown*: 16–22 weeks; *overwintered*: 40–46 weeks
HEIGHT 45–60cm (18–24in)
AVERAGE YIELD 450g (1lb) per 30cm (12in) run
VARIETIES 'Balaton', 'Bedfordshire Champion', '(The) Kelsae', 'Owa', 'Sturon', 'Turbo'; *red-skinned*: 'Long Red Florence', 'Red Baron'; *Japanese and overwintered varieties*: 'Radar', 'Senshyu Yellow'

Shallots

Allium cepa Aggregatum Group

These are multiplier onions with a distinctive flavour both fresh and pickled. They are easy to grow, from seed (sown like ordinary onions to produce a single solid bulb) and also as sets, each of which splits into several new ones.

HOW TO GROW Shallots need a long growing season and are traditionally planted on the shortest day for harvest after the longest day, or in late winter for colder regions and heavy soils. Treat in the same way as bulbing onions. Harvest when leaves start to die back, drying the clusters on the soil surface for a few days before separating and storing. Bulbs from healthy plants can be saved and replanted the next season.

WHEN TO SOW/PLANT Early winter to early spring
SPACING 20cm (8in) square, or 15cm (6in) in rows 23cm (9in) apart
TIME TO MATURITY 26 weeks
HEIGHT 38–40cm (15–16in)
AVERAGE YIELD 8–12 bulbs per planted set; 1 bulb per seedling
VARIETIES 'Hative de Niort', 'Pikant'; *spring planting only*: 'Golden Gourmet', 'Sante'; *seed*: 'Ambition'

Shallots 'Golden Gourmet'

Leeks *Allium porrum*

An easily grown and mildly flavoured crop that can be left in the ground for autumn and winter harvest as required. Slim, fast-growing varieties are available for early use, while hardier kinds mature from early winter onwards. Like onions, spacing affects size and at the closest distances plants make mini-leeks like salad onions. Plants enjoy moist soils with plenty of humus, but good drainage is vital for winter crops.

HOW TO GROW Sow early varieties under glass and prick out singly, or multi-sow in modules and transplant clusters intact; sow later maincrops in a seed bed and transplant when pencil-thickness. Mini-leeks are sown direct and thinned to 2cm (¾in) apart. Transplant into dibber holes 15cm (6in) deep (see *page 191*), dropping a seedling in each; water in but do not refill the hole with soil, as the leek stem swells to fit this. Water regularly in dry weather, and mulch to keep plants moist.

WHEN TO SOW Spring
GERMINATION 2–3 weeks at 7°C (45°F) minimum
SPACING 8–15cm (3–6in) in rows 30cm (12in) apart
TIME TO MATURITY 26–40 weeks according to variety
HEIGHT 30–45cm (12–18in)
AVERAGE YIELD 450g (1lb) per 30cm (12in) run
VARIETIES *Early*: 'King Richard', 'Startrack', 'Titan'; *maincrop*: 'Alcazar', 'Autumn Mammoth', 'Musselburgh'; *late*: 'Apollo', 'Natan', 'St Victor'

Leeks 'Musselburgh'

Salad onions 'White Lisbon'

Salad (spring) onions
Allium cepa

Also known as bunching onions or scallions, these crops grow fast and may be used as an intercrop for harvest almost all year from successional sowings. Older salad varieties eventually form small bulbs that can be pickled, but plants are usually harvested while young for their slim white or red stems. True pickling onions are sown in late spring and left to grow until the foliage turns yellow. Sow salad varieties every 3–4 weeks from early spring, ending with a winter-hardy variety in late summer. Thin if necessary to 2.5cm (1in) apart, and start harvesting when 15cm (6in) high, pulling alternate plants to let others develop.

WHEN TO SOW/PLANT Early spring to late summer
GERMINATION 2–3 weeks at 7°C (45°F)
SPACING Unthinned in drills or 8cm (3in) wide bands 15cm (6in) apart
TIME TO MATURITY 8–10 weeks
HEIGHT 15–30cm (6–12in)
VARIETIES 'Crimson Forest', 'Guardsman', 'Ishikura', 'Ramrod', 'White Lisbon', 'White Lisbon Winter Hardy'

Garlic *Allium sativum*
An easy crop, provided you choose a planting variety that suits your locality's day length and typical temperatures (bulbs bought for eating are often from hot regions, and may also carry virus diseases). Each planted clove develops into a new bulb. For large bulbs, garlic needs several weeks' cold conditioning, so cloves are usually planted in autumn (in pots where soils are heavy or wet), although some varieties prefer spring planting. Four bulbs provide enough cloves for a 3m (10ft) run.
HOW TO GROW Plant cloves point uppermost 5–10cm (2–4in) deep, the greater depth for light soils, and grow like onion sets. Harvest when leaf tips yellow, lifting carefully with a fork and drying and storing like onions. Healthy bulbs saved for replanting will adapt to your conditions over several years.

WHEN TO PLANT Late winter and early spring, and late autumn
SPACING 15cm (6in) square, or 10cm (4in) in rows 30cm (12in) apart
TIME TO MATURITY 24–36 weeks
HEIGHT 60cm (2ft)
VARIETIES 'Cristo', 'Solent Wight', 'Thermidrome'; *spring planting*: 'Printanor'

Garlic 'Solent Wight'

pumpkin family

The Cucurbitaceae, which is the botanical name for the pumpkin or gourd family, includes squashes, courgettes, marrows, cucumbers and melons. They are all tender, fleshy fruits that come from hot climates, and share a love of warm and lavish growing conditions.

Squashes

Cucurbita species & hybrids

The term 'summer squashes' usually applies to immature soft-skinned fruits that are eaten fresh, while 'winter squashes' have darker, more strongly flavoured flesh and hard, ripened skins for long storage. There are bush, trailing and semi-trailing varieties. Trailing kinds may be grown as groundcover between tall vegetables or on top of compost heaps; they also look decorative when stems are trained up trellis, wigwams and arches.

RIGHT **Squash 'Butternut'**
FAR RIGHT **Squash 'Crown Prince'**

HOW TO GROW Prepare individual planting sites by digging out a hole 45cm (18in) deep and wide. Mix the excavated soil with a large bucketful of compost or rotted manure. Refill the hole, leaving the surface gently mounded for good drainage.

Sow seeds on edge, 1cm (½in) deep in 8cm (3in) pots, about 4–5 weeks before frosts end, and germinate at 15–18°C (60–65°F). Harden off and plant out after the last frosts, no deeper than the plants were previously. Cover with cloches if cold. Pinch out growing tips of trailing kinds when 30–38cm (12–15in) high to stimulate sideshoots. Mulch plants when large enough, and water every week in dry weather. (See also *pages 191–2*.) Pull up and destroy plants with the yellow leaf streaks and mottling of virus.

Harvest summer squashes when they are large enough for use (about 8 weeks after planting). Squashes for keeping are cut when their stems start to dry, and should be cleared before the autumn frosts; ripen their skins (see *page 204*) before storing.

WHEN TO SOW Spring
GERMINATION 5–10 days at 15°C (60°F) minimum
SPACING *Bush and trained plants:* 90cm (3ft); *as groundcover:* 1.8m (6ft)
TIME TO MATURITY 8–12 weeks
HEIGHT 90–180cm (3–6ft)
AVERAGE YIELD 3–4 fruits per plant
VARIETIES 'Atlantic Giant', 'Butternut', 'Crown Prince', 'Jack be Little', 'Lady Godiva', 'Twonga', 'Uchiki Kuri'

RIGHT **Courgette 'Burpees Golden'**
OPPOSITE **Squash 'Jack be Little'**

Courgettes & marrows
Cucurbita pepo

These tender annuals are grown in the same way as squashes (see left). Courgettes are the young fruits of marrows and should be harvested regularly when they are 10–15cm (4–6in) long. Harvest marrows when they are large enough for use (about 8 weeks after planting). The single stem of a courgette is often too weak to support the plants, so keep them upright by tying them like cordons to stakes. Staking also improves air circulation, which helps prevent powdery mildew.

WHEN TO SOW Mid-spring to early summer
GERMINATION 5–10 days at 15°C (60°F)
SPACING *Bush:* 90cm (3ft) each way; *trailing:* 1.8m (6ft) apart each way
TIME TO MATURITY 8–12 weeks
HEIGHT *Bush:* 90cm (3ft); *trailing:* 1.8m (6ft)
AVERAGE YIELD *Courgettes:* 12–20 per plant; *marrows:* 3–4 per plant
VARIETIES *Courgettes:* 'All Green Bush', 'Burpees Golden', 'Gold Bush', 'Tempra'; *marrows:* 'Custard White', 'Green Bush', 'Long Green Trailing'

Outdoor cucumbers
Cucumis sativus

Unlike greenhouse or 'frame' types (see *page 173*), outdoor, or 'ridge', cucumbers will grow satisfactorily at only 15°C (60°F). Traditional varieties produce short, rough-skinned fruits (gherkins are small versions of these), but hybrids and Japanese kinds have fruits that are smooth and long or round. There are bush varieties and tall vining kinds for growing like trailing squashes. Fertilization does not result in a bitter flavour, so there is no need to remove the male flowers.

HOW TO GROW Plants are grown in the same way as squashes, but germinate the seeds at 21–26°C (70–80°F) and then grow the seedlings at 15°C (60°F). Mulch bush and trailing plants to keep the fruits clean. Water regularly around (not over) the plants. Harvest each fruit when long enough, at the same time pinching out the shoot tip to encourage further branching. Pull up plants that develop virus symptoms or mildew in autumn, and clear crops before the last frosts, pickling any small or surplus fruits.

WHEN TO SOW Spring
GERMINATION 1 week at 21°C (70°F) minimum
SPACING 75cm (30in)
TIME TO MATURITY 12–14 weeks
HEIGHT *Bush*: 60cm (2ft); *vining*: 3m (10ft)
AVERAGE YIELD *Bush*: 3–4 fruits per plant; *vining*: 8–12
VARIETIES 'Burpless Tasty Green', 'Bush Crop', 'Kyoto', 'Masterpiece'

Cucumber 'Masterpiece'

Melons *Cucumis melo*

This is a sun- and heat-loving crop for growing outdoors where 90 or more warm summer days can be guaranteed. Elsewhere it is grown in a cold frame or cold greenhouse if you choose a cantaloupe or ogen variety, or a heated house for other kinds such as the large musk and honeydew kinds. Heat is essential for successful germination, or you can buy chitted seeds.

HOW TO GROW Sow melons in the same way as squashes (see *page 86*) 6 weeks before the last frost, and germinate at 21°C (70°F). Pot on if plants become rootbound, and pinch out growing tips after 4–5 true leaves

to encourage sideshoots. Plant in prepared sites outdoors under plastic tunnel cloches, in the centre of a cold frame or in a greenhouse border or growing bag.

Train the sideshoots, one to each corner of a frame, or two in opposite directions in a greenhouse or under cloches. Stop these after 5 leaves: subsequent sideshoots bear flowers and are stopped 2 leaves beyond a swelling fruit (allow one per shoot). Train stems vertically on nets or strings in a greenhouse, and use these to suspend ripening melons in nets (see picture, right). You may need to fertilize female flowers under glass. Water and feed with a general fertilizer every 10–14 days, and ventilate whenever possible. Cut fruits when cracks appear at the base of the stalk and they give off their distinctive sweet aroma.

WHEN TO SOW Spring
GERMINATION 1 week at 21°C (70°F)
SPACING 90–150cm (3–5ft)
TIME TO MATURITY 3–4 months
HEIGHT 3m (10ft) or more
AVERAGE YIELD 2–4 fruits per plant
VARIETIES 'Adonis', 'Ogen', 'Sweetheart', 'Tiger'

Melon 'Adonis'

selecting your crops

leaves & salads

Loose-leaf lettuce 'Bijou'

Most salad and loose-leaf crops like spinach will fit in wherever there is space, often as a catch- or intercrop (see *page 142*). Although easy-going and tolerant of varied soil conditions, none should be grown in the same place in successive years – this is a precaution against soil pests and nutrient deficiencies.

Lettuce *Lactuca sativa*

The essential salad plant for most gardeners, available all year with a careful choice of different types and varieties (see table, below). The main distinction is between loose-leaf kinds, which are often decorative and can be cropped repeatedly over a long period (see *page 176*), and heading or hearting varieties, which include soft butterheads or 'flats', tall upright cos

or romaine lettuces, and round crunchy crispheads or 'icebergs'. Some tolerate short days and low light levels, and may be grown under glass for winter use; crispheads prefer plenty of summer heat. All need consistently moist growing conditions. Modern varieties may be pest- or disease-resistant, heat-tolerant or slow to bolt.

HOW TO GROW Sow 1cm (½in) deep, in drills for thinning according to size, or in modules for transplanting with the least possible root disturbance. Keep the lowest leaves of transplants just above soil level, as deeper planting can cause rotting. Water freely whenever dry (but keep plants under glass on the dry side and well ventilated), keep weed-free, and mulch summer crops on light soils. Start cutting heads while small, as plants often mature simultaneously;

SOWING TIMES FOR YEAR-ROUND LETTUCE

VARIETIES	SOWING TIME	HARVEST TIME	NOTES
Early summer e.g. 'Little Gem', 'Tom Thumb', loose-leaf kinds	Late winter and early spring	Late spring to early summer	Sow under cloches or indoors
Summer e.g. 'Oakleaf', 'Sioux', 'Vienna', 'Webb's Wonderful'	Early spring to midsummer every 3–4 weeks	Early summer to late autumn	Sow in situ; cloche late sowings in autumn
Winter e.g. 'May King', 'Valdor', 'Wendel'	Late summer and mid-autumn	Late autumn and all winter	Sow indoors; transplant under glass
Spring e.g. 'Rouge d'Hiver', 'Winter Crop', 'Winter Density'	Late sumer and early autumn	All spring	Sow in situ; cloche all winter; thin in spring

MUSTARD & CRESS

The salad garnish of mustard and cress is a popular container crop for window sills and greenhouses. The seeds are usually supplied in separate packets owing to their different growth rates. Sow cress evenly in a tray lined with 2-3 layers of moist absorbent paper, and over-sow 3-4 days later with an equal amount of mustard seed. Keep the seeds moist throughout. Cut the seedlings with scissors when 4-5cm (1½-2in) high, about 3-4 weeks after sowing. Seeds can also be sown separately, and outdoors in a fine seedbed.

Iceberg lettuce 'Sioux'

pick a few leaves at a time from loose kinds or cut down completely to leave a stump for regrowth.

Lettuce seeds become dormant above 25°C (77°F), crispheads a few degrees higher, which can impair summer sowings. Counter this in hot weather by sowing in late afternoon as temperatures fall, and cover drills with wet newspapers for 24 hours afterwards. Keep pots of seeds cool and shaded.

WHEN TO SOW See table, left
GERMINATION 1-2 weeks at 10-25°C (50-77°F)
SPACING 15-30cm (6-12in) square
TIME TO MATURITY 8-12 weeks
HEIGHT 10-25cm (4-10in)
VARIETIES See table, left

Chicory *Cichorium intybus*

There are two main kinds of chicory: heading and forcing.

Heading chicory, which includes numerous radicchio (red) and sugar loaf varieties, can be grown like lettuce to produce refreshing, slightly bitter crisp leaves or complete heads most of the year.

Forcing chicory, sometimes called Belgian, Brussels or Witloof chicory, is sown in rows 30cm (12in) apart in late spring and thinned to 20cm (8in). Roots can be left in for covering in late winter under 15cm (6in) ridges of soil to force and blanch 'chicons' for spring use. Alternatively, dig up roots and force indoors during winter (see *page 208*) for cutting 4-6 weeks later. Large roots can be dried and ground like coffee - 'Magdeburg' is a selected variety for this purpose.

WHEN TO SOW *Forcing*: late spring; *heading*: early spring to midsummer
GERMINATION 1-2 weeks at 10°C (50°F)
SPACING *Forcing*: 20cm (8in) in rows 30cm (12in) apart; *heading*: 15-30cm (6-12in) square
TIME TO MATURITY *Forcing*: 26 weeks + forcing time; *heading*: 8-12 weeks
HEIGHT 15-30cm (6-12in)
VARIETIES *Forcing*: 'Apollo', 'Dura', 'Magdeburg', 'Zoom'; *heading*: 'Catalogna Frastagliata' (a form of 'asparagus' chicory), 'Grumolo Verde', 'Rossa of Treviso 2'

Radicchio 'Rossa of Treviso 2'

Endive *Cichorium endiva*

Similar to heading chicory in flavour and performance, but larger. Frizzy or 'crispa' types have narrow, deeply toothed leaves; escarole or Batavian endive is a hardy, broad-leaved kind. Hardiness varies, so check catalogue descriptions carefully. Much of the bitterness can be removed by blanching. Loosely tie the leaves of upright varieties with raffia and then cover with a pot or bucket; lay an upturned dinner plate on the centre of spreading varieties. Leave in place for a week before cutting.

WHEN TO SOW *Frizzy endive*: early spring to late summer; *broad-leaved*: late summer plus early autumn under cloches
GERMINATION 1–2 weeks at 10°C (50°F)
SPACING 30–40cm (12–16in)
TIME TO MATURITY 12–16 weeks
HEIGHT 15–30cm (6–12in)
VARIETIES *Frizzy*: 'Pancalieri', 'Wallonne'; *broad-leaved*: 'Blonde Full Heart', 'Grobo'

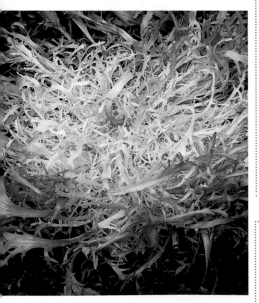

Endive 'Pancalieri'

Corn salad *Valerianella* species

Also called lamb's lettuce or mâche, this is a hardy mild-flavoured annual to sow in spring and autumn for harvesting as a complete rosette of basal leaves before the flower stems develop. Self-seeds freely.

WHEN TO SOW Late summer and early autumn; modern varieties such as 'Vit' also in late spring
GERMINATION 2 weeks at 10°C (50°F)
SPACING 10–15cm (4–6in)
HEIGHT 8–10cm (3–4in)
TIME TO MATURITY 8–10 weeks onwards
VARIETIES 'Verte de Cambrai', 'Vit'

Corn salad 'Vit'

a more peppery perennial, which is less likely to bolt on dry soils. Sow at 4–6 week intervals from late spring to early autumn, and thin to 15cm (6in) apart. Make the last sowing in a cold frame for winter use. Gather leaves as needed or cut whole plants while they are still small, leaving the stumps to grow again. Self-seeds well.

WHEN TO SOW Late spring to early autumn; to late autumn under glass
GERMINATION 2 weeks at 10°C (50°F)
SPACING 15cm (6in) apart each way
TIME TO MATURITY 6–8 weeks
HEIGHT 30–45cm (12–18in)
VARIETIES No special varieties

Land cress *Barbarea* species

A peppery leaf crop, similar in appearance to water cress, that grows easily from a spring or late summer sowing in moist shade. Pick odd leaves or harvest whole plants, but leave a few to flower and self-seed.

WHEN TO SOW Spring and late summer
GERMINATION 1–2 weeks at 10°C (50°F)
SPACING 20cm (8in) in rows 30cm (12in) apart
HEIGHT 20cm (8in)
TIME TO MATURITY 8 weeks onwards
VARIETIES None

Rocket *Eruca vesicaria* subsp. *sativa*

The spicy, slightly nutty flavour of the cultivated annual salad rocket has been a favourite since classical times. Wild rocket (*Dipsotaxis tenuifolia*) is

Claytonia *Montia perfoliata*

Miner's lettuce, or winter purslane, is ready in 12 weeks from late spring, midsummer and early autumn sowings for cutting all year round.

Harvest whole plants, leaving stumps to resprout, pick a few of the mild succulent leaves or snip with scissors as a seedling crop.

WHEN TO SOW Spring to early autumn
GERMINATION 2 weeks at 10°C (50°F)
SPACING 15cm (6in) in rows 30cm (12in) apart
TIME TO MATURITY 10-12 weeks onwards
HEIGHT 15-20cm (6-8in)
VARIETIES None

Spinach *Spinacia oleracea*

A range of leaf crops can be grown as spinach substitutes (see below and *page 186*), but true spinach is a distinctive vegetable, often with remarkably intense colouring. Many varieties such as 'Emilia' grow fast but are suitable only for summer and autumn use, while others ('Giant Winter', for example) are hardier and best used outside the summer months. Modern kinds like 'Whale' are dual-purpose, slow to bolt and resistant to mildew. 'Monnopa' is low in oxalic acid, which causes the bitterness that some people find unpalatable.

HOW TO GROW Sow summer spinach in light shade, 2.5cm (1in) deep in rows 30cm (12in) apart, starting in early spring and repeating every 3-4 weeks; sow hardy kinds in late summer and early autumn. Thin seedlings to 8cm (3in) apart, and pull up alternate plants when they are large enough to use; crop the others by cutting individual leaves. Water freely in dry weather, especially in hot summers when plants easily bolt if they are stressed.

WHEN TO SOW Early spring to early autumn
GERMINATION 10-14 days at 10°C (50°F), after soaking in water for a few hours
SPACING 8-15cm (3-6in) in rows 30cm (12in) apart
TIME TO MATURITY 10-12 weeks
HEIGHT 15-30cm (6-12in)
VARIETIES 'Emilia', 'Galaxy', 'Giant Winter', 'Monnopa', 'Palco', 'Tetona', 'Veneto', 'Whale'

Perpetual spinach & chard *Beta vulgaris* Cicla Group

These leaf beets, which are grown for their foliage and leaf stalks, are an excellent alternative to true spinach (see also *page 186*). Perpetual spinach (spinach beet) has large soft leaves that are used like true spinach,

'Perpetual Spinach'

while chard (seakale beet) has glossy savoyed foliage with broad white, yellow or red midribs that are often eaten as a separate vegetable. Both kinds are hardy, robust and long-lasting, even on drier soils. A spring sowing will often remain usable until the following year, although sowing a further batch in late summer will ensure winter crops, especially if some seedlings are transplanted to a cold frame.

HOW TO GROW Sow in rows 45cm (18in) apart in light shade, and thin to 23cm (9in).

WHEN TO SOW Early spring to late summer
GERMINATION 2-3 weeks at 7°C (45°F)
SPACING 23cm (9in) in rows 45cm (18in) apart
TIME TO MATURITY 12 weeks
HEIGHT 45-60cm (18-24in)
VARIETIES 'Perpetual Spinach'; *chard*: 'Bright Lights', 'Charlotte', 'Rainbow Chard', 'Ruby Chard', 'Swiss Chard'

Chard 'Ruby Chard'

stem & perennial vegetables

Celery & celeriac

Apium graveolens

Traditional celery is planted in a trench (see *page 214*) and progressively earthed up to blanch its stems (see *page 198*). Green and self-blanching celery varieties are grown on the surface, close together in blocks to encourage paler stems (planting in a cold frame is even more effective). All celeries need very rich, moist conditions, and on poorer soils celeriac is more successful, forming useful swollen roots even in dry seasons; with generous feeding and watering, the crisp, juicy roots can be enormous.

HOW TO GROW Sow all kinds indoors about 10 weeks before the last frosts, prick out into pots and harden off for planting out when they have 5–6 true leaves. Cover with a cloche in cold weather, or hold plants back, trimming to 8cm (3in) high to delay growth. Water generously every week, mulch with straw or compost, and give a general feed in midsummer. Harvest whole celery plants when large enough (about 12 weeks after planting), and clear before the frosts. Trench celery is hardier and tastes better after frost. Dig celeriac as needed, or clear in late autumn and store like carrots (see *page 160*).

WHEN TO SOW Late winter and early spring in heat

GERMINATION 3 weeks at 10°C (50°F) minimum

SPACING *Celery*: 23cm (9in) apart each way; *celeriac*: 30cm (12in) apart each way

TIME TO MATURITY *Self-blanching celery*: 26 weeks; *trench celery*: 40 weeks; *celeriac*: 30 weeks

HEIGHT *Celery*: 45–60cm (18–24in); *celeriac*: 30cm (12in)

VARIETIES *Celery*: 'Celebrity', 'Giant Red', 'Giant White', 'Golden Self-blanching', 'Greensleeves', 'Hopkins' Fenlander', 'Lathom Self-blanching', 'Victoria'; *celeriac*: 'Diamant', 'Iram', 'Marble Ball', 'Monarch', 'Prinz', 'Tellus'

Celeriac 'Prinz'

Celery 'Celebrity'

Florence fennel

Foeniculum vulgare var. *azoricum*

This is quite different from the perennial herb fennel, although the feathery leaves have the same sweet aniseed flavour. Florence fennel is grown for its crisp white stem base, swollen like a bulb and capable of reaching 0.4kg (1lb) in warm fertile soil. Modern hybrids can be sown from mid-spring, but older kinds tend to bolt if sown much before

Florence fennel 'Sirio'

midsummer. Sow in situ and thin to distance, or indoors in small pots or modules to avoid root disturbance. Plant out when seedlings have 3–4 leaves, water regularly and mulch. Harvest the 'bulb' when the size of an apple, cutting it to leave a 2.5cm (1in) stump to produce leafy sideshoots for flavouring.

WHEN TO SOW Mid-spring to midsummer, late summer for growing under glass
GERMINATION 2 weeks at 10°C (50°F)
SPACING 15cm (6in) in rows 30cm (12in) apart
TIME TO MATURITY 10–12 weeks
HEIGHT 45–60cm (18–24in)
VARIETIES 'Amigo', 'Perfection', 'Pronto', 'Romanesco', 'Sirio', 'Zeva Fino', 'Zeva Tardo'

Globe artichokes
Cynara scolymus

This is a perennial crop (see *page 31*) with handsome sculptural foliage and large blue 'thistles' on 1.5m (5ft) stems: the unopened flower head, or 'choke', is the part used. Plants can be raised from seeds, sown in a nursery bed in spring, but results are variable – select the best and propagate from offsets. Otherwise, buy named plants and space them 90cm (3ft) apart in rich, well-drained soil in full sun. Water and mulch in a dry summer. Cut the main head while it is still tight, followed by the sideshoots. Hardy prickly kinds normally survive winter unaided,

Globe artichoke 'Green Globe'

but in cold gardens, choice varieties like 'Gros Vert de Laon' should be thickly mulched while dormant.

WHEN TO SOW/PLANT Early to mid-spring
GERMINATION 2–3 weeks at 7°C (45°F)
SPACING 90cm (3ft) apart each way
TIME TO MATURITY 18 months from seed
HEIGHT 90–150cm (3–5ft)
VARIETIES 'Green Globe', 'Gros Vert de Laon', 'Purple Globe', 'Purple Roscoff', 'Violetta'

Jerusalem artichokes
Helianthus tuberosus

These sunflower relatives are grown for their large clusters of starch-free tubers. Although perennials, they can become weedy unless planted and harvested as an annual crop.

HOW TO GROW Plant tubers in early spring, 10cm (4in) deep and 30cm (12in) apart. Grow as a windbreak or screen, and support the 1.8–3m (6–10ft) stems on exposed sites. Dig tubers as needed, clearing crops in spring and selecting smaller tubers for immediate replanting in fresh ground.

WHEN TO PLANT Early spring

SPACING 30cm (12in) apart in single rows

TIME TO MATURITY 26 weeks

HEIGHT 1.8–3m (6–10ft)

VARIETIES 'Boston Red', 'Dwarf Sunray', 'Fuseau', '(Smooth) Garnet'

Asparagus *Asparagus officinalis*

A decorative perennial fern that remains productive for 30 years or more if self-set seedlings are prevented from taking over.

HOW TO GROW Plants can be raised from seed in a nursery bed (see *page 127*), or you can save time by planting 1- or 2-year old crowns 45cm (18in) apart each way in a sunny, well-drained position. Keep plants well weeded, water (young plants only) in a dry season, and feed with general fertilizer in early spring and again when harvesting finishes. Gather spears when they are 15–20cm (6–8in) long, cutting them with a knife about 5cm (2in) below the surface. Take 1–2 spears per plant in the first 2 seasons, and cut freely thereafter for about 8 weeks

Asparagus 'Lucullus'

until the longest day. Cut and clear the fern when it turns yellow in autumn. Modern F1 hybrids like 'Franklim', 'Grolim' and 'Jersey Knight' are all-male, producing numerous extra-large spears and with no risk of seedlings.

WHEN TO SOW Late spring (after soaking in water for 48 hours)

GERMINATION 3–4 weeks at 10–15°C (50–60°F)

SPACING 45cm (18in) apart each way

TIME TO MATURITY 2–3 years from seed

HEIGHT Up to 1.5m (5ft)

VARIETIES 'Cito', 'Connover's Colossal', 'Franklim', 'Grolim', 'Jersey Knight', 'Lucullus', 'Martha Washington'

Rhubarb *Rheum x hybridum*

This perennial vegetable provides the first 'fruit' of the season. Although reliable in the poorest soil, it responds to rich, well-drained conditions and annual autumn manuring with huge crops of tender juicy stems that can be forced for early use (see *page 208*).

HOW TO GROW Plant crowns 90cm (3ft) apart with their buds just below the surface. Water liberally in dry weather. Cut off the stately 2.4m (8ft) spikes of creamy flowers before they set seed, to avoid exhausting the crowns. Gather stems by pulling them off at the base: always leave 3–4 on each plant, and stop harvesting around midsummer. All available kinds are good; 'Timperley Early' and the various 'Stockbridge' cultivars are best for forcing.

WHEN TO PLANT Late autumn or late winter

SPACING 90cm (3ft) apart each way

TIME TO MATURITY 1–2 years after planting

HEIGHT 90cm (3ft); flowers up to 2.4m (8ft)

VARIETIES 'Glaskin's Perpetual', 'Hawke's Champagne', 'Stockbridge Arrow', 'The Sutton', 'Timperley Early', 'Victoria'

summer-fruiting vegetables

A number of tender warm-climate crops are popular with allotment gardeners and regularly do well even in poor summers, provided suitable varieties are chosen and started early in the season. This usually means sowing indoors in temperate regions for transplanting outside after the last frosts or for keeping under glass throughout; in warmer areas, with a longer frost-free growing season, direct sowing outdoors is successful. Be guided by experienced neighbours and local climate data. More informative catalogues often include recommended temperature regimes and the number of days' growth that the different varieties need.

Outdoor tomatoes

Lycopersicon esculentum
Plants grow and fruit best at 21°C (70°F) or above, and greenhouse culture is recommended where average summer temperatures tend

Tomatoes 'Summer Sweet'

to be cooler (see *pages 172-3*). Most varieties are tall and are trained as cordons with all their sideshoots removed (see also *page 188*); on bush varieties, the sideshoots grow instead of the main stem, with each sideshoot producing more sideshoots as soon as a flower truss develops. Very dwarf bushes like 'Totem' and 'Tumbler' do well in containers, baskets and window boxes. Tomatoes rotate best with root vegetables (see *pages 32-5*), but keep well away from potatoes, as they share the same ailments.

The fruits have a wide range of shapes, colours and flavours that vary according to their balance of sugars and acids. Good flavour depends as much on culture as choice of variety, and plenty of sunlight plus moderation in watering and feeding can enhance the quality of the most humdrum tomato. Grow F1 hybrids for uniformity and predictability, heritage varieties for *joie de vivre*.

HOW TO GROW Sow indoors 8 weeks before the last frosts, prick out into 11cm (4in) pots, and harden off for planting out, ideally before the first flower truss shows colour. Mulch in early summer with compost (or straw to keep the fruits of bush kinds clean). Train cordons by tying the main stem to a strong post and pinching out all sideshoots; remove the growing tip in late summer to hasten ripening. Water every week in dry weather. Gather fruits as they colour, and clear crops before the frosts for ripening indoors (see *page 202*).

Tomatoes 'Tumbler'

WHEN TO SOW Mid- to late spring
GERMINATION 1-2 weeks at 15°C (60°F) minimum
SPACING *Bushes*: 60cm (24in); *cordons*: 45cm (18in)
TIME TO MATURITY 16-20 weeks
HEIGHT *Bushes*: 45-60cm (18-24in); *cordons*: 1.2m (4ft) or more
AVERAGE YIELD Up to 4.5kg (10lb) per plant
VARIETIES 'Golden Sunrise', 'Harbinger', 'Marmande', 'Summer Sweet', 'Tigerella', 'Tornado', 'Totem', 'Tumbler' and hundreds of heritage varieties

Peppers *Capsicum* species

Sweet and hot peppers enjoy the same culture as tomatoes, but prefer slightly higher temperatures and moister, more acid soil conditions. Sweet peppers, paprikas and mild chillies are all forms of *Capsicum annuum*, ready from about 12 weeks after planting. Very hot cayenne peppers and pungent bird chillies (*C. frutescens*) need a further month to ripen, preferably above 21°C (70°F), so they are often more successful under glass or as container plants to bring indoors in late summer.

HOW TO GROW Sow and grow like tomatoes, space plants 45cm (18in) apart, and in dry weather give each plant 9 litres (2 gals) of water every 2 weeks; feed regularly with a high-potash fertilizer. Pinch out the growing tips if sideshoots are slow to form, and stop these once they set fruit. Gather sweet peppers while they are green or when they turn colour, and hot peppers when fully ripe. Clear crops before the frosts, hanging entire plants under glass to finish ripening.

WHEN TO SOW Late winter to mid-spring

GERMINATION 2–3 weeks at 15°C (60°F) minimum

SPACING 45cm (18in) apart each way

TIME TO MATURITY 18–20 weeks

HEIGHT 60–90cm (2–3ft)

AVERAGE YIELD *Sweet*: from 4–10 per plant; *hot*: up to several dozen per plant

VARIETIES *Sweet*: 'Bell Boy', 'Fiesta', 'Madison', 'Redskin', 'Sweet Nardello'; *hot*: 'Early Jalapeno', 'Friar's Hat', 'Habanero' (*C. chinense*), 'Hungarian Hot Wax', 'Ring of Fire'

Sweet pepper 'Madison'

Chilli pepper 'Friar's Hat'

Aubergine 'Moneymaker'

Aubergines *Solanum melongena*

Also known as eggplant or brinjal, this tropical perennial is grown as an annual, and produces variable fruits that may be long or round, normally deep purple but sometimes white, yellow or greenish. It needs plenty of heat and often does best under glass.

HOW TO GROW Sow and grow like tomatoes, plant out 45cm (18in) apart, and water and feed like peppers. Pinch growing tips when plants are 30cm (12in) high, and stop all sideshoots on large-fruited kinds once 4–6 fruits develop. Harvest these when fully coloured and still shiny.

WHEN TO SOW Late winter to mid-spring

GERMINATION 2–3 weeks at 15°C (60°F) minimum

SPACING 45cm (18in) apart each way

TIME TO MATURITY 18–20 weeks

HEIGHT 50–150cm (20in–5ft)

AVERAGE YIELD 4–6 fruits per plant

VARIETIES 'Black Beauty', 'Long Purple', 'Moneymaker', 'Rosa Bianca', 'Slice-Rite', 'Snowy'

Sweetcorn *Zea mays*

This is an important and popular crop to grow yourself: flavour declines soon after picking as the sugars turn to starch, so the cobs need eating while they are still very fresh. Varieties range from fast early-maturing kinds, which are ready as soon as 50 days after planting, to maincrops that need 16 weeks or more of warmth before they are ripe. 'Super-sweet' and 'sugar-enhanced' varieties have a superior flavour but they must be grown on their own to avoid cross-pollination with standard kinds.

HOW TO GROW Sow indoors in pots or modules 5–6 weeks before the last frosts, and harden off well before planting out in blocks to aid wind pollination. Choose a warm, sunny position sheltered from the coldest winds, and well-drained, fairly fertile but not recently manured soil. Take care when weeding because sweetcorn roots are very near the soil surface. Water if dry when the flowers appear, and again while the cobs are swelling. Pick cobs when the silks at the tip begin to shrivel, but test the cobs first by peeling back the husk and pressing your nail into a grain – milky contents indicate readiness.

WHEN TO SOW Mid-spring
GERMINATION 10–14 days at 10°C (50°F) minimum
SPACING 30–45cm (12–18in)
TIME TO MATURITY up to 18 weeks
HEIGHT 90–240cm (3–8ft)
AVERAGE YIELD 1–2 cobs per plant
VARIETIES 'Conquest', 'Double Standard', 'Kelvedon Sweetheart', 'Sundance', 'Swallow'

Sweetcorn 'Swallow'

BABY SWEETCORN

Varieties like 'Minipop' and 'Minisweet' (right) produce several immature cobs per plant for use as baby sweetcorn. Raise in the same way as ordinary sweetcorn but plant 15cm (6in) apart each way. Harvest cobs when they are 10–15cm (4–6in) long with brown silks.

key culinary herbs

Culinary herbs are essential partners of the food crops you grow, and most cooks agree they have the best flavour and aroma when freshly gathered. The choice is vast – especially if you include cosmetic, medicinal and dye plants as well – and their needs vary, from the dry, sun-baked conditions enjoyed by thyme and rosemary to parsley's cool light shade. But there is room on the busiest allotment for a basic collection of classic and favourite kinds.

Whether you allocate all your herbs a special corner or bed, or disperse perennials as edging plants and annuals as intercrops, you need to ensure their essential requirements are met. Few herbs survive for long in acid soils, deep shade or heavy ground with poor drainage. A raised bed is the best solution for a sticky waterlogged site. Add some mild organic material for leafy herbs – garden compost, mushroom compost or leafmould, for example, but never manure – and thoroughly clear weed roots from sites for perennial herbs.

The maintenance of herbs is minimal. Leafy herbs such as parsley enjoy a mulch of compost, plus water whenever they are dry; aromatic woody and Mediterranean herbs can be mulched with grit or gravel to accelerate drainage. Trim perennials into shape after flowering. Harvest leaves and shoot tips (a form of pruning) for regular use, and shear plants wholesale for preserving just before or during flowering, when their flavour is the greatest. (See also Rejuvenating perennial herbs, *page 184*.)

Basil *Ocimum basilicum*

A tender bushy annual with warmly aromatic foliage and a range of subtly different flavours, colours and leaf shapes, depending on the variety. Plants need sharp drainage and a sunny spot sheltered from cold winds. Sow indoors in spring, pot up seedlings individually and plant out 15–20cm (6–8in) apart. For late use, sow again in midsummer. In cold areas, keep in pots or grow under cloches. Avoid splashing the leaves while watering. Harvest the shoot tips regularly to encourage further branching and delay flowering.

Basil (*Ocimum basilicum*)

Bay *Laurus nobilis*

The glossy leaves of this evergreen tree or shrub are picked as needed all year round, or they can be gathered at pruning time for drying slowly in darkness. Plants are slightly tender

Bay (*Laurus nobilis*)

while young, so screen from cold winds after planting, but they are reasonably hardy once established. Plant in autumn or spring, and trim to shape (simple topiary is an option) during early summer. In cold areas, grow as a container plant and bring under glass or wrap with insulation in winter.

Chives *Allium* species

Common chives, with its clumps of grassy foliage and mauve flower heads, is the best known of several alliums used to add hints of onion or garlic to dishes. Others include Chinese or garlic chives, Welsh or bunching onions, and the slightly eccentric tree onion. All are available as plants or bulbils, or they can be raised from seed sown in modules in spring. Plant 23cm (9in) apart in moist fertile soil, in sun or light shade. Use the leaves and flowers as needed, or freeze just before flowering. Divide every few years, and pot up divisions in autumn for winter use indoors.

Coriander *Coriandrum sativum*

There are two distinct strains of this popular annual: the simple species and varieties like 'Moroccan' are bred for seed production, while 'cilantro' types such as 'Chechnya' and 'Leisure' yield several cuts of leaves before finally flowering and seeding. Early batches and those sown in late summer are less likely to flower prematurely. Sow both kinds direct in mid-spring and thin to 5cm (2in) for seeds, 23cm (9in) for leaves; sow leaf crops again at 5–6 week intervals until early autumn, cloching this last sowing for early spring use. Cut early and late leaf crops when 15cm (6in) high and leave to regrow; pull up complete maincrop plants, as these usually flower if they are cut. Harvest seed crops in late summer just before they are ripe, and dry the heads in paper bags.

Coriander (*Coriandrum sativum*)

Chives and thymes growing in small pathside blocks are handy for frequent picking.

Dill *Anethum graveolens*

A dual-purpose annual herb for sunny sites and light soils. Varieties like dwarf 'Fernleaf', 'Tetra' and sturdy 'Vierling' are leaf crops, whereas 'Mammoth' and seeds sold for cooking produce plants that flower quickly with good seed yields. Grow like coriander (see *page 101*). Support the fragile stems with twiggy sticks in windy positions and water leaf crops generously in dry weather.

Fennel *Foeniculum vulgare*

This large, 1.8m (6ft) tall, graceful perennial has green and bronze forms, both of them ornamental, attractive to insect allies and treasured for their sweet anise flavour. One plant is usually enough and will fatten into a dense clump that benefits from dividing and replanting every 3–4 years. Plant young bought specimens in well-drained soil in full sun, or sow pinches of seed in spring in small pots, and plant complete potfuls 60cm (24in) apart. Gather young shoots and leaves as needed. Remove flower stems to prolong leaf crops, or allow to flower and harvest the aromatic seeds in late summer. (For Florence fennel, see *pages 94–5*.)

Lemon balm *Melissa officinalis*

A sweetly fragrant Mediterranean perennial with golden and variegated forms, simpler to buy as plants than to raise from seeds or cuttings; alternatively, beg a spare division from someone else, since plants can spread wantonly and usually need thinning. Grow in full sun, and gather the refreshing, intensely lemon-flavoured leaves while young. Cutting down growth before seeds set stimulates a further crop of useful foliage as well as restraining invasiveness.

Mint *Mentha species*

There are many species and even more cultivars of this spreading perennial but, for culinary use, apple or round-leaved mint (*M. suaveolens*), spearmint (*M. spicata*) and peppermint (*M. x piperita*) are most popular. Grow as bought plants or root divisions, planted 30cm (12in) apart in moist, fertile ground where they will not be invasive, or in large containers to confine the branching roots. Harvest the leaves and shoot tips as needed or just before flowering for preserving, and trim some stems to ground level in midsummer for fresh supplies in autumn. Water well in dry weather, and divide clumps every 3–4 years.

Mint (*Mentha* x *villosa*)

Oregano *Origanum species*

The most popular forms of this diverse, pungent genus are sweet marjoram (*O. majorana*), hardier pot marjoram (*O. onites*) and, spiciest of all, wild marjoram or oregano (*O. vulgare*). Sweet marjoram is usually grown as an annual, but the others are reliably perennial. All need full sun and well-drained soil. Buy plants or sow indoors in spring, in modules for

Oregano (*Origanum vulgare*)

planting out 45cm (18in) apart. Use the leaves as needed, just before flowering for preserving. Mulching and cloching sweet marjoram in late autumn can help it survive winter frosts.

Parsley *Petroselinum crispum*

With two sowings (mid-spring and late summer) you can have fresh parsley all year round (see also *page 204*). Sow in situ, in moist, rich soil in dappled sun or light shade, and thin seedlings 15cm (6in) apart, or start in modules for transplanting. Keep moist in dry weather. Curly varieties like 'Favourite' are decorative garnishes; plain-leaved French and Italian parsleys have a stronger flavour for cooking. Harvest the complete stems as needed, grow in pots or a frame for winter use, and leave a few plants to flower and self-seed.

Curly parsley (*Petroselinum crispum* 'Favourite')

Common sage (*Salvia officinalis*)

Sage *Salvia officinalis*

The common form of this aromatic evergreen shrub is hardier and better flavoured than its various ornamental cultivars (but pineapple sage, *S. rutilans*, is an irresistible scarlet winter-flowering species for a frost-free container). Sow in pots in spring or take soft cuttings in summer, and plant 60cm (24in) apart in a sunny well-drained spot. Pinch out growing tips for bushy growth, and trim after flowering. Use the leaves any time, and gather for drying just before flowering. Propagate and replace leggy plants when 4–5 years old.

Savory *Satureja* species

The leaves of savory, with their bitter, thyme-like flavour, are often used in recipes with pulses to aid digestion and reduce flatulence; the herb has traditionally been grown close by for gathering with peas and beans. The annual summer savory (*S. hortensis*), which has the finest flavour, is a tender 30cm (12in) high plant, sown in early spring on the surface of small pots; prick out and transplant 15cm (6in) apart after the last frosts. The bushier perennial winter savory (*S. montana*) is hardy and usable over a longer period. Sow like annual savory or buy young plants. Both kinds like full sun and well-drained soils. Pick fresh leaves any time and harvest summer savory for drying just before it flowers.

Tarragon *Artemisia dracunculus*

Half-hardy French tarragon is the species to grow (not the ill-flavoured Russian subspecies). The widely spreading roots of this tall perennial can be invasive, so grow like mint in a bed of its own, a pot or bottomless bucket, or allow to romp in a wild corner. Plant 30cm (12in) apart in a small group in a warm, dry position, and mulch after the stems die down in late autumn. Pick as needed, using the upper sprigs to encourage further branching. Divide and replant elsewhere every 3–4 years.

TENDER HERBS

All but the largest herbs can be grown in pots for greenhouse or window-sill culture and for harvest out of season. A few, though, are traditionally kept indoors, either because they make attractive houseplants or because they are too sensitive to flourish outside.

Lemon verbena (*Aloysia triphylla*) ▶
This elegant deciduous shrub has possibly the strongest and most refreshing lemon flavour of all herbs, and is commonly distilled for perfumery. Grow in a 20cm (8in) pot in a sunny, well-ventilated position. Water regularly and give a house plant feed every month in summer. Trim to shape after flowering and again in autumn; keep nearly dry and above 4°C (40°F) in winter. Harvest the leaves any time for immediate use.

Lemon grass (*Cymbopogon citratus*)
A tropical grass that can fatten into an impressive clump in a large container of soil-based compost. It needs to be kept above 7°C (45°F), and nearly dry in winter. Buy fresh stems undamaged at the base, and root in a little water. After

Thyme *Thymus* species

There are many desirable cultivars – some with variegated foliage, others with distinctive flavours – but common thyme, *T. vulgaris*, is the usual culinary form. All are short-lived woody perennials, best bought as young plants and then renewed by layers or summer cuttings when 4–5 years old. Plant 23cm (9in) apart in dry soil in sun, or collect various kinds in a strawberry tower pot. Harvest shoot tips as needed, during flowering for drying, and shear to shape when the flowers finish.

a week or two, pot up by burying the base 2.5cm (1in) deep in the compost, and keep in a warm sunny position. Gather young stems by pulling or cutting them free from a strong clump. Repot annually, and divide in spring.

Ginger (*Zingiber officinale*)
Reed-like leaves and occasionally spikes of white and purple flowers are produced from fat, branching rhizomes. Grow in a 30cm (12in) container, above 13°C (55°F) with plenty of humidity in summer; in winter, keep almost dry to prevent dormant plants from rotting. Buy fresh root ginger with several good swollen buds, and bury horizontally just under the surface. Divide every spring, repotting young root segments and keeping the rest for use.

selecting your crops

fruit

For cultural purposes, fruit falls into two main types: tree, or top, fruit and soft fruit.

Tree fruit
Fruits like apples, pears, plums, peaches and apricots make the largest plants and live longest. They are often available in a range of forms, from full-size standards down to slim cordons or genetically dwarf bushes, depending on the particular fruit. Some, such as apples, pears and cherries, are grafted on rootstocks that control size and vigour. These restricted forms need special (but not complicated) training and pruning.

Soft fruit
This group, which includes all the berries and currants, is perennial but usually less permanent: strawberries need renewal every 3–4 years, and most experts recommend replacing crops like raspberries and blackcurrants every 7 years or so to counter declining yields from viruses and other disorders. Most can be trained: for example, gooseberries and redcurrants in special forms like dwarf standards or cordons, and blackberries and raspberries on wires or poles to save space and often increase yields.

Growing requirements
The various types of fruit are so versatile that even a small planting area can yield a profitable crop. Fruits are also easy to please, provided you consider a few essentials at the planning stage. In order to get fruit, blossom must set well. This means

Blueberries 'Bluecrop'

protecting flowers from frosts and cold winds: avoid frost hollows, screen on exposed sites, and choose late-flowering and early-ripening varieties if the growing season is short. Although certain fruits such as redcurrants tolerate some shade, most need sun to mature the crops and ripen the stems that bear the fruit buds. Where possible, align plants on a north-south axis, and make sure that screens, hedges and windbreaks do not cast direct shade.

Most need well-drained soil, but moisture is important for the flowers and developing fruits, so add plenty of organic matter when preparing sites and mulch to prevent drying out in summer – grass clippings are ideal because they encourage the slight acidity preferred by all except stone fruits (plums, cherries, for example). Wrapping fruit tree trunks with grease bands offers protection from pests (see *page 204*).

Unlike most vegetables, fruits are perennial and generally permanent, so plan sites carefully. Choose varieties you enjoy. Some have special cultural qualities – for example, apple 'Sunset' resists scab, gooseberry 'Invicta' is immune to mildew, blackcurrant 'Ben Sarek' takes up little space – but flavour is usually paramount. Thinning fruit (see *page 192*) is also desirable. Some fruits also do well under glass (see *page 175*).

Visit fruit-tasting festivals, try other plotholders' varieties and buy named produce to find the kinds you like.

PRUNING As well as limiting size, pruning also redirects growth: the top bud on a pruned stem usually grows first, in the direction in which it points, so that you can guide any new growth where you want it.

Trained forms like cordons, fans and espaliers are partially pruned in summer (see *page 196*) to stimulate fruit buds, and finished in winter (see *page 212*) to restrict size. As a guide, summer prune sideshoots to 5 leaves and winter prune to 2 buds.

Train and tie new stems when young, while still soft and supple to avoid injury. Check old ties regularly to make sure they are secure but not cutting into thickening stems.

Keep pruning tools very sharp, always cut just above a bud, and clear away prunings to avoid inviting diseases (or use them for cuttings, see *page 135*). When pruning to control diseases, dip the tools in sterilizing solution during and after work.

Apples *Malus* species

Not all allotment sites allow fruit trees, so check the rules first. Apple trees are popular, with hundreds of kinds available, and they are also the most versatile, thanks to a range of rootstocks on which the selected variety can be grafted. A very vigorous kind (MM111 in the UK, for example) can produce a tree 6m (20ft) tall and wide on poor soil, while very dwarfing M27 and M9 stocks are used for bushes and cordons only 1.8–3m (6–10ft) in size but these need good growing conditions. Dwarf trees start cropping 2 years after planting, large forms take 4–6 years. Heavy crops need thinning (see *page 192*).

There are hundreds of classic apple varieties in collections that can often be propagated to order. Some grow best in specific localities, others where the climate is cooler or wetter than average. All have special qualities and are worth exploring wherever samples are available. The varieties listed below are reliable for most sites.

PLANTING POSITIONS Consult a good catalogue or fruit handbook when deciding where to site apples and the best form: a single semi-dwarf tree will provide shade and structure, and potentially yield 90kg (200lb), while cordons can be planted 75cm (30in) apart in a line, occupying as much room as a row of runner beans and allowing a number of different varieties to be grown, each yielding about 3kg (7lb). You also need to check a variety's credentials – when it flowers and fruits, whether it is disease-resistant and suitable for your soil and climate, if it needs one or more partners nearby for effective cross-pollination, and whether it is an eating or cooking variety, for storing or to use straight from the tree.

WHEN TO PLANT Bare-root trees are planted while dormant, ideally in autumn; container-grown trees can (in theory) be planted any time of the year, although planting during the growing season entails much more care with watering in a hot or dry summer. Prepare the planting site thoroughly: dig or fork the ground two spits deep, clear out all weeds, and work in plenty of compost or rotted manure. Provide support before planting: short stakes for specimen trees, horizontal wires for cordons, fans and espaliers. Plant firmly and control weeds for the first few years to eliminate competition. Water young trees when dry, giving about 22 litres/sq.m (4 gals/sq.yd) every 7–10 days, and mulch with compost or rotted manure 5cm (2in) deep each spring.

VARIETIES *Dessert*: 'Adam's Pearmain', 'Ashmead's Kernel', 'Discovery', 'Egremont Russet', 'Holstein', 'Lord Lamborne', 'Red Falstaff', 'Spartan', 'Sunset'; *culinary*: 'Annie Elizabeth', 'Golden Noble', 'Grenadier', 'Newton Wonder'

Apples 'Lord Lamborne'

Pears 'Conference'

Pears & quinces

Pyrus communis & Cydonia oblonga

These are grown in a similar way to apples, but they flower earlier and like more heat to crop well: they are a gamble where summers are cool or wet, and on very light soils. Although they have no very dwarfing rootstocks, they can be trained in the same forms as apples. Timing the harvest is critical because most varieties are picked early to ripen in store. Always test fruits as they change colour to see if they part easily from the tree when lifted. They then need storing in boxes or on shelves in a cool place until almost ready (keep quinces apart from other fruits to avoid cross-flavours). When the fruits colour fully or give under light pressure near the stalk, bring them into warmth indoors. Quinces are usually cooked and may be used while still firm. Almost all pears need cross-pollination with another compatible variety (see Apples); quinces are self-fertile.

VARIETIES *Pears*: 'Beth', 'Beurré Superfin', 'Concorde', 'Conference', 'Merton Pride', 'Onward', 'Thompson's'; *quinces*: 'Champion', 'Meech's Prolific', 'Vranja'

Peaches, nectarines & apricots *Prunus persica, P. persica var. nectarina & P. armeniaca*

Easier to grow than many people suspect, these luscious fruits only need warmth and shelter at flowering and ripening times to have a good chance of fruiting well outdoors. In cooler regions they are best grown in pots and beds in a greenhouse, where they can be trained as fans up into the roof, helping to shade the contents in summer. Genetic dwarf kinds grow only 1.5–1.8m (5–6ft) tall, and do well as bushes in containers outdoors or under glass. All varieties are self-fertile, so a single tree will crop fully on its own, but you may need to pollinate the early spring blooms of indoor plants by dabbing their centres with a small soft paint brush – on mild days, simply open the door and vents for early bees to do the job for you.

Plant and tend as for apples, water regularly during growth, and mulch well. Thin fruits to leave individual specimens about 10–15cm (4–6in) apart. Test ripening fruits when they feel soft near the base of the stalks to see if they come away easily, and handle gently to avoid bruising. Prune like acid cherries (see right) by renewing fruited stems after harvest with new young shoots.

VARIETIES *Peaches*: 'Bellegarde', 'Bonanza' (dwarf), 'Duke of York', 'Peregrine', 'Redhaven', 'Royal George', 'Saturne' (Chinese peach); *nectarines*: 'Early Rivers', 'Elruge', 'Humboldt', 'Lord Napier', 'Nectarella' (dwarf), 'Pineapple'; *apricots*: 'Aprigold' (dwarf), 'Flavourcot', 'New Large Early', 'Tomcot'

Cherries *Prunus avium & P. cerasus*

These fruits are a great favourite with birds, so always choose a variety grafted on a dwarfing rootstock that will produce an easy-to-net tree. Cherries like similar conditions to plums but will tolerate lighter soils; acid (pie or cooking) varieties fruit as well in cool shady positions as in sunny warmth. All varieties can be trained as fans, which are easier to protect from frost and birds than large free-standing trees.

Plant and tend in the same way as apples (see *page 105*). On dry soils water consistently while fruits are developing, to prevent splitting. Pick or cut fruits with their stalks as soon as ripe. These are stone-fruits, so prune in spring and summer, treating sweet cherries like plums (see *page 196*). Acid cherries crop on young wood, so cut out fruited shoots after harvest; the following spring thin out young shoots to leave an equivalent number of replacements to bear the new crop. Only a few varieties are self-fertile and most need specific pollen partners, so read the catalogues carefully.

VARIETIES *Sweet*: 'Bradbourne Black', 'Early Rivers', 'Merton Bigarreau', 'Stella', 'Sunburst', 'Sweetheart'; *acid*: 'Morello', 'Nabella'

Cherries 'Stella'

Plums, gages & damsons

Prunus domestica & P. insititia

These are popular and choice fruits, easily grown where the soil is deep and moist for most of the year; they prefer clay to sandy soils, and (like all fruit with stones) crop best in slightly alkaline conditions, up to about pH7.2. Give them a sunny position away from exposed or low-lying ground, sheltered from winds when their early blossom appears. Damsons are the hardiest plums, whereas gages need warmth and are best grown against a sunny wall or fence. Rootstocks range from semi-dwarfing for bushes, pyramids and fans to vigorous for full-size trees. Plant and tend in the same way as apples. Depending on the variety and season, the fruits may set heavily or not at all – thin the heaviest sets to prevent brittle branches from breaking. Lightly prune to limit size and spread in spring and summer, while growth is active and wounds heal fast. Harvest fruit for cooking and preserving when it develops a surface bloom, for dessert fruit when fully ripe and tender – check the fruits regularly, as they do not ripen simultaneously. Some varieties are self-fertile, but almost all benefit from cross-pollination with a suitable neighbour.

VARIETIES *Plums*: 'Czar', 'Early Rivers', 'Kirke's', 'Marjorie's Seedling', 'Opal', 'Victoria'; *damsons*: 'Farleigh Damson', 'Merryweather'; *damson/plum cross*: 'Shropshire Prune'; *gages*: 'Count Althann's Gage', 'Denniston's Superb', 'Early Transparent Gage', 'Oullin's Golden Gage'

Plums 'Victoria'

Figs *Ficus carica*

Hardy except in very cold areas – where the top growth may be injured by severe frost – figs are vigorous, aristocratic trees that do best in large containers to limit their growth and stimulate more prolific fruiting. They can be trained as fans against a wall or inside a large greenhouse. The classic partnership of fig and grape vine makes a perfect shady bower for sitting and cooling under after working in the summer sun.

Prepare the ground as for apples (see *page 105*), and plant in spring. Water in dry weather while the fruits are swelling, but not to excess or they may split. Harvest in late summer or early autumn as the colour of the fruits deepens and they bend downwards with a drop of nectar at their tip. Prune in spring, removing frost-damaged shoots and any that cross or overcrowd the main branches.

VARIETIES 'Brown Turkey', 'Brunswick', 'White Marseilles'

Currants & berries

Ribes species & *Vaccinium corymbosum*
Redcurrants (with their white-fruited cousins) and gooseberries are prolific

Gooseberries 'Whinham's Industry'

Redcurrants 'Red Lake'

fruits that crop on a permanent framework of branches, so they can be grown as bushes, cordons, fans or short ornamental standards to make decorative screens around vegetable beds. Blackcurrants are greedy feeders for rich conditions, and only grow as bushes because they are pruned by removing one-third of the old stems each year to stimulate new stems that give the best crops. Blueberries need acid soil and should be grown in containers or raised beds where this is not available; they are only grown as bushes (see *page 180* for pruning), and for top yields two different varieties should be grown together. All tolerate some shade, and benefit from an annual mulch of compost in spring, together with an occasional soaking (with rainwater for blueberries) in dry weather while fruits develop.

VARIETIES *Redcurrants*: 'Fay's Prolific', 'Jonkheer van Tets', 'Red Lake'; *whitecurrants*: 'White Grape', 'White Pearl', 'White Versailles'; *blackcurrants*: 'Ben Lomond', 'Ben Sarek', 'Laxton's Giant'; *gooseberries*: 'Careless', 'Invicta', 'Whinham's Industry'; *blueberries*: 'Bluecrop', 'Herbert', 'Sunshine Blue'

Brambles *Rubus* species

Blackberries and their various hybrids such as loganberries and tayberries are vigorous, spreading plants, although up-to-date varieties are often more restrained. They can be trained on posts and horizontal wires as fences and screens, or allowed to ramble into existing hedges, while thornless varieties look and crop well trained on arches and pillars. Mulch in autumn with compost or rotted manure. Canes are produced one year and crop the next, after which they are cut out and replaced with the young green canes that are still developing. Early, maincrop and late varieties of blackberries can extend the harvest.

VARIETIES *Blackberries*: 'Fantasia', 'Oregon Thornless', 'Waldo'; *hybrid berries*: 'Thornless Boysenberry', 'Thornless Loganberry', 'Tayberry'

Raspberries *Rubus idaeus*

There are summer-fruiting varieties that crop heavily around midsummer, and autumn-fruiting kinds to extend the harvest from late summer until the first frosts. Fruits are generally red but

Raspberries 'Heritage'

may be yellow, black or purple. These cool-climate crops like a little shade on hot sites, and need moist growing conditions, so add compost at planting time and mulch liberally every spring. New canes are spaced about 45cm (18in) apart in a row and trained on horizontal wires. Cut out summer-fruiting canes immediately after harvest, autumn types in late winter; in a warm season, the autumn variety 'Heritage' will also crop in summer if canes that fruited in autumn are left unpruned until after a further summer crop. Check maturing fruits every 2–3 days, as they soon spoil once ripe.

VARIETIES *Summer fruiting*: 'Glen Moy', 'Malling Admiral', 'Malling Jewel'; *autumn fruiting*: 'Autumn Bliss', 'Fallgold', 'Heritage'

Strawberries *Fragaria* species
An easy and popular crop, usually grown together in a bed (see *page 198*) and rotated around the plot every 3–4 years as the short-term plants pass their peak. Maincrop kinds, which fruit from late spring to midsummer according to variety, are planted one year to give their best yield the next (but see *page 179*), after which size

Strawberries 'Cambridge Late Pine'

and quality gradually decline. Perpetual (remontant or everbearing) varieties fruit mainly from midsummer to mid-autumn, as do alpine strawberries. The large-fruited kinds produce runners bearing young plants used to make new beds or for forcing (see *page 196*); alpines are generally non-running and form compact plants that are multiplied by division and often used for edging. Flavour varies widely with variety, and older kinds like mid-season 'Royal Sovereign' and perpetual 'Aromel' are thought by many to be superior to modern varieties, which are firmer and often disease-resistant.

VARIETIES *Maincrop*: 'Cambridge Late Pine', 'Gariguette', 'Royal Sovereign'; *perpetual*: 'Aromel', 'Flamenco', 'Rapella'; *alpine*: 'Alexandria', 'Baron Solemacher', 'Fraises des Bois'

Grapes *Vitis* species
These are favourite allotment fruits, with dessert kinds growing well in a greenhouse (see *page 212*), and wine

varieties outdoors on posts and wires. Careful pruning and training are vital to limit the often rampant growth and redirect energy into fruit production, although a more relaxed regime can result in an ornamental vine over an arch or arbour with some fruit as a bonus. All varieties need sun and fertile, well-drained soil, together with a manure mulch in spring for best crops. Choose appropriate varieties to suit indoor or outdoor sites, for dessert or wine purposes, and plant during autumn or winter. Flowers on indoor plants need fertilizing by hand, plus careful ventilation and humidity control during fruiting.

VARIETIES 'Bacchus', 'Leon Millot', 'Muscat Hamburgh', 'Phoenix'

Grapes 'Bacchus'

fruit

ornamental & edible flowers

Classic kinds like gladioli and dahlias are raised for cutting or show, and a more ecological approach has led to the introduction of companion and attractant plants to help create a balanced and healthier growing environment. If your plot is the only garden you have, there is no justification for an old-fashioned narrow insistence on using an allotment solely for growing food. Many flowers are edible, anyway!

Flowers for cutting
These have traditionally been allocated space in kitchen gardens as crops to grow for convenience in rows alongside vegetables. This is still the best way for tall flowers that need support from canes or wires to keep their stems straight and upright, and for annuals sown in batches for succession – remember to thin them to about 23cm

FLOWER TIME
By studying their habits, botanists noticed that particular flowers regularly open or close their blooms to time, and they compiled lists for every hour of daylight. You could use this knowledge to pace your day on the plot. For example, dandelions open at about 7am, scarlet pimpernel at 9am; at noon, morning glories close, while evening primroses open at 6pm; and, in case you are working late, dandelions finally close at 9pm. Flowers ignore local Summer Time.

(9in) apart for superior blooms. Many perennials do equally well in ornamental groups dispersed around the plot, to punctuate the business beds with colour and frivolity. Explore varieties developed specially for the cut flower trade, such as tall antirrhinum 'Sky Rocket', small straight-stemmed 'Sonja' sunflowers (*Helianthus*) or the Japanese range of double *Chrysanthemum coronarium*.

SEASONAL SUGGESTIONS
Spring Anemones, honesty (*Lunaria*), lily of the valley (*Convallaria*), narcissi, stocks (*Matthiola*), tulips, wallflowers (*Erysimum*)
Summer Antirrhinums, calendulas, columbines (*Aquilegia*), cornflowers (*Centaurea cyanus*), pyrethrum, sweet peas (*Lathyrus odoratus*), sweet Williams (*Dianthus barbatus*)
Autumn Chrysanthemums, cosmos, dahlias, gladioli, heleniums, rudbeckias, sunflowers (*Helianthus*)
Winter Hyacinths, narcissi, snowdrops (*Galanthus*) – all forced under glass.

Flowers for eating
A wide range of flowers was eaten in ancient Greece and Rome, a practice that is becoming popular once more. Some can be eaten whole, while only the petals of others are used. Most are added to salads or desserts. Pick early on a dry day, rinse in cold water and use at once, as they rarely keep well. Make sure none have been sprayed with chemicals.

EAT WHOLE (except for stalks and any green parts): angelica, basil, catmint (*Nepeta*), chives, courgettes, dill, elder, evening primrose, mint, rosemary.

PETALS ONLY (but do not eat any green parts, the central pistil, stamens and white bases to petals): bergamot, borage, chicory, chrysanthemum, cowslips and primroses (*Primula*), fuchsia, hollyhocks (*Alcea*), lavender, nasturtiums (*Tropaeolum*), pinks and carnations (*Dianthus*), pot marigolds (*Calendula*), roses, scented pelargoniums, sweet Williams (*Dianthus barbatus*), violets (*Viola*).

ATTRACTING WILDLIFE
Growing flowers is a simple and certain way to attract birds, bees and other beneficial insects to your plot. Many single or old-fashioned garden flowers are as effective as wild flowers for this, and it is easy to find space for a few plants of achillea, centaurea, Michaelmas (*Aster novi-belgii*) and Shasta daisies (*Leucanthemum* x *superbum*), golden rod (*Solidago*) or valerian (*Centranthus*), for example. Infiltrate hedges with honeysuckle (*Lonicera*), buddleja, thornless blackberries and elderberries, and train virginia creeper (*Parthenocissus*) and ivy (*Hedera*) on sheds for honey bees and birds. If permitted, include some favourite wild flowers like corn marigold (*Xanthophthalmum segetum*), lady's smock (*Cardamine pratensis*) and field scabious (*Knautia arvensis*), or sow a small patch with a bumblebee or butterfly mixture, but make sure your flowers do not self-seed over other plots.

CLASSIC ALLOTMENT FLOWERS

Plenty of space and dedicated individual attention are fundamental to raising these plants well, whether as cut flowers or for exhibition. They fit uneasily into a domestic garden community, whereas on the allotment they can share the intensive care normally given to vegetable crops.

SWEET PEAS For supreme quality these are normally sown in autumn and overwintered in a cold frame for planting out in spring in well-spaced, trenched rows. Each plant is trained as a cordon, secured to a tall cane with wire rings. Sideshoots and tendrils are removed regularly to concentrate energy in stem growth and flowers, which are larger and more numerous on extra-long stalks.

CHRYSANTHEMUMS The season starts in late winter, when dormant stools are revived to produce a batch of cuttings. These are potted on into large containers, which are finally stood outdoors once frosts are past, although early-flowering varieties are often planted in the open ground. Plants are trained on canes, with their growing tips pinched out on specific dates to encourage a set number of sideshoots that will bloom at a given time.

DAHLIAS These need an early start, too, either from cuttings or divisions of tubers. They are planted out after the frosts in well-prepared and enriched sites with plenty of space. Like chrysanthemums, a limited number of stems are encouraged by pinching and thinning, and special care must be devoted to singling the buds on each stem so that those remaining produce the largest blooms. Plants need copious watering and regular feeding.

GLADIOLI There are countless named large-flowered varieties producing tall plants that look out of place in a garden, but make magnificent cut blooms. Corms are planted in rows, often in successive batches for continuity, and each developing flower spike is tied to a stake. Regular feeding begins as buds form, and continues until the foliage dies down, so that good strong corms for the following year are produced by the autumn, when the corms are lifted for storing.

cultivating your allotment

Seeds and young plants are naturally endowed with vitality and resilience. By encouraging them with a favourable growing environment and a regime of sensitive care, you can ensure their successful progress from seedbed to maturity and triumphant harvest.

the soil

SOIL CHARACTERISTICS

LIGHT SOIL	LOAM (IDEAL SOIL)	HEAVY SOIL
large particles	medium-sized particles	small particles
gritty or grainy	crumbly	greasy and pliable
holds little water	stays evenly moist	easily waterlogged
fast drainage	well drained	slow drainage
often infertile	good fertility	fertile when cultivated
easily worked	workable when not wet	hard to work
warms quickly	warms steadily	cold, and slow to warm
dusty when dry	stable and friable	dries hard and cracks

The importance of soil

Soil is one of the Earth's more precious resources, and probably the most important raw material at a gardener's disposal. Seldom perfect for cultivation and often taken for granted, neglected or even abused, it is nonetheless alive and can be managed or amended over the seasons until even the least promising plot is coaxed into supporting high yields of top-quality crops.

Over many thousands of years weathering and erosion reduce rock to mineral fragments, which range in size from coarse grains of sand to the finest particles of clay. These rock fragments are the largest component of almost every soil type and determine its character. As generations of plants flourish and die, their decaying remains form humus, the spongy organic material concentrated in varying amounts in the upper few centimetres, or 'topsoil'. Cultivated soil also contains water and air in quantities that mainly depend on the proportion of humus and the size of the mineral particles. Finally, soil is home to countless organisms, from moles and earthworms to microscopic bacteria. Their diversity and numbers are directly related to soil quality: impoverished ground can seem depopulated compared to the teeming life of well-tended soil.

Getting acquainted
Once you are familiar with the lie and aspect of your plot, turn your attention to the nature of the soil, because this will determine future plans and activities. Check for three main qualities: whether

2 Empty a couple of cans of water into the hole. If the water disappears quickly or steadily, drainage is unlikely to be a problem, but if it takes hours (or even days) to vanish, you may need to undertake some preliminary drainage of at least part of the site to avoid waterlogging in wet weather (see *page 116*)

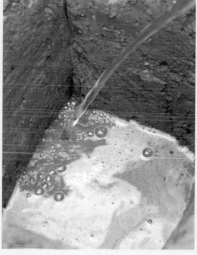

1 Skim off any weeds with a spade and then dig a neat hole about 45cm (18in) across and deep. This will reveal the soil 'profile': the depth of dark friable topsoil and the quality of the lower subsoil, which may be heavy and solid, implying slow drainage, or porous stony or gravelly material on ground that drains quickly.

3 Take a handful of moist topsoil and squeeze it into a ball. If the ball keeps its shape and feels sticky and can be polished with your thumb, the soil is heavy with a high clay component, especially if you can mould it into other shapes. If it falls apart readily again, the soil is light and sandy or silty

the soil is heavy or light (see above), if it drains well (see *page 116*), and whether it is acidic or chalky (see *page 125*). Also note its organic content, as thin, pale soils low in humus can be relatively infertile and uncooperative, while very organic soils – usually dark, crumbly and fibrous or 'peaty' – will need careful water and nutrient management.

Starting cultivation You will
first need to clear any neglected and overgrown sites, but if you are lucky enough to take over a clean, well-tended plot with no obvious problems such as poor drainage, you can start preparing the ground for your planned layout. Even if you intend to adopt a

minimal- or no-digging routine (see *page 36*), it is a good idea to first dig over all or part of the plot during autumn or winter. This will give some experience of handling the type of soil, reveal less obvious features such as buried roots or variations in texture and structure, and allow you to incorporate plenty of manure or compost if you plan to concentrate on surface cultivation later.

Single digging should be adequate at this stage, but where drainage is bad or deep beds planned, double digging may be preferable, at least locally. Rotavating (see *page 123*) is a useful alternative, especially if you are starting in summer on a weedy plot and have the whole season at your disposal: repeated

rotavation at fortnightly intervals in dry weather can destroy most perennial weed roots, provided they are raked off the surface after each session. However, this treatment can temporarily damage soil structure and may cause drainage problems on clay subsoils. Light soil soon dries out once disturbed, so in spring or summer dig over only as much as is needed for immediate use. Heavy ground benefits from being roughly dug in autumn and left for rain and frost to break it down.

SEE ALSO ▶ Exploring your plot
page 25 Single digging *page 124*
Double digging *page 124*

the soil

Improving your soil

Most allotment soils are some form of loam, a mixture of light sand and heavy clay particles. Depending on the proportions of these mineral ingredients, your soil may be a sandy loam or clay loam, and its texture will vary accordingly.

TEXTURE This textural quality is important because the size of the soil particles determines the amount of empty spaces, or 'pores', that can be filled with air or water, both vital for healthy soil organisms and strong plant growth. Very sandy soils have large particles and pores, so they drain and dry out quickly, whereas the fine grains of clay leave tiny pores that can absorb huge quantities of water but release it again only very slowly.

Improving your soil depends on understanding these differences in behaviour. Clay remains wet for a long time in spring and is therefore slow to warm up enough for you to start sowing, but if you increase the size of the soil pores, the clay will drain and warm up faster (see *page 118*). Sand, on the other hand, has large pores that make light soils airy and difficult to keep moist in hot dry weather, but the addition of plenty of organic material (see *page 118*) will help retain moisture for longer, as well as binding the loose grains into a more stable structure.

DRAINAGE The pores of badly drained ground are often full of water to the exclusion of air, a condition that can cause nutrient deficiencies and poor growth; in extreme cases oxygen depletion is lethal to plant roots and soil organisms. Puddles lingering long after rain, holes filling with water, soil smelling sour and stagnant, and the presence of rushes, sedges and moss are all indications of waterlogged ground that needs improvement.

Very often regular cultivation and the addition of organic material will cure the problem. On level ground, creating slightly raised narrow beds (see *page 36*) will provide extra depth of drained soil for crops, while a sloping site can be contoured so that water drains from higher cultivated ground to the lowest point, where a pond or bog garden could be made.

For more all-round improvement, dig a rubble drain across the site, about 60cm (2ft) deep and 30–45cm (12–18in) wide, and gently sloping to a soakaway in one corner. A soakaway is a pit 1.2–1.5m (4–5ft) across and as deep as possible – it must be at least 1.2m (4ft) to be effective. Fill this with stones and builder's rubble, covered with a layer of gravel. Top off with turf or use the space for a water tank, seat or similar feature.

MAKING YOUR OWN COMPOST

Every allotment and household produces organic waste that can be turned into a free, renewable source of humus and fertility containing a balanced and good range of plant nutrients. Turning this waste into compost need not be a sophisticated art: dead organic materials decompose naturally, and compost-making merely exploits this characteristic under more controlled conditions.

A simple heap of waste in a corner of the plot will eventually rot into compost, but a bought or home-made container can generate more heat, accelerating the process in less space. Given enough heat, all plant and

Garden compost is full of nutrients and ideal for improving the soil. This simple heap is piled high with lawn mowings and annual weeds.

WORMERIES

A bought or home-made wormery, housing thousands of compost worms (ordinary garden worms cannot be used) steadily recycling vegetable waste into a rich friable source of fertility, is the ideal solution where compost material is available little and often: large volumes can overwhelm the worms and cause problems. Stand the wormery in a warm but shaded place, on the soil for liquids to drain away safely unless there is an integral reservoir. Use the compost solids to feed greedy crops such as squashes, for top-dressing containers or for making potting compost. Use the liquid as a compost heap activator or dilute it for using as a general feed.

animal waste can be composted, but under normal conditions common sense will suggest that pet manures, meat residues and diseased plants may attract rodents or transmit infection, and should therefore be excluded.

Too much of any single waste material will delay decomposition and make the resulting compost unbalanced, so aim for a good mix of ingredients. These can be divided into 'green' waste (weeds, vegetable trimmings, lawn mowings, soft prunings), which supply nitrogen, and 'brown' (paper, tree leaves, straw, eggshells, vacuum cleaner contents), which provide carbon. Equal quantities of green and brown ingredients make the best compost.

When the container is full, make sure the contents are moist and cover them with an insulating layer of sacking or old mats and a sheet of plastic or a rainproof lid. Leave to mature for several weeks in summer, longer in winter. Emptying and remixing the contents once or twice accelerates decay, as will the addition of a stimulant such as poultry manure in autumn and winter heaps. Start using the finished compost from the bottom or middle, whichever is more accessible; undecayed material from the sides and top can be used to start another heap.

Quick compost Mix torn newspapers and thin card with an equal volume of lawn mowings in a black plastic bag. Water the contents with urine as an activator, seal the top of the bag, and leave in a sunny place. The contents can be ready for digging in after 3–4 weeks in warm weather.

SEE ALSO ▶ Compost bins *pages 52-3* Adding organic matter *page 118* **Making leafmould** *page 208*

MAKING A COMPOST TRENCH

A trench filled with compostable material such as kitchen waste and then left for at least two months will produce very fertile soil for hungry crops such as peas or beans. Trenches are usually made in winter to be ready for planting or sowing in the spring. They are not suitable for heavy or badly drained soil, as they tend to become waterlogged.

1 Mark a strip 45–60cm (18–24in) wide along a bed or across the plot.

2 Dig out a section at one end of the strip to at least a single spade's depth. Put the soil to one side.

3 Loosen the bottom of the trench with a fork and then gradually fill to half its depth with compost material, such as kitchen waste, as this becomes available.

4 Cover with soil from the next section, and continue to the far end of the strip, which will be filled with the soil put aside from the first section. Leave for at least 2 months before planting or sowing with peas or beans for a bumper crop.

the soil

SOIL IMPROVEMENT CHECKLIST

LIGHT SOILS

▶ Dig or fork in plenty of compost or manure to prevent rapid drying out and to add body to the light texture.

▶ Dig only when prepared ground is needed because loosened soil dries out faster.

▶ Do not cultivate in windy weather, when loose topsoil can blow away.

▶ Tread the surface firm if you are sowing or planting immediately after digging.

▶ Avoid leaving ground bare for long periods: mulch the surface or grow a green manure such as mustard, crimson clover or lupins.

▶ Hoe or prick over the soil with a fork after prolonged heavy rain, which can seal the surface with a hard cap.

▶ Top up fertility levels every spring, as the heavy rains in winter quickly leach out soluble nutrients.

HEAVY SOILS

▶ Try to dig as much spare ground as possible during autumn, to allow winter weather to crumble the soil.

▶ Do not cultivate while the soil is very wet – treading on wet clay causes compaction, drainage problems and poor aeration.

▶ Mulch after the soil dries and warms in spring, to prevent hot sun setting and cracking the surface.

▶ Grow deep-rooted green manures such as buckwheat, fenugreek and grazing rye to open up the structure.

▶ Add lime to clay (see below).

▶ Add compost or manure annually to physically open up clay, admit more air and aid drainage.

▶ Consider dividing the plot into raised or narrow beds to limit treading on cultivated ground.

▶ Restrict the use of mechanical cultivators, as these can produce an impenetrable buried 'pan' of soil.

IMPROVING CLAY SOIL WITH LIME

Careful management and a regular leavening of organic material will help loosen clay soil and improve its texture. You can also alter its mechanical behaviour with garden lime, which binds the sticky clay particles together into larger, more manageable crumbs by a process called 'flocculation'.

In the autumn, spread 400g/sq.m (12oz/sq.yd) of lime on the surface of the soil; for serious cases, repeat the treatment in the spring. There should be an improvement in the texture of the soil after two years, when you can reduce the rate to 65g/sq.m (2oz/sq.yd) twice annually.

Keep applications of lime and manure several weeks apart to avoid a chemical reaction. Note that adding lime will alter the soil's pH status (see *page 125*): to avoid increasing the levels of alkalinity, mix 1 part dolomite (magnesium limestone) with 4 parts gypsum (calcium sulphate) and use this instead at the same rate.

ADDING ORGANIC MATTER

Sound cultivation focuses on feeding the soil, rather than the plant. The vitality of any soil depends on a flourishing population of microscopic bacteria, which, in turn, rely for survival on humus, a crumbly, dark brown material made of decomposing organic remains. Adding 'bulky' organic material such as compost and manure fortifies humus levels, feeding these organisms and contributing to improved soil structure and fertility. You need to replenish organic matter annually, either dug in and mixed with the soil or applied as a mulch, because humus is constantly being broken down into minerals and nutrients, and cropping makes huge demands on this store of essential plant foods.

SOURCES OF HUMUS Anything that will rot readily can supply humus. The most common materials for allotment use are as follows:

Animal manures These are usually bought by the trailer-load in autumn for digging in, or in bags at any time for improving small areas. Fairly high in nutrients, they are best sourced from non-intensive farms to avoid unwelcome chemical residues, and should be stacked for a year to decay unless already well rotted (see Making a hot bed, *page 53*).

Garden compost Easily made on-site or at home from garden and domestic waste, this is a free and renewable resource containing good levels of nutrients, and available all year round once a composting routine has been established.

Spent mushroom compost This useful waste material is based on rotted straw, available regularly from mushroom growers. As it is usually alkaline, it is good for brassica beds, but can contain chemical residues

Phacelia, a popular green manure that also attracts beneficial insects.

unless from an organic source. It may produce occasional mushroom crops!
Other suitable materials These include proprietary bagged manures, which are composted animal and plant wastes, and are often expensive. Straw is good for mulching and then digging in once partly decayed; leafmould, although low in nutrients, is an excellent soil conditioner and mulch; and worm compost, the rich product of a wormery (see *page 116*), is best used for potting compost and targeted feeding.

MULCHING A mulch is a blanket of material, applied to insulate the soil from extreme weather, suppress weeds by denying them light, and help reduce evaporation of soil moisture. Organic mulches also supply plant foods, encourage earthworms and gradually improve soil texture as they are incorporated. Inorganic and deep organic mulches can be used to clear weedy ground.

All the organic materials dug in to supply soil humus can be used for mulching, together with grass clippings, shredded prunings and other woody waste, bracken and bark. If dug in, these extra undecayed materials can deplete the soil as they rot, but they are excellent as mulches on the surface, where they start to decompose safely. Mulches of organic materials not only stabilize existing soil conditions but also absorb a lot of moisture, so are applied only to moist soil that has warmed up in spring.

GREEN MANURES A green manure is a cover crop of plants sown for digging in as a soil improver. Several kinds are leguminous and can boost soil fertility, storing atmospheric nitrogen in their roots and then releasing it as they decay. Others have strong roots that penetrate and aerate heavy subsoils, and can transfer minerals from the depths to the topsoil for use by later crops. All stabilize and protect the soil surface from

unwelcome weathering, help smother weeds and prevent nutrients from leaching out of the soil. Before digging in, sprinkle the green manure crop with nitrogen-rich poultry manure to speed up decomposition, and dig in before flowering if you want to avoid volunteer seedlings later. Unobtrusive clumps of clover, phacelia and buckwheat left to flower attract bees and hoverflies.

Choosing the best green manure will depend on the season, the type of soil you have and the time available for the crop to grow. Popular types include:
Alfalfa (lucerne) Long taproot for hard ground; sow spring or autumn; 12 months to grow.
Buckwheat Good for light soils; sow spring to late summer; 2–3 months to grow.
Field (winter) beans Add nitrogen to heavy soils; sow autumn; 4–6 months to grow.
Crimson clover Adds nitrogen to light soils; sow spring to late summer; 2 months or more to grow.
Fenugreek Strong taproot for poor subsoils; sow spring onwards; 3 months to grow.
Lupin Nitrogen-fixer for light soils; sow spring and summer; 3–4 months to grow.
Mustard Fast brassica for most soils; sow spring to autumn; 4–6 weeks to grow.
Phacelia Leafy crop for most soils; sow spring to autumn; 2–3 months to grow.
Trefoil Adds nitrogen to light soils; sow spring to late summer; 3–4 months to grow.
Winter tares Winter-hardy nitrogen-fixer for heavy soils; sow spring to autumn; 2 months or more to grow.

SEE ALSO ▶ Mulching weeds away *page 122* Fertilizers & feeding *pages 150–1*

SOIL FERTILITY

In an allotment context, fertility – the potential of the soil to support plant growth – is determined by a number of factors, including the soil's healthy structure and population of beneficial organisms, its pH status (levels of calcium, see *page 125*), and its store of available plant foods.

The various nutrients essential for growth must not just be present but also accessible. Plants absorb food in solution and therefore need adequate water, together with nutrients in a dissolved form. Chemical fertilizers are concentrated and easily soluble, which is why they act fast, but they can only feed plant growth and have little beneficial effect on the soil. Bulky organic manures and compost physically improve the ground and support growth as they are broken down by soil organisms into simple soluble chemicals.

SUPPLYING NUTRIENTS

A balanced supply of the chemical elements, or nutrients, is essential for healthy plants (see *page 150*). Several, called trace elements, are required only in minute quantities, whereas larger amounts of major nutrients such as nitrogen (N), phosphorus (P) and potassium (K) need to be readily available and regularly replenished. Crops depend heavily on them for energy and development, while their solubility means their residues are continuously leached from the soil by rain.

Ground that is sensitively cultivated and regularly replenished with organic material will often contain enough accessible nutrients to sustain plants through to maturity without further feeding with supplementary fertilizers, and it is possible to maintain allotment crops by digging in large

SIGNS OF LOW FERTILITY

All ground should be routinely manured or composted, depending on the crop, but some areas or soils may require more urgent amendment. This chart lists the most common symptoms to watch out for and indicates the likely causes.

SYMPTOMS	LIKELY CAUSE
Generally poor, slow or pale growth	Inadequate soil structure; unsuitable pH; low soil organism activity; nutrient depletion
Stunted growth; pale or yellow leaves; small fruits	Nitrogen shortage
Poor root development; blue-tinted leaves; low fruit yields	Impaired drainage or phosphate deficiency
Leaf mottling; small crops; poor-quality fruits	Insufficient potassium
Root rots; mosses; spiderworts; surface algae; sour smell	Poor drainage; excess acidity (low pH); soil compaction

Leaf mottling.

amounts of manure or compost initially and then mulching or top-dressing annually with an 8cm (3in) layer of the same materials.

Poorer soils, sandy soil that is rapidly depleted, and heavily cropped ground at the end of a wet winter may be seriously impoverished, however, and supplementary feeding (see *pages 150–1*) can then turn disappointment into success. When using fertilizers, always target the plants in need rather than distribute them over a wide area where much will go to waste, and avoid over-application, which can cause plant disorders.

Before deciding to boost growth with fertilizers, it is worth exploring alternative sources of fertility. Companion planting with leguminous species can be surprisingly productive: trefoil sown between sweetcorn plants, for example, will share some of its root-fixed nitrogen with the crop and can then be left as winter groundcover to dig in as a green manure in spring.

The leaves of comfrey, a potash-rich perennial, laid alongside crops will provide all the benefits of a mulch and supply nutrients as they rot.

SEE ALSO ▶ **Companion planting** *page 35* Checking soil acidity *page 125* **Fertilizers & feeding** *pages 150–1*

the soil

121

clearing the plot

cultivating your allotment

Planning your approach

You may have the good fortune to take over a well-tended plot or one that was recently abandoned. If so, you will probably only need to clean away crop remains for composting and dig in annual weeds as green manure (see *page 119*). A long-neglected allotment, however, needs a more planned approach before you can start sowing and planting. Over time, annual weeds are infiltrated and eventually dominated by perennials that can be much harder to eradicate.

Starting the work in autumn allows the whole winter for steady clearance, but if you take over the allotment during the growing season, it would be sensible to identify the least overgrown or most accessible part of the plot and clear this first, simply controlling the rest by mowing or strimming until you can work on it later. If the prospect seems daunting, you could enlist family members to share out the work. Neighbouring plot-holders will often help new tenants make a start (but you should return the favour to other newcomers).

Unless you have plenty of time and stamina, adopt a gradualist strategy: remember Nature abhors a vacuum, and a large cleared area will soon host more weeds if left unused.

THE WORST WEEDS Although many weeds can be tolerated, even eaten (see *page 153*), others can be a problem and need firm control. Tenacious villains include species like lesser celandine (*Ranunculus ficaria*) with easily dispersed bulbils, and those that spread by persistent underground rhizomes or stolons: couch grass (*Agropyron repens*), ground elder (*Aegopodium podagraria*) and bindweeds (*Calystegia* and *Convolvulus*), for example. Overlooked bulbils and root fragments soon grow back, and only the hottest compost heap will kill the roots.

Fork out plants and roots wherever they intrude, and dispose of them safely. They are rich in minerals that are lost if they are burnt or binned, however. A more thrifty plan is to dry the roots in the sun on a sheet of plastic until brittle and then crumble the remains in the compost heap. Alternatively, gather the roots in a woven bag and steep them in water to make liquid fertilizer (see *page 151*).

STRIPPING TURF If the weed cover comprises mainly grass and shallow-rooted perennials, you can cut and skim off the top 5cm (2in) of matted roots in turves. This is valuable fibrous topsoil, so arrange the turves upside down in a stack and wrap this securely in black plastic for a year or two. When this has rotted well, the stack can be dug in to supplement humus levels in the soil.

OVERGROWN PLOTS How you tackle the reclamation of overgrown plots depends on available tools, long-term plans and personal inclination. Always explore the plot carefully, especially before using machinery, because obstacles could be concealed in the topgrowth, and proceed cautiously: depending on the season, there may be bulbs, asparagus, rhubarb and other perennial plants dormant below ground.

Cutting down Where the topgrowth is more than about 15cm (6in) high, cut it down with a sickle, slasher, strimmer or pair of shears. Compost the cut material or, if it contains woody stems and brambles, stack it in a corner to rot and provide a wildlife habitat. You may then be able to rotary-mow the site more closely.

MULCHING WEEDS AWAY

All but the toughest weeds can be killed if you smother them with a sheet mulch. Cover the mown weeds with pieces of overlapped cardboard or a thick layer of newspapers, and then spread a 10–15cm (4–6in) layer of manure or compost on top. Leave for a few weeks – all winter if possible – before making planting holes with a dibber through the sheet for a robust crop such as potatoes, beans, sweetcorn or squashes. Use old potting compost or friable soil from elsewhere to fill in the holes. Yields will be acceptable, and you will be left with a fertile and weed-free bed when the mulch is turned in.

Inorganic mulches, such as black plastic film, woven plastic groundcover sheet and black mulching paper, can also be used to clear weedy ground. In addition, they protect the soil and are useful for crops such as strawberries, potatoes and onions, which are planted through slits or holes cut in the material. Used with care, these mulches will last for several seasons.

RIGHT Sacking, planks of wood and plastic sheets left on the ground for at least a year will smother most weeds. BELOW As well as clearing a plot of weeds, a rotavator can also be used to loosen compacted ground.

Rotavating A rotavator is a petrol-powered machine used primarily to clear weeds but it can also turn manure or compost into cleared ground. Rotavating is efficient and undemanding, but liable to multiply perennial weeds from root cuttings. Rake off all unearthed roots and thoroughly fork through areas needed for cultivation to make sure few root fragments are left.

Digging & forking This is a strenuous but thorough option for clearing an overgrown plot. Chop an area into manageable strips with a spade and carefully fork it through, shaking off as much loose soil as possible. Loosen the soil around deeper weeds with a fork and try to remove all the roots A mattock (heavy broad-bladed hoe) is useful for grubbing out nettle and bramble roots.

Herbicides Even if you intend to garden organically, you might decide to use a systemic weedkiller such as glyphosate initially to clear heavy weed infestations. Be aware of the disadvantages of this method (see *page 153*), especially the risks to adjacent plots. A sound compromise might be to clean beds by another method, and treat only intervening paths with a herbicide.

Smothering Depriving weeds of light is a slow but certain way to destroy them. If you can leave an area uncultivated for at least a year by covering it with old carpets or black plastic sheeting, overlapped and securely pegged to the ground, you will kill all but the most tenacious weeds, which can then be dug or forked out. Some managements consider this method unsightly, so check the regulations first.

SEE ALSO ▶ Tools *pages 54–5* Mulching *page 119* **The case for weeding *pages 152–3***

doing the groundwork

Preparing the soil Ground that is cleared and, where necessary, drained ready for cultivation will need digging or forking over to produce the conditions that are suitable for planting or sowing. If the plot has been well maintained, it may be sufficient to fork the surface and then level it for immediate use. Otherwise dig it over by one of the methods described below.

SINGLE DIGGING This is digging to a single spade's depth ('spit') and is adequate for most purposes, such as loosening new ground and turning in manure or weeds. You can either dig out a spadeful of soil and invert it with a twist of the handle so that it falls back in its original position or take out a trench.

DOUBLE DIGGING This is a strenuous undertaking that disturbs the soil two spits or more deep, and is used to prepare raised or 'no-dig' beds, amend poor drainage and improve poor ground.

FORKING This is digging with a full-size fork, which can be easier than with a spade on stony ground and is useful for breaking down rough-dug soil, turning well-tended ground, freeing weeds and working in manure or compost. Use the fork to its full depth for maximum results, or simply prick over the soil with the tips of its tines to aerate and loosen the surface.

RAKING The final stage of soil preparation involves the levelling and breaking down of clods of earth by raking vigorously to and fro, and then combing the surface with the rake, holding it in a more upright position, to skim off any stones and weed fragments.

HOEING Although hoeing is used mainly for the routine control of weeds between growing plants, a Dutch, or push, hoe is also valuable for loosening a caked surface immediately before sowing and planting.

HOW TO DIG

1 Moving backwards, dig the first trench to a spit deep and a spit across. Deposit the soil in a wheelbarrow and take it to the far end of the plot (this soil is for filling in the last trench). Square up the trench, removing all the loose crumbs of soil from the bottom.

Timing cultivation Clay soils are best dug in autumn and left rough to expose the greatest area to frost and prevent compaction from heavy rainfall. The soil can then be broken down to a finer tilth just before sowing or planting. Light ground is best dug in spring, leaving its vulnerable surface protected from rain and wind over winter by a covering of green manure, annual weeds or a mulch of leafmould. Leave light soils for a few weeks to settle after

2 If you wish to improve the texture and fertility of the topsoil, spread manure or compost in the bottom of the trench, together with any annual weeds skimmed off the next strip to be dug.

cultivating your allotment

cultivation, or lightly tread any areas that are going to be used immediately to prevent evaporation. Digging waterlogged or frozen soil damages its structure, and is unnecessarily difficult on very dry ground.

Checking soil acidity
Calcium is an important element (see *page 150*) that determines how easily plants absorb other nutrients. Levels of calcium in the soil may be low (as in acid soils), high (as in alkaline soils) or, more commonly, about midway.

MEASURING CALCIUM You can measure the amount of calcium in your plot with a simple electronic tester or a chemical kit according to a pH scale of 0–14: readings below 7.0 (neutral) are increasingly acid, above 7.0 more alkaline. Crops differ in their calcium requirements, but most have a fairly wide tolerance within the range of pH6.5–7.0. Cabbages and other brassicas, however, prefer more alkaline conditions.

LIMING Adding lime to the soil will make it more alkaline: applying 270g/sq.m (8oz/sq.yd) on sandy soils or 2–3 times that amount on clay can raise the pH by approximately 1.0 (one unit). (Making soils more acid is harder, and involves adding sulphur, iron sulphate, grass clippings or leafmould over the course of several seasons.)

In most cases, liming brassica beds (see *page 74*) at the start of the season is sufficient, provided you rotate these annually to maintain an acceptable pH status over the whole plot. Annual soil tests are usually unnecessary, but testing when you first take over is wise because deficiency problems arise in extreme soils, especially where there has been excessive liming, which is difficult to correct.

SEE ALSO ▶ **Crop rotation** *pages 32–5* No-dig beds *page 36* **Tools** *pages 54–5* Green manures *page 119* **Preparing a tilth** *page 126* Making leafmould *page 208*

4 Finally, dig a second trench alongside the first, and throw this topsoil into the first trench; make sure that the topsoil and subsoil are not mixed together. Repeat down the plot until the last trench is filled with the heap of excavated topsoil from the first.

3 Where the soil is poor, shallow or infertile, loosen the subsoil in the bottom of the trench to the full depth of a digging fork (use a pickaxe on compacted ground) and work plenty of manure into this second spit.

DIGGING HINTS
▶ Divide the work into comfortable sessions, and stop before you become tired.
▶ Pace yourself: rest at the end of rows to clean your spade.
▶ Digging large areas that you have divided into manageable strips is psychologically more rewarding.
▶ Never cultivate in wet or frosty conditions.
▶ Hold the spade upright to work the maximum depth.
▶ Loosen the edges of each spadeful by chopping cleanly through the surface.
▶ Turn in annual weeds but remove perennial roots as you go.
▶ Twist the handle as you invert each spadeful, to loosen soil and weed roots.
▶ Never bring the pale subsoil to the surface.
▶ Roughly level the surface as you go, to save work later.

the final stages

Making a seedbed The final cultivation step before the ground is ready for sowing is to reduce the soil to a 'tilth' (see panel, below).

A tilth is an even layer of well-broken crumbs of soil approximately 2.5–5cm (1–2in) deep that will provide the best environment for germination. The ground should be moist, but dry enough to crumble readily. Prepare only enough ground for immediate use, as the fine surface is vulnerable to heavy rain, wind or hot sun if it is left exposed.

PREPARING A TILTH

Dig or fork over the area if it is not already in a workable condition, and shatter large clods with a fork. If the surface is compacted or weathered, loosen it with a fork or hand cultivator, and remove any weeds and stones. The rest of the preparation can be carried out with a garden rake. Although not essential, a wide wooden hay rake is an excellent aid to final levelling, especially on narrow beds.

2 Light puffy soils may need firming, especially for growing crops like onions and brassicas. Either tread lightly over the surface if the soil is fairly dry, or tamp it down with the rake held vertically.

1 Roughly rake the area level with a firm to-and-fro action that helps break down the lumps of soil even further. Rake off any weeds and stones, and spread any base dressing of fertilizer (see *page 151*).

3 Rake the soil level once more – the bed is now ready for larger seeds such as peas and beans. For small seeds, gently comb coarser crumbs off the soil surface holding the rake almost upright to leave a fine finish.

STALE BEDS Even clean, well-maintained soil will contain dormant weed seeds, and recently cleared ground very many more. Weed species excel at fast germination, often emerging well before crop seedlings and crowding them out. You can reduce this competition by preparing the seedbed 3–4 weeks before you need it, allowing the weeds to appear first (water the bed in dry weather to encourage them). Hoe them off and level the surface again just before sowing. The few weeds that appear later will be easier to remove.

WARMING THE SOIL The majority of vegetable seeds will not germinate in soil temperatures below 7°C (45°F). This is a level sometimes only reached in late spring, which is long after you want to start sowing, and it is a particular problem on heavy soils that warm and dry slowly.

The soil in these raised beds has been thoroughly worked over to produce a tilth suitable for sowing larger seeds such as peas and beans.

Covering the bed or seed patch with cloches or plastic film 3–4 weeks before you are ready to sow will make several degrees' difference, and can allow first sowings to be made as soon as late winter on well-drained ground. Keep the covers in place after sowing to avoid losing the benefits of early warming.

This kind of protection also helps dry out soil that is too wet to break down and cultivate for sowing. It will also help maintain a prepared seedbed until you are ready to use it, although you may need to water, as rain is excluded and the soil may dry quickly.

Nursery beds
Many vegetables are sown where they are to grow, but you will almost certainly need to reserve a special temporary area for sowing transplanted crops and for the various other stages before final planting out.

A nursery or waiting bed is prepared in the same way as a seedbed for starting brassicas, perennials and follow-on crops, and a little less thoroughly for other plants.

Use it for successional sowings to be thinned and moved out when the seedlings are large enough, and for 'parking' young plants until growing space is available. It is a useful place to root hardwood cuttings and strawberry runners, and for heeling in fruit until you are ready to plant (see *page 141*) or winter crops like the last leeks and parsnips at the end of the season.

SEE ALSO ▶ The case for weeding *pages 152–3* Sowing for succession *page 185* **Propagating strawberries *page 190–1*** Propagating new fruit *pages 206–8*

DEALING WITH STONES
Although a few, smaller stones in the soil help it drain and warm up, too many can impede cultivation, especially when hoeing or sowing fine seeds, and also spoil the quality of root crops. Always remove large stones from the surface and wherever they appear during the season – more migrate to the surface in the natural course of cultivation. Smaller stones should be raked off when preparing seed and nursery beds. Cleared stones can be used for a number of purposes.

▶ Lose them in the bottom of tree planting holes on heavy ground.

▶ Add them to soakaways and drainage trenches.

▶ Heap them in a corner for newts and other reptiles.

▶ Rake them into drainage gullies at the end of raised beds.

▶ Pack them as a mulch around fruit trees and container plants.

▶ Use as a drainage layer in containers and pots.

▼ Spread them like gravel on paths.

growing from seed

Choosing seeds Most allotment plants are grown from seed. Whether you buy your seeds from a reputable dealer or save them from your own plants, they need to be fresh or still viable after storage if they are to germinate promptly and evenly. Good seeds give plants the best start in life, so it is worth selecting them with care.

The range of types and varieties of seed can be bewildering. The quality of bought vegetable seeds is regulated by legal standards of purity and germination, so you can usually sow confident that the majority will grow. All varieties are available as normal 'naked' seeds. Some may be pelleted: individually enclosed in clay to make them easier to handle. Keep these moist after sowing to help the coating break down.

Seed tapes can eliminate the need for thinning, as seeds are embedded at even distances in the biodegradable ribbon. Chitted seeds are pre-germinated and need to be sown immediately, usually under glass. Note that some seeds, particularly sweetcorn and beans, may be dressed with a chemical fungicide to prevent rotting during germination.

Varieties of a particular crop can differ widely in performance, so check that your choice suits the climate, soil and time of year, and whether it is early or maincrop, dwarf or tall, hardy, self-blanching and so on. Good flavour is another important factor, and can depend on seed type as much as sound cultivation, so be prepared to explore unfamiliar varieties. Try growing two varieties of a crop for comparison to find the one you prefer, and test this the following year against another new one.

F1 varieties, bred by crossing parents with desirable virtues to produce hybrids with predictable performance, are worth their higher cost if you want consistency, uniform cropping or high pest and disease resistance. Non-hybrid varieties are randomly pollinated and usually more variable, but many have stood the test of time because of some remarkable quality such as flavour or yield, and always merit consideration, especially as you can save their seeds for future seasons. Old 'heritage' varieties are the cream of these non-hybrid kinds: the result of generations of careful selection, they depend for survival mainly on gardeners who keep them in existence for their unique and valuable qualities (see Resources, *pages 216–18*).

SAVING YOUR OWN SEEDS

Collecting the seeds of F1 hybrid crops is rarely successful because the seeds tend to revert and produce unpredictable plants, but most gardeners save seeds from non-hybrid crops. By selecting the best plants over several seasons or an outstanding specimen with some special feature such as survival after a hard winter or disease attack, you can eventually develop a reliable strain that is adapted to your particular plot or taste, as well as saving money. For general purposes, simply let the best plants flower and develop seed pods or heads, and leave these until fully ripe. Shell or shake out the ripe seeds, remove any seed case debris and store the seeds in labelled packets.

▶ To avoid accidental loss, open heads of small seeds are best enclosed in paper bags before they mature; then shake the ripe seeds free in the bags.

▶ Some gardeners prefer to save seeds from a random sample of plants, rather than only the best, to maintain diversity and a broader genetic base.

▶ Cross-pollination with nearby crops may occur, so check if isolation from other plants is necessary when saving seeds from heritage or special varieties.

STORING SEEDS

Seeds deteriorate with age, particularly if they are exposed to moisture and warmth, so keep all packets in airtight tins or jars in a cool, dry place. Intact foil or vacuum packs suspend ageing for a few seasons, but once opened their contents gradually lose their viability. Tightly seal opened packets and label them with the date when bought or used. Enclosing sachets of dessicant silica gel with seed packets will protect them against moisture – these turn pink when damp but can be dried in a warm oven for reuse. The shelf life of seeds varies considerably:

4 years or more: aubergines, celeriac, celery, cucumbers, melons, onions, peppers, radishes, squashes, tomatoes

3 years: beetroot, brassicas, carrots, chicory, endive, leaf beet, leeks, lettuces

2 years: beans, peas, spinach, sweetcorn

1 year: salsify, swedes, turnips

Use at once: parsnips, scorzonera

TESTING OLD SEEDS Germination rates of seeds may be noticeably lower even after one year's storage, and many packets should be thrown away after 2–3 seasons. To check if old seeds are worth sowing, test a sample by sprinkling them on moist absorbent paper on a saucer. Cover with plastic film and leave in a warm place, in light or darkness according to type. If more than half germinate, sowing the same season could be worthwhile, if only as green manure. Discard the packet if fewer, or none, germinate within about 2 weeks.

SEE ALSO ▶ Keeping your plants healthy *pages 154-7*

growing from seed

sowing seeds

Ideal conditions Starting seeds off and watching the resulting plants emerge is always exciting, however many years you have been gardening. Don't waste all that promise by taking shortcuts at this stage – care during sowing and the critical days that follow are vital for success.

Seeds need to be in close contact with moisture and air to start growing quickly and evenly. Thorough seedbed preparation and evenly moist soil will provide the right environment for germination, but they also need warmth, ideally a soil temperature of 10°C (50°F). Few seeds will germinate below 7°C (45°F). Test the seedbed with a soil thermometer, and where necessary warm the soil before sowing (see *pages 126–7*), or wait a week or two: late sowings usually grow faster and catch up.

Do not sow tender crops like runner beans, tomatoes and sweetcorn outdoors more than about 4 weeks before the last expected frost, unless you can protect them during a cold snap, and keep some seeds in reserve to sow replacements. Some vegetables, such as lettuce, do not germinate well in high temperatures, so choose a shaded spot for midsummer crops and sow late in the afternoon as the heat declines. Early and late sowings do best in a sheltered but sunny position.

Sowing methods Most outdoor vegetables can be sown in the bottom of straight, narrow furrows, or 'drills'. Other methods include broadcasting, sowing in wide drills and station sowing. Sowing indoors (see *pages 134–5*) extends the growing season.

BROADCASTING Many salad greens and small fast-growing vegetables can be sown in blocks or patches by scattering, or 'broadcasting', the seeds evenly on the surface of the soil. Afterwards, gently rake in several directions to bury the seeds, or sieve a light covering of fine soil or old potting compost over them.

WIDE DRILLS Peas, beans and small-seeded vegetables like carrots and radishes can be grown in bands 23cm (9in) or more wide to save space. Take out a shallow channel with a spade or draw hoe, space large seeds evenly along the row or broadcast smaller seeds, and cover in the usual way.

STATION SOWING Plants that need plenty of room, like marrows or sweetcorn, can be sown at spaced stations (see below), using a line for guidance. Alternatively, space out the seeds in drills, and sow radishes or a similar fast catch crop in the intervening spaces.

Sowing depth One of the commonest causes of failure is sowing too deeply. Small seeds have less stored energy than larger kinds and must be sown closer to the surface so they reach the light quickly. Aim to cover small seeds like onions and carrots with no more than 1cm (½in) of soil; medium-size seeds such as brassicas and sweetcorn seeds germinate best about 2.5cm (1in) deep, and large seeds like beans 5cm (2in) deep.

Germination time The interval between the sowing and the emergence of seeds varies widely according to the particular crop: radishes, for example, can appear almost overnight, whereas parsnips take several weeks. The wait may be prolonged by environmental factors such as a deterioration in the weather. Most seedlings will start emerging after 7–10 days. If nothing appears after about 2 weeks, scrape the soil aside to see if seeds are germinating. If necessary, sow a fresh batch of seed.

When station sowing, make holes with your finger or a dibber (above left) at the required distances, and drop in 2–3 seeds in each hole (above right). Then cover the seeds with loose soil.

SOWING IN NARROW DRILLS

1 Mark out the row with a taut garden line. If the ground is heavy, stand on a plank to avoid compressing the adjacent soil.

2 Use the corner of a hoe or rake to drag out a shallow, level drill. Remove any stones and weed roots.

3 Pour a small amount of seeds from the packet into one hand, and thinly but evenly sprinkle a pinch at a time along the drill with the other hand. Large seeds, such as peas and beans, and pelleted seeds can be spaced out individually. Sow extra after you finish to fill any gaps.

4 Draw some of the loosened soil back to cover the seeds and leave a level finish. On light soils gently firm the surface with the head of the rake. Remember to label the end of the row with the variety, sowing date and any other important information.

TRY THIS

▶ If the soil is dry, flood the open seed drill with water before sowing and leave to drain; cover the seeds with dry soil or sieved leafmould.

▶ On heavy ground, stand on a plank when sowing, to avoid consolidating the adjacent soil.

▶ In a dry season, water sown drills every few days with a fine spray, or cover with damp newspapers until seedlings appear.

▶ Stretch wire netting or a web of black cotton over drills where birds or cats are a problem; watch out for slugs.

▶ Instead of shaking seeds straight from the packet into the drill (this is certain to produce uneven or overcrowded seedlings), pour a small amount into your hand and sprinkle them a pinch at a time.

▶ Thin seedlings at an early stage, to avoid overcrowding (see *page 138*).

▲ Small amounts of seed, such as successional batches of lettuce, can be sown in circular drills pressed into the soil with an inverted 13cm (5in) pot.

SEE ALSO ▶ **Crops for your allotment** *pages 56–111* Final stages *pages 126–7* **Combining crops (catch crops)** *page 142*

sowing seeds

131

sowing & planting times

This chart shows the recommended sowing and planting times, as well as the spacing requirements, for some of the most popular allotment crops.

CROP	ROW SPACING	PLANT SPACING	HEIGHT	EARLY SPRING	LATE SPRING	EARLY SUMMER	LATE SUMMER	EARLY AUTUMN	LATE AUTUMN	EARLY WINTER	LATE WINTER
beans, broad	25cm (10in)	25cm (10in)	1.2–1.8m (4–6ft)	S	SH	H	H		S	S	(S)
beans, climbing	60cm (24in)	15cm (6in)	1.8–3m (6–10ft)	(S)	S	S	H	H			
beans, dwarf	45cm (18in)	10cm (4in)	30–45cm (12–18in)	(S)	S	SH	SH	H	(H)		
beetroot	23–30cm (9–12in)	10cm (4in)	15–30cm (6–12in)	S	S	SH	SH	H	H		(S)
broccoli, sprouting	60–75cm (24–30in)	60–75cm (24–30in)	90–120cm (3–4ft)	H	SH	T					H
Brussels sprouts	60cm (24in)	60cm (24in)	45–120cm (18–48in)	SH	SH	T		H	H	H	H
cabbage, autumn	35–45cm (14–18in)	35–45cm (14–18in)	25–38cm (10–15in)	S	ST	T		H	H		
cabbage, Chinese	30cm (12in)	30cm (12in)	25–38cm (10–15in)			S	ST	TH	H		
cabbage, spring	30cm (12in)	10–25cm (4–10in)	25–38cm (10–15in)	H	H	H	S	T			
cabbage, summer	35–45cm (14–18in)	35–45cm (14–18in)	25–38cm (10–15in)	ST	ST	H	H	H			(S)
cabbage, winter	50cm (20in)	50cm (20in)	25–38cm (10–15in)	H	S	ST	T		H	H	H
calabrese	30cm (12in)	15–23cm (6–9in)	38–60cm (15–24in)	SH	SH	H	SH	SH			
carrots, early	15cm (6in)	8–10cm (3–4in)	23–38cm (9–15in)	(S)	S	SH	SH	H			
carrots, maincrop	15cm (6in)	5–8cm (2–3in)	23–38cm (9–15in)		S		H	H	H		
cauliflower, summer	50cm (20in)	50cm (20in)	30–45cm (12–18in)	(S)	T		H	H			
cauliflower, winter	75cm (30in)	75cm (30in)	30–45cm (12–18in)	H	H	S	T			H	H
celery, self-blanching	30cm (12in)	23cm (9in)	30–60cm (12–24in)	(S)	(S)	T	H	H	H		
chard	45cm (18in)	30cm (12in)	45cm (18in)	H	SH	H	SH	H	H		H
cucumber, outdoors	45–75cm (18–30in)	45–75cm (18–30in)	60–300cm (2–10ft)		(S)	T	H	H			

S = sow   (S) = sow under glass
P = plant   (P) = plant under glass
T = transplant   (T) = transplant under glass
H = harvest   (H) = harvest under glass

CROP	ROW SPACING	PLANT SPACING	HEIGHT	EARLY SPRING	LATE SPRING	EARLY SUMMER	LATE SUMMER	EARLY AUTUMN	LATE AUTUMN	EARLY WINTER	LATE WINTER
kale	30–60cm (12–24in)	30 60cm (12–24in)	45–120cm (18–48in)	H	S	T			H	H	H
leeks	30cm (12in)	15cm (6in)	30–45cm (12–18in)	SH	SH	T	T	H	H	H	H
lettuce	15–30cm (6–12in)	15–30cm (6–12in)	15–25cm (6–10in)	(S)	S	SH	SH	SH	H	(H)	
melons	90 150cm (3–5ft)	90–150cm (3–5ft)	90–180cm (3–6ft)		(S)	S(T)	T	H	(H)		
onions, bulbing	30cm (12in)	5–8cm (2–3in)	45–60cm (18–24in)	SPT	SP	H	SH	PH			(S)
onions, salad	10cm (4in)	1–2.5cm (½–1in)	30–38cm (12–15in)	SH	SH	SH	SH	H	H		(S)
parsnips	20–30cm (8–12in)	10 15cm (4–6in)	38–45cm (15–18in)	SH	SH	S	H	H	H	H	H
peas	45–60cm (18 24in)	8–10cm (3 4in)	30–150cm (1–5ft)	S	S	SH	H	H	(S)(H)		
peppers	30–50cm (12–20in)	30–50cm (12–20in)	38–120cm (15–48in)	(S)	S	T	H	H			
potatoes, early	45cm (18in)	30cm (12in)	45–90cm (18–36in)	P	P	H	H				
potatoes, maincrop	75cm (30in)	38cm (15in)	45–90cm (18–36in)		P		H	H	H		
radish	15cm (6in)	2.5cm (1in)	10 15cm (4–6in)	SH	SH	SH	SH	SH	H	(H)	(S)
shallots	23cm (9in)	15cm (6in)	38cm (15in)	P			H			P	P
spinach, summer	30cm (12in)	8–15cm (3–6in)	15–20cm (6–8in)	S	S	SH	H	H			
spinach, winter	30cm (12in)	8–15cm (3–6in)	15–20cm (6–8in)	H	H			S	H	H	H
squash	90–180cm (3–6ft)	90–180cm (3–6ft)	60–180cm (2–6ft)	(S)	S(T)	SH	H	H			
sweetcorn	30–60cm (12–24in)	30–60cm (12–24in)	90–240cm (3–8ft)	(S)	(S)(T)	ST	H	H	H		
tomatoes, outdoor	25–45cm (10 18in)	25–45cm (10–18in)	30–180cm (1–6ft)	(S)	(S)(T)	T	H	H	(H)		
turnips	15–23cm (6–9in)	15–23cm (6–9in)	30–45cm (12–18in)	S	SH	SH	SH	H	H	H	(S)

BREAKING THE RULES

Although trials have established optimum spacings, growing temperatures and sowing dates for different crops (see *pages 132–3*), most crops are, in fact, very flexible and forgiving.

Recommended distances between rows and plants, for example, usually assume that standard varieties are planted in rows on average soil during the main growing season. But compact varieties or plants for harvesting young can be grown closer together, especially on fertile ground and in raised beds or under cloches. Plants grown in squares (see *page 36*) or interplanted with another crop may tolerate different spacings

from row crops, and early or dwarf varieties can often be planted closer than maincrops.

Similarly, sowing dates can vary according to variety. Spring cabbage, for example, is normally sown in late summer for transplanting about 6 weeks later, but a variety such as 'Duncan' can be sown in succession to crop almost all year round.

It is always worth experimenting to find a method that suits your own soil, routine or microclimate, and you can usually hedge your bets by resowing, keeping some plants back in reserve, or testing a sample under different conditions. Remember that you are the one in charge.

Sowing indoors

Although it is perfectly feasible to have produce available all year round without the aid of glass or plastic, growing under cover can extend the natural growing season by several weeks, and helps avoid the hazards of late spring or early autumn frosts. Tender and slow-maturing crops like French beans or sweetcorn can be started 6 weeks earlier than outdoors, for example, allowing a month's growth and a further 2 weeks for hardening off. Sowing methods indoors are straightforward, and you have greater control over growing conditions.

SOWING IN TRAYS Make sure you use an appropriate clean tray or pot for the quantity and size of seeds, and a fresh supply of moist seed compost at indoor temperature.

▶ Fill the container to the top, strike off the excess with a board, and tap the container on the worktop to settle the contents. Soil-based composts also need gentle firming with a flat piece of wood for trays or a jam jar for pots. Water with a very fine rose and leave to drain.

▶ Scatter tiny seeds thinly and evenly all over the surface, or in rows; larger ones can be spaced at regular distances apart. Then sieve a light sprinkling of compost over the seeds, except for any that need light: these are simply pressed into the surface.

▶ Label with variety and date, and cover with a piece of glass; if the seeds need darkness, cover this with a piece of newspaper. Stand the container in a warm place. Turn the glass daily to reduce condensation, and remove both glass and paper when seedlings emerge.

Sow seeds thinly and evenly all over the surface of the compost.

▶ If the compost dries out before seedlings appear, stand the container in about 2.5cm (1in) of water at indoor temperature until damp patches appear at the surface.

PRICKING OUT Soon after their emergence in trays and pots, seedlings need more space to develop or they will suffer the ill-effects of overcrowding: competition, lack of air and the rapid transmission of disease. Wait until their seed leaves are fully expanded and you can handle them easily.

▶ Fill a full-size tray with fresh, moist universal or seedling compost, level and settle the contents by tapping; firm evenly if using a soil-based mix.

▶ Holding them by their leaves (the stems are easily crushed), ease out seedlings with a dibber or table fork and transfer them singly, about 5cm (2in) apart, to holes in the surface of the new tray.

▶ Make sure their roots fit easily, and gently firm them upright. Water completed trays with a fine rose and stand them indoors, in full light but shaded from bright sun until they are growing strongly.

USING MODULES You can avoid the brief checks seedlings experience from root disturbance during pricking out and transplanting outdoors by sowing in modules. These are plastic or polystyrene trays divided into separate cells, although the term is also loosely used for soil or rockwool blocks and biodegradable pots (see Making your own pots, *page 214*) that are buried at planting time to disintegrate in the ground.

Seeds can be started in modules by using seed compost and sowing in each cell a tiny pinch of small seeds or 2–3

HANDY HINTS

▶ Try to provide the recommended amount of warmth until seedlings emerge, when cooler surroundings are preferable.

▶ Always keep seedlings in good light to avoid thin, weak growth that is susceptible to diseases.

▶ Water seeds and seedlings with tap water, as stored water from butts and tanks can encourage damping-off disease.

▶ Do not start root crops such as parsnips and long carrots indoors, as their long taproots resent pricking out and transplanting.

larger ones; resulting seedlings are singled by carefully removing all but the strongest. Alternatively, seedlings may be sown conventionally and then pricked out from the seed trays into modules to reduce root disturbance when transplanted outside.

MULTI-SEEDING Some vegetables can be sown in modules and left unthinned for planting out and growing as a cluster of plants. This can save time, minimize root disturbance and economize on space indoors. Sow a pinch of about 6-8 seeds in each pot or cell and grow as normal, but do not thin or prick out the seedlings. Harden off (see *page 139*) and plant out complete clusters 30-38cm (12-15in) apart - this distance allows individual plants to make their own space as they grow. Suitable crops include beetroot, leeks, salad and maincrop onions, parsley, and round varieties of carrot and turnip.

SEE ALSO ▶ **Growing under glass *pages 170-5* Propagating new fruit *pages 206-8***

OTHER METHODS OF PROPAGATION

Creating new plants by vegetative propagation instead of with seeds may be faster, more reliable or the only method of propagation. For example, Jerusalem artichokes and potatoes are grown from tubers (see Chitting potato tubers, below); rhubarb and asparagus from young plants or 'crowns'; onions, shallots and garlic as 'sets' (bulbs or segments of bulbs). Most perennial herbs can be propagated by softwood cuttings, while many bush fruits are multiplied from hardwood cuttings. Seed-raised crops like tomatoes are also available as growing plants, which can often save you time and the need to supply extra heat for germination.

Propagating fruits Provided they are vigorous and completely healthy, many fruits are easily multiplied to create extra plants or replacements. Raspberries are normally propagated by lifting and replanting suckers, and occasionally by taking soft tip cuttings in summer. Burying the ends of young bramble canes in late summer will induce tip rooting by the following spring. Strawberry runners bear new plants that are potted up or transplanted to a fresh bed (see *pages 190-1*). Most other soft fruits are propagated from hardwood cuttings prepared in autumn: trim a length of new stem to about 30cm (12in) long and bury the lower half firmly in the ground, where it will root ready for transplanting the following autumn. Top fruits are normally grafted or budded, techniques easily mastered but needing care, precision and suitable rootstocks. It is probably best to leave this to the professionals and buy new disease-resistant stocks.

Softwood cuttings The tips of young shoots on active plants are packed with growth hormones and will often root as cuttings in spring and summer. Choose a strong healthy plant and pull off a sideshoot or cut off its tip, about 4-8cm (1½-3in) long - small cuttings root faster, but a long one can be trimmed short for a second attempt if the base rots before it roots. Trim the bottom of the cutting just below a leaf joint and remove the lower leaves. Some cuttings root easily in a jar of water, alternatively, insert to half their depth in a pot of moist cuttings compost and keep warm inside a plastic bag to maintain humidity. This technique can be used on a host of plants, even tomato sideshoots and the growing tips of raspberries.

CHITTING POTATO TUBERS

Sprouting, or chitting, potato tubers in mid-winter helps promote early growth. Check that the tubers (seed potatoes) are healthy and undamaged. Arrange them side by side in a box or tray, with their rose ends (the one with the most eyes) uppermost. Keep in a frost-free place, well lit but out of direct sun. Shoots will sprout from the eyes and should be about 2.5cm (1in) long at planting time. For large potatoes, rub off all but the 2-3 strongest shoots before planting. (See also *page 179* for pre-planting ideas.)

sowing seeds

allotment story
SEEDS OF HOPE

'Our hospital with the blue sky' is how a group of asylum seekers describe their allotment on a site in north London. They are part of a project called 'Natural Growth', first set up by a psychotherapist working with victims of torture and persecution, such as Ahmed, an Iraqi Kurd. Since it started, the allotment project has provided many displaced persons with not only food on the table but also a safe and welcoming therapeutic place in which to work through personal traumas.

As in Germany, where the International Gardens Association in Göttingen has been helping Bosnian women refugees adapt to life in exile, the north London therapists noticed that a number of their patients talked about the farms, gardens and local crops they had left behind. Since many were not responding to conventional therapy, it was decided that an allotment project might be more successful.

At first only the more physically fit were involved because the sites generally needed a lot of hard work before they were cleared for cultivation. This in itself can have positive results, but usually it is the sowing of seeds that starts the healing process. Growing vegetables and fruits from their original home countries is familiar and reassuring, whereas discovering that not everything will thrive in cooler conditions is the first step for many of them in coming to terms with their new environment.

caring for young plants

Ensuring success
The first few weeks after sowing are critical to a crop's success. Weeds and native plants are well adapted to struggle, and survival of the fittest is in their long-term interest, but vegetable varieties are sophisticated hybrids and selections, bred for quality as much as for performance, and they need care and protection if they are to fulfil their promise.

THINNING SEEDLINGS Even the most sparsely sown row of seedlings will usually need thinning out to allow each plant its own space to develop without competition. Always thin in several stages as insurance against losses as plants develop. With outdoor sowings in situ, start when the whole row has emerged but while seedlings are still small. Pinch off surplus seedlings at soil level to leave survivors just clear of each other (see below). Repeat whenever seedlings look crowded, leaving them at progressively greater distances apart until they are at recommended spacings.

Clear and compost the thinnings to avoid attracting pests and diseases, and water or firm the row afterwards in case you have loosened any roots. Crops that withstand transplanting can be thinned by carefully lifting unwanted seedlings with a fork or dibber for replanting elsewhere. Seedlings in pots can be treated in the same way. Thin brassicas sown in a nursery bed once or twice before planting out, or lift them all with a fork and transplant 8–10cm (3–4in) apart elsewhere in the bed.

GROWING ON In the first few weeks of growth, weeds, especially annual ones that grow very fast, can be a threat to outdoor seedlings. Hoe regularly, or spread a thin organic mulch, making sure this does not touch the seedlings.

Watch out for sudden cold spells, particularly at night, and be prepared to cover plants with fleece, newspaper or cloches; jam jars and clear, bottomless plastic bottles are useful for station-sown plants. Before they are exposed to the elements, plants sown in situ under cloches or fleece, and those started indoors, need hardening off (see right).

Seedlings and young plants are a gourmet dish for slugs and other pests, so guard them with traps and deterrents. They also have little resistance to diseases at first, so give them air and space, make sure plant debris and mulches do not touch them, and do not overfeed.

Young plants under glass are sensitive to scorch from bright sun, especially soon after pricking out, so cover them for the first days with sheets of newspaper in sunny weather (keep the paper handy for cold nights). If the weather turns warm for any length of time, consider moving plants to a cold frame, which may be easier to shade and ventilate.

WATERING & FEEDING Seedlings have very immature root development while they are still small, and can quickly dry out in hot weather. Soil that has been well fortified with organic material should shield outdoor sowings from stress, but seedlings on impoverished and light sandy soils will benefit from a light mulch of leafmould or grass clippings to reduce evaporation.

Good soil will also supply all the nutrients they need for the first few weeks, as will poorer ground prepared with a base dressing of fertilizer (see *page 151*). Feeding, in fact, can be distinctly harmful, encouraging soft sappy growth that is vulnerable to infection and lacks the resilience needed to cope with adverse weather. Only young plants in trays, ready for

Select a surplus seedling and pinch it carefully close to the soil. Remove it gently, to give the remaining seedlings space to grow.

Clear, bottomless plastic bottles, slotted around wooden stakes, protect station-sown broad bean seedlings. As plants, they will use the stakes as supports.

final planting out but delayed for some reason, will benefit from a dilute feed of general fertilizer to prevent deterioration and to check growth.

HARDENING OFF Plants raised in warmth – whether indoors, in a cold frame or under cloches – need to be acclimatized gradually to outdoor conditions before they can withstand full exposure.

▸ Move greenhouse plants to the coolest part of the house for 2–3 days, and then transfer them to a cold frame. Keep the frame closed initially and protect with sacking or mats whenever frost threatens.

▸ After a couple of days, gradually admit air to the frame for longer periods each day until, after about 2 weeks, it is fully ventilated, at first only by day. Finally, leave the frame open all the time.

▸ If you have no frame, stand plants in a sheltered place outdoors on mild days, returning them to the greenhouse by night. Towards the end of the second week leave them outside for a few nights.

▸ Cloches can be partially ventilated like a frame, but do not simply remove the ends as this turns them into a wind tunnel. Eventually uncover plants completely, but keep the cloches alongside for a few days in case the weather deteriorates.

SEE ALSO ▸ Cold frames, covers & cloches *pages 48–9* Keeping plants healthy *pages 154–7* **Slug & snail protection** *page 178*

PLANTING OUT INDOOR SOWINGS

Lightly fork over the area, removing all weeds and raking in some sieved garden compost or a base dressing of general fertilizer (see *page 151*) to stimulate root activity. Leave the ground level but not as fine as for a seedbed.

1 Plants in seed trays can be loosened by knocking each end of the tray and then carefully tossing the intact contents on the ground. Alternatively, remove plants individually with a trowel.

2 Make a hole for each plant, large enough to take the rootball comfortably with the lowest leaves just above surface level. Use a measured stick to ensure accurate spacing.

3 Holding the plant in one hand, replace the soil all round the roots with the other, gently firming the stem upright with your fingers. Water and mulch lightly as you complete each row.

TRY THIS

► Where the ground is dry or drains very freely, set large plants a little deeper than normal and contour the surface down the stem to leave a shallow dish for holding water.

► On shallow or poorly drained soils, bury the rootball more shallowly and pile the soil up to the original planting mark on the stem to leave a gentle mound.

► In very dry weather, especially on light soils, 'puddle in' plants by flooding them in their holes before refilling and firming.

► For the first few days, protect leafy transplants in hot sunshine by covering each with an upturned flower pot during the day.

► With the exception of transplanted leeks, always use a trowel rather than a dibber for making planting holes.

PLANTING OUT
LARGER SPECIMENS

When planting out larger specimens prepare the ground in the same way as for planting out indoor sowings (see left) but over an area twice the diameter of the plant. Make sure plants have been watered and left to drain.

► Use a trowel or spade, depending on the size of the plant, to take out a hole that is large enough to hold the rootball at the depth it was growing before.

► Loosen the soil in the bottom with a fork, and mix in plenty of well-rotted garden compost or bought tree compost.

► If you are planting a tree or larger shrub, firmly drive in any supporting stakes before planting, to prevent any root damage.

cultivating your allotment

TRANSPLANTING Even though you can sow all crops where they are to grow and thereby avoid transplanting them to another position, this can limit choice and greatly reduce the length of the cropping season. You can extend both the harvest period and the diversity of produce available by sowing early indoors, moving late sowings under glass and starting successional crops in a nursery bed, but all these strategies involve moving plants while they are actively growing.

Some plants positively benefit from being moved. Winter brassicas, for example, develop stronger root systems if they are transplanted, first from seed to nursery bed and again to their final positions 4–6 weeks later. Moving root crops, on the other hand, usually results in losses and distorted roots.

Most plants tolerate transplanting well, provided they are still young and

Heeling in bare-root plants such as raspberry canes will keep them in good condition until they are ready to be planted.

- ▶ Knock the plant from a rigid pot by tapping the rim upside down on the spade handle; soft plastic containers can be carefully cut or torn away.
- ▶ Cleanly trim off any tangled, damaged or spiralling roots with secateurs or a sharp knife.
- ▶ Centre the rootball in its hole, test that it is level by laying a stick across the hole, and then refill all round, crumbling any lumps of soil as you go.
- ▶ Shake bare-root plants gently to settle the soil in any cavities, and consolidate all round with your fingers or by lightly treading.
- ▶ Level the ground, water and mulch, keeping the surface material about 5cm (2in) away from the stem. Label and tie to supports where necessary.

conditions are ideal. To avoid serious checks to growth, choose a dull or day or showery evening, with the ground evenly moist and the weather neither very cold nor hot and dry. Make sure the plants have been hardened off (see *page 139*) if necessary, and water them well just before you start.

When transplanting from open ground, water the plants in the seedbed and also water the new site before starting. Lift a small handful of seedlings with a fork and carefully separate them into a tray, keeping them covered to prevent their roots drying out. Trowel out a hole a little larger than the roots, centre the plant in the hole (handling the plant only by its leaves), and replace the soil so the lowest leaves are just above surface level. Firm in and water.

HEELING IN Where planting has to be delayed, keep bare-root plants in good condition by temporarily 'heeling' them into a spare piece of sheltered ground. You can do this with fruit and brassica plants, and also with left-over winter crops that occupy needed space. Dig out a trench or hole that will accommodate the roots comfortably,

lean the plants close together against one side, and refill with soil, lightly firming it all round.

PLUG PLANTS Bought seedlings and larger plug plants require immediate care if they are to stay in good condition. Prick out or pot up small seedlings and mini-plugs, and grow them on under cover until they are large enough to harden off and plant out.

Larger ('jumbo' or 'maxi') plug plants can be potted up or planted straight out, depending on where you intend growing them, but if the weather is unsuitable or you doubt whether they are fully hardened off, pack them in trays or boxes for a few days and keep in a cold frame or cool place indoors until they are ready or conditions improve. Water regularly, and foliar feed if planting is delayed, especially if the leaves turn yellow.

SEE ALSO ▶ Managing water *pages 148-9* Fertilizers & feeding *pages 150-1* **Sowing for succession** *page 185*

spacing vegetables

Traditional spacing

The traditional way to grow vegetables is in straight, widely spaced rows, an arrangement intended to allow easy access for hoeing and other cultural routines. This is neither the most economical nor the most profitable method, however, and experience with narrow beds and other intensive layouts that can be maintained without walking between plants shows that crops can be grown successfully at greater densities.

Productive spacing

The most productive arrangement is to space plants at an equal distance from their neighbours, staggered in parallel rows. Plants make the best use of the available water and nutrients, and have enough space to develop without competition from neighbours; when mature they almost touch, thus shading the ground to reduce moisture loss as well as suppressing weeds. On newly reclaimed plots, however, wide spacings will allow you room to keep on top of vigorous weed regrowth – competition from weeds between rows is a greater threat than from those growing in a row among plants.

Flexible spacing

Spacing is sometimes flexible and a matter for personal choice because distance apart can affect size as well as overall yield. Summer cabbages, for example, can be spaced 35 x 35cm (14 x 14in) apart for a maximum yield of small heads, but 45 x 45cm (18 x 18in) apart will give the same total weight of larger, more

solid hearts from one-third fewer plants. Alternatively, space at maximum densities and use alternate plants while they are small, leaving the others to grow on to maturity.

SEE ALSO ▶ **Choosing the bed system** *pages 36–7* The case for weeding *pages 152–3* **Sowing for succession** *page 185*

COMBINING CROPS

Instead of planting a single crop at close spacing, you can often maximize yields from an area by pairing and partnering crops that mature at different times or complement each other.

▶ Fast-maturing radishes, dwarf peas or small lettuces can be grown as catch crops between fully spaced vegetables such as parsnips or sweet corn, and will be cleared before their slower-growing neighbours need the extra room.

▶ Winter brassicas need plenty of space, but you can intercrop a row of fast summer cabbages between rows of winter varieties that take longer to mature, and also fit a summer cabbage between every pair of winter plants to harvest before the latter are very large.

▶ Tall crops such as runner beans or raspberries cast shade that can benefit shy and shade-tolerant crops like summer cauliflowers, soft lettuces or alpine strawberries growing close by, especially in midsummer when it can be extremely hot.

▶ On very fertile ground, try matching together several crops with different needs. In the 'three sisters' arrangement, sweetcorn is planted at full spacing, 2–3 climbing bean seeds are sown beside each plant to twine up its strong stem, and trailing marrows or squashes are interplanted as groundcover.

▶ Try growing early carrots between rows of widely spaced maincrop varieties. Either sow them at the same time to harvest first, or several weeks later to pull after the maincrop has been lifted for use or storage.

▶ Grow plants of different habits, like carrots and onions, as companions or intercrops to make full use of space and light. Round lettuces fit neatly between slim upright plants like leeks or sweetcorn; slim cos lettuces combine well with larger, slow-maturing iceberg or butterhead varieties; and loose-leaf or 'cut and come again' lettuces can be sown around heading varieties to crop after the latter are finished.

▶ Gain time and space with successional sowings of lettuce, kohlrabi, spinach or mini-cauliflowers by sowing the follow-on crop in a pot plunged at the end of the row of earlier plants. Time the sowing so that the seedlings are ready to move out as the preceding crop is harvested.

▶ Sowing carrots, spinach, beetroot and leaf lettuce in broad bands up to 90cm (3ft) wide can save a lot of space. Broadcast seeds (see *page 130*), and thin seedlings to a few centimetres apart by combing through them with a wire rake. Peas sown in this way can be spaced out and do not need thinning.

allotment story
FOOD FOR THE SOUL

The Garden Gate, a 1-hectare (2½-acre) organic community garden – which is run by the mental health charity Thanet Mind, founded by the late Betty Barber – is for adults experiencing mental health issues in the seaside town of Margate in Kent. Since one in four people will suffer from mental illness at some point in their lives, effective kinds of therapy are important, and taking care of an allotment is a wonderful form, offering a purposeful occupation and the opportunity to make friends in safe and supportive surroundings.

There is no pressure to work but everyone is able to contribute in some way. 'Some people arrive thinking they can't do anything and then prove to themselves they can. It's rewarding to see people blossom,' Paul, the project leader, explains. Three times a week, he cooks a lunchtime feast for everyone, using whatever is in season. 'Everything is picked from the allotment and cooked within 30 minutes,' he says proudly.

Over half the site is dedicated to raising vegetables and fruit, and there is also a young planted woodland, already attracting wildlife, from hedgehogs to naturalized parakeets. There are masses of flowers too, mixed in with the cabbages, chard, sweetcorn and purple-podded beans. 'It's great fun, and nice for the visitors to take home flowers and a share of the produce – vegetables always taste better when you've grown them yourself,' Paul sums up.

nurturing your plants

Routine care Once seedlings and young plants have been transferred to their final positions and have settled in, they will be less vulnerable and dependent on your care than when they were growing under cover or in a nursery bed. Nonetheless, they still need routine attention and will benefit from a regular weekly inspection, if only to confirm that all is well. Make a mental list of points to check, and for specific details see the individual plant entries in Crops for your allotment (*pages 56–111*).

PROTECTION Simple precautions to shield susceptible plants from hazards can make the difference between success and disappointment. Extreme or unexpected weather can ruin a crop if some kind of protection is not kept handy. Plants may need shielding from hot sun, drying winds or sudden cold snaps, so gather together an arsenal of fleece, large pots, jam jars, bottomless plastic bottles, plastic film or cloches to meet every hazard. Emerging seedlings, young transplants, and tender crops (especially at either end of the season) are all particularly vulnerable. In emergencies, simply covering plants with a few sheets of weighted down newspaper will often save the day. Remember, it is always wiser to take precautions rather than chances, even if the threat does not materialize.

SUPPORT Climbing vegetables and many kinds of fruit need sturdy canes or stakes provided at planting or sowing time, but other plants can also benefit from support, which helps them grow more strongly and occupy less space. Bush tomatoes and dwarf

An upturned basket lifts pumpkins off the ground, supporting their weight.

peas produce cleaner crops if their branches are propped up with twiggy sticks or netting; broad bean varieties, Brussels sprouts, dahlias and gladioli

Bottomless plastic bottles protect young lettuces from slugs and snails.

A makeshift cloche shields courgette plants from adverse weather.

Wire netting tied to wooden stakes creates a barrier against rabbits.

Removing the tips of broad beans speeds up ripening.

THINNING CROPS It may seem wasteful to reduce the quantity of fruit on a plant, but thinning can improve quality where more fruits have been set than a plant can ripen successfully, and in some cases it will prevent injury, especially where overladen branches can break and introduce the risk of disease. Limiting the number of fruits by removing misplaced or misshapen fruits and thinning clusters to well-spaced individuals is an important routine with apples, pears, peaches, plums and other tree fruits, as well as crops like peppers, melons, grapes and many exhibition vegetables and flowers.

EARTHING UP This is the technique of mounding up soil around a plant with a rake or draw hoe. In windy situations tall plants like Brussels sprouts and sprouting broccoli are more stable if their stems are earthed

Thinning out plums will improve the quality of the remaining fruits.

may need strong canes to keep them upright and undamaged; and even courgette plants are healthier if their lax stems are tied to stout stakes. Provide support early to avoid a disheartening salvage task later, especially on light soils and windy sites.

TRAINING Pruning, training and pinching out are all ways to fit naturally exuberant or spreading plants into a limited space, and can also redirect a plant's energies from extending growth into producing a better crop. Pinching out is a kind of light pruning that is used to remove growing tips to stimulate or eliminate sideshoots (cucumbers, melons, cordon tomatoes, woody perennial herbs), encourage ripening (strawberries, broad beans, outdoor tomatoes), or avoid major pruning later in the season on fruits. Pruning is important for all permanent woody-stemmed herbs and fruit, and is often combined with training on supports where plants are grown in restricted forms.

Earthing up potato plants prevents light from turning the tubers green.

up in autumn and firmed upright; sweetcorn benefits from the same attention and will develop buttress roots in the fresh layer of soil for additional support. The stems of potato plants are earthed up several times, partly to stimulate more growth but mainly to prevent light from turning tubers green and inedible. Crops like trench celery and sweet fennel are blanched by earthing up to keep their stems pale, crisp and tender. For best results always earth up while the soil is moist, and clear any weeds as you go.

HARVESTING This is the climax of the growth cycle. Many maturing crops need frequent checking to make sure produce is gathered at its best and to extend the harvest.

SEE ALSO ▶ **Key culinary herbs** *pages 100–3* Fruit *pages 104–9* **Harvesting & storing** *pages 160–3* Summer pruning *page 196* **Winter pruning** *page 212*

managing water

The importance of water

After soil, water is the gardener's most precious natural resource – it is essential for healthy soil and all active stages of plant growth. However, it is frequently wasted, often misused and sometimes in short supply. Managing water wisely depends first on well-planned collection and conservation strategies, and secondly on its efficient use around the allotment.

ECONOMIZING For much of the year, sufficient water for plant growth is stored in the soil from accumulated rainfall, and improving this capacity can postpone the need to water. Add plenty of organic material, such as compost and manure, to boost humus levels, and mulch bare surfaces to delay evaporation. The foliage of plants shades soil and reduces water loss, so close spacing and underplanting crops at wider distances help stabilize moisture levels, especially on lighter soils. If experience shows that watering becomes a problem, reassess your choice of crops and methods: for example, a single sweetcorn plant requires 225 litres (50 gals) to produce a cob, herbs rarely need watering, plants in east–west trenches stay cool and shaded, and locally saved seed in dry regions is often more drought-resistant.

TARGETING PLANTS In the absence of useful rainfall, plants need varying amounts of water at different stages of their lives. When the available water is inadequate, growth slows and disorders develop. Overwatering also causes serious problems, so it is important to know when, how, and how much to water plants.

Concentrate on the plants that benefit most, rather than watering the whole plot or bed indiscriminately: there is no point giving water to plants that do not need it. Many crops only really require watering during certain stages of growth. Early potatoes, for example, prefer consistently moist soil from start to finish, whereas maincrops need one or two good soakings when the tubers are marble-size (about the time they come into flower).

Crops that should be kept evenly moist throughout include all leafy vegetables such as brassicas, salads

Onions may need watering during bouts of hot, dry weather, even if they have been planted in well-prepared soil.

SIGNS OF DROUGHT

The first indications that plants are not receiving enough water are subtle.

► Lustrous leaves look dull.
► Leaves and stems feel less resilient.
► Growth rate slows down.

As time passes, the symptoms become more obvious:

► Stems flag and leaves droop.
► Flowering falters or stops.
► Fruits stop swelling or turn yellow and fall.

TRY THIS

► Water in the evening or on dull, still days to reduce evaporation.
► Loosen trodden soil before watering to aid penetration.
► Mulch after watering to conserve ground moisture.
► Terrace sloping sites and edge beds to prevent run-off.
► Control weeds, which compete for scarce water supplies, and keep fruit trees weed-free after planting (see When to plant, *page 105*).
► Leave seed drills lower than the surrounding soil to confine water.
► Restrict water to a necessary minimum to improve the flavour of tomatoes and carrots.
► Use taller plants, hedges or temporary screens to shelter vulnerable plants from the drying effects of wind.
► Underplant widely spaced crops with squashes, New Zealand spinach or a green manure as groundcover.

and spinach, because water stimulates leaf growth. Root vegetables also like consistent watering, but only enough to sustain growth without producing excessive foliage. Target other crops during their most critical stages: all seedlings, transplants and newly planted specimens; seed and fruit crops like pulses, tomatoes and sweetcorn while flowering and when fruits are swelling. Plants in shallow soils and next to walls need extra watering in dry spells, while those in containers and under glass should be checked frequently to make sure they never dry out.

Ideal quantities vary depending on the crop, soil type and time of year. Avoid watering little and often, which only dampens the surface and encourages superficial rooting. Instead, give plants a thorough soaking, aiming for about 5 litres/sq.m (1 gal/sq.yd), twice that amount at critical stages, and apply this weekly on light soils, every 10–14 days on clay.

Never allow the soil to dry out completely. After watering, test how far down the water has penetrated using your fingers or a trowel to expose the soil nearby to about 10–15cm (4–6in) down; if the soil is moist, watering has done the job. Afterwards, mulch the bare soil to prevent loss from evaporation.

To target the roots of a particular plant, push a flower pot into the soil beside the plant and fill the pot with water several times.

METHODS OF WATERING

Coupling a hosepipe to the communal tap is almost certainly antisocial, and may be difficult or expressly forbidden, so in most cases watering will involve using a can or buckets. If you do use a hose, connect this to a seep hose or spray line laid between plants to deliver a gentle trickle at the roots rather than to a sprinkler, which wastes enormous quantities of water.

A watering can is the most precise means of delivery, even if the most laborious (plastic is lighter than galvanized metal). Use a fine rose for seedbeds and seedlings, otherwise aim a stream from the spout at the base of individual plants. Another way of targeting thirsty plants like runner beans and squashes is to push a flower pot, upturned bottomless bottle or length of pipe into the soil beside the plant and direct water to the roots (see left). Explore automatic watering devices like capillary mats and drip systems with reservoirs for containers, growing bags and greenhouse beds.

SEE ALSO ► Watering equipment *page 52* Improving your soil *pages 116–19*

fertilizers & feeding

What fertilizers do Intensive cropping gradually exhausts the plant foods in the soil unless they are regularly replenished. Annual dressings of compost and manure are an important means of restoring fertility, allowing many crops to mature successfully without supplementary feeding. But sometimes you need to top up nutrient levels, especially when repairing neglected or impoverished soil, and this is when concentrated fertilizers may be valuable. Remember, though, that they do nothing for soil structure or long-term fertility, and should always be used with discretion: excessive or unnecessary use can block the uptake of other nutrients and even cause local pollution by leaching into water supplies.

Types of fertilizer Nutrients come in many different guises. They may be organic (concentrated seaweed, for example) or inorganic (sulphate of ammonia); fast-acting or slow-release; straight (a single ingredient like the potassium in rock potash) or compound (a balanced or 'general' mixture). They also come in a variety of forms, such as powder, tablets, granules and liquids.

Which fertilizer you decide to use depends on the reason for feeding and also your personal philosophy. For organic gardeners, chemical

THE ROLE OF NUTRIENTS

MAJOR NUTRIENTS	ACTIVITY	DEFICIENCY SYMPTOMS
Nitrogen (N)	Fuels growth and photosynthesis	Stunted growth; pale or yellowish leaves
Phosphorus (P)	Promotes healthy roots and fruits	Blue-tinted leaves; low fruit yields
Potassium, potash (K)	Boosts nitrogen; sustains health	Leaf mottling; low yields of small fruits
Calcium (Ca)	Adjusts acidity and nutrient access	Die back; fruit disorders
Magnesium (Mg)	Vital for germination and chlorophyll	Dead leaf patches; early leaf drop or tinting
MINOR NUTRIENTS	**ACTIVITY**	**DEFICIENCY SYMPTOMS**
Iron (Fe)	Helps form chlorophyll	Pale foliage, especially on chalky soils
Manganese (Mn)	Supports the action of iron	Pale leaf patches; bright green veins; leaf rolling
Boron (B)	Helps plants absorb nutrients	Rough fruit/leaf patches; brown hearts in vegetables
Molybdenum (Mo)	Makes nitrogen readily available	Distorted leaves and shoot tips
Copper (Cu)	Improves general nutrition	Young leaves or shoots wilt and die off
Zinc (Zn)	Balances growth processes	Distorted leaves and shoots, brown buds

LIQUID FEEDS

All solid sources of fertility such as weeds, manures and compost plants like comfrey are easily distilled into liquid feeds. Simply pack the material (comfrey is shown here) into a net or woven bag, and immerse in a bucket or tank of water. Leave for two weeks, prodding or squeezing the bag occasionally. The resulting liquid can be diluted to the colour of weak tea for foliar feeding. Be warned: it will stink!

fertilizers will not be an option – they are, in any case, environmentally costly to produce and, because they are highly concentrated and readily soluble, their residues often leach quickly from your plot into the surroundings. Bought organic feeds can also be ethically dubious, as their production and supply may involve pollution (mining of rock potash, for example), inhumane practices (poultry manure from battery

units) or high energy and transport costs (seaweed meal).

Many gardeners prefer to produce their own fertilizers at home or on the allotment. Garden and worm composts are a balanced source of nutrients for general and targeted feeding, while green manures, especially nitrogen-rich leguminous crops like alfalfa and clover, add fertility as well as humus-forming bulk. Some plants accumulate minerals from deep in the soil, and if they are cut or pulled up and composted, they are a concentrated source of fertility for less talented plants (see Fertilizer plants, above right). For the fastest results, soak these plants in water to make a foliar feed. Comfrey, for example, can be cut 4–5 times per year and used fresh as a source of potassium. Grow it among fruit bushes, cut the leaves when full-size and spread them around bushes as a mulch.

THE MAIN NUTRIENTS

Fertilizers are rated according to their content of the main nutrients for growth: nitrogen (N), phosphorus (P) and potassium (K). A general fertilizer with an NPK ratio of 7:7:7 contains 7 per cent of each nutrient, while bonemeal (NPK 3:20:0) is a rich source of slow-release phosphates, plus a little nitrogen but without any potassium.

Feeding time
Whether you buy fertilizers, produce them on the allotment or use a combination of both sources, knowing when they should be applied means that you will use them efficiently and avoid waste.

Base dressing General fertilizer spread and raked into a bed after cultivation, especially on light soils after heavy rainfall, to boost soil fertility and give plants a good start.

Top-dressing A general, high-nitrogen or high-potash feed spread around plants during the lifetime of a crop to boost development or revive growth after winter.

Foliar feed Liquid fertilizer sprayed or watered onto plants, usually to aid rapid recovery after a setback such as drought, or to amend a nutrient deficiency.

SEE ALSO ▶ Supplying nutrients
pages 120–1

the case for weeding

Controlling weeds There is never enough room to grow everything on the allotment, and gardening of any kind involves being selective. Weeds are opportunist species that persist in muscling into the plot, menacing the plants you want to grow, and dealing with these intruders firmly and efficiently is a key part of providing allotment crops with the best living conditions.

WHY CONTROL WEEDS?

Unless weeds have value as groundcover or green manure, they need to be controlled. In addition to taking up valuable space, weeds compete with cultivated plants for available light, water and nutrients.

Many are also alternative hosts for various pests and diseases. Fat hen, for example, can support black and green aphids over winter as well as various mosaic virus diseases; groundsel will transmit the main fungal diseases such as blight and mildew; and charlock and other crucifers host brassica clubroot disease.

THE DIFFICULTIES It is impossible to eliminate weeds altogether. Seeds of annual weeds can lie buried for 30 years or more and still germinate when cultivation brings them to the surface. Fresh seeds can arrive on the wind and soon colonize clean cultivated ground, sometimes flowering and shedding their own seeds several times in a single season. Many perennials spread both by seed and by underground methods such as rhizomes, bulbils and creeping stems that soon regenerate if damaged or separated during clearing and cultivation.

Any plant becomes a weed if it is tenacious, self-sufficient, prolific and a born survivor. On allotments, this might include volunteer potato plants from a previous crop, salsify, good king henry, blackberries and similar self-seeders, as well as more obvious weeds such as thistles, buttercups and ground elder. A combination of prevention and prompt treatment will reduce the numbers of these almost inevitable competitors to manageable levels.

ABOVE Spear thistles, like most weeds, should be dug up as soon as they are noticed, otherwise they will become increasingly difficult to remove.
LEFT Although delicious to eat, cooked or uncooked, brambles are born survivors, and so prolific that their numbers need to be kept at a manageable level on the allotment.

Herbicides can usually be avoided if weeds are routinely dug up.

AVOIDING HERBICIDES

Using weedkillers on an allotment is unnecessary, and may be considered positively antisocial where it proves difficult to avoid splashes or spray drifting onto adjacent plots. Weedkillers are expensive, leave unwelcome or dangerous residues for varying lengths of time, and they often disrupt the activities of soil organisms; as with all chemical inputs, their regular use can lead to a build-up of resistance. For routine maintenance, a variety of manual controls combined with patience will usually succeed. Only perhaps where a badly overgrown plot needs clearing might the careful application of a systemic herbicide be justified.

USING YOUR WEEDS
If you start to treat weeds as plants to appreciate or even harvest, then weeding can become less of a chore. Chickweed, blanched dandelion leaves and young nettle tips are all edible and nutritious. Like all plant species, weeds absorb nutrients from the soil, often from deep down, so they are also a valuable boost to the compost

WEED CONTROL
PROGRAMME

▶ Take your time clearing an overgrown plot (see *pages 122–3*), especially if it is infested with perennial weeds. If time presses, though, thoroughly prepare a small area for immediate sowing or planting, then work on the rest of the plot.

▶ Sow as many crops as possible in a weed-free seed- or nursery bed for transplanting, and continue clearing the final growing areas as weed seedlings or root fragments appear.

▶ Liberally mulch growing plants (see *page 119*), as this will suppress many annual weed seedlings, and remnants of perennial weeds will be easier to pull up.

▶ Prepare beds well in advance of sowing and leave as stale beds (see *page 126*) to eliminate later weeds as they germinate.

▼ Try using deterrent methods, such as planting crops through plastic or paper mats, and growing smother crops like clover and nasturtiums to suppress weeds in between taller plants. Outdoor tomato plants have been found to kill couch grass

heap. Perennial weed roots are a rich source of minerals (see *page 122*), while the foliage of nettles and comfrey can be steeped in water to make a balanced liquid feed (see *page 151*).

▲ Shallow-hoe bare ground and between rows while weeds are small and the soil dry. Pulling or forking up larger weeds is easier when the ground is moist.

▶ Never leave uprooted weeds lying on the surface where they will often continue growing and set seed in moist conditions. Tackle larger weeds before they flower, mowing or shearing them down if necessary.

IDENTIFYING SOIL
BY WEEDS

Prevalent weed species can help you identify your soil type. Black bindweed, cinquefoil, corn marigold, daisy, foxglove, horsetail, shepherd's cress, sorrel and wild pansy are typical of acid soils, whereas alkaline soils are preferred by black medick, campanulas, greater hawkbit, pennycress, stonecrop, tansy and valerian. A wide mixture of vigorous weeds indicates that you have good fertile soil, as well as plenty of work ahead of you.

SEE ALSO ▶ **Green manures**
page 119 Clearing the plot *pages 122–3*
Mulching weeds away *page 122*
Keeping your plants healthy *pages 154–7*

keeping your plants healthy

Pests & diseases Just like weeds, pests and diseases are fundamental facts of allotment life. Essential actors in the natural drama of plant growth, decay and death, they cannot be avoided completely, and their arrival is not necessarily cause for trepidation or evidence of some mistake or oversight in cultivation. You do have a lot of choice, however, in the way you anticipate and respond to their appearance. The most realistic approach is to encourage robust plants, take effective precautions, and aim for a tolerable, low level of incidence rather than total elimination. Chemical treatments should be used, if at all, only in emergencies.

CULTIVATING GOOD HEALTH
You can reduce the risk of trouble from pests and diseases by supporting and strengthening the good health of your plants. Keep the soil well drained and in good heart with annual dressings of humus-forming organic material, cultivate the surface between crops to expose soil pests for birds and other predators, and mulch growing plants to reduce stress from drought.

Practise crop rotation (see *pages 32–5*) to prevent soil problems from becoming endemic, and keep on top of weeds, which can handicap your plants by competing ruthlessly for nutrients and transmitting disorders. Avoid unnecessary cultural risks like sowing in cold conditions, skimping on hardening off, mishandling transplants and leaving diseased material to spread infection.

AVOIDING PESTS Both neglect and overprotection can promote weak growth that succumbs more easily to trouble than sturdy, self-sufficient plants fortified by sensible precautions.

Choosing tolerant or resistant seed varieties is a sound preliminary measure, especially if plants are also regularly rotated in well-prepared soil or dispersed among unrelated crops that camouflage their presence. Interplanting adjacent rows of carrots with two rows of onions, for example, or undersowing brassicas with clover can confuse or deter carrot flies and cabbage root flies respectively. Try

Growing lettuces between rows of cordon tomatoes makes good use of the available light and space.

intercropping a susceptible vegetable with flowers like gaillardias and limnanthes to attract insect predators (see Friends & foes, opposite).

Check bought and gifted plants for pests: they are a common source of transmission, as are all overwintered crops, which can shelter and feed a reservoir of pests. Become familiar with the behaviour and habits of pests so you can install barriers, traps and deterrents like carrot fly fences and slug traps in strategic places at the right time of year. Finally, inspect plants regularly: vigilance and early treatment can save major urgent attention later.

SIMPLE SOLUTIONS Only a small minority of pests cause serious or general trouble. Many, like froghoppers ('cuckoo spit'), are little more than a cosmetic nuisance, while others – asparagus beetle, currant clearwing moth – are either highly crop-specific or seldom met. Very often the simplest or most obvious treatment is also the most effective: brassica seedlings can shrug off flea beetle attacks if they are sown early and watered in dry weather; manually catching and despatching slugs or caterpillars in a jar of brine is fast and efficient; squashing leaf miner larvae at the end of their leaf tunnels is instant; and leaving a ring of raked-off stones around the bed acts as a *cordon sanitaire* to deter slugs and snails.

SEE ALSO ▶ Crop rotation *pages 32–5* Companion planting *page 35* **Combining crops** *page 142* Slug & snail protection *page 178*

PEST	DESCRIPTION	DAMAGE CAUSED	TREATMENT
Aphids	Soft sap-sucking black, green or grey mealy insects, sometimes winged.	Weaken and distort growth, carry virus diseases and excrete sugary honeydew that supports sooty mould.	▶ Grow susceptible crops under fleece. ▶ Encourage birds and insect predators. ▶ Rub off early colonies, or blast off with a spray of clean water. ▶ Spray with insecticidal soap.
Caterpillars & grubs	Larvae of moths, butterflies, sawflies, etc. Some very visible and seasonal; others live or hibernate in the soil.	Variously feed on leaves, stems, fruits or roots.	▶ Pick off visible larvae and destroy. ▶ Spray with 60g (2oz) salt in 4.5 litres (1 gal) water, or with *Bacillus thuringiensis* (specific fungal preparation). ▶ Cultivate soil to expose larvae like cutworms for birds.
Slugs & snails	Soft-bodied molluscs that feed widely on many plants, mainly at night and in damp situations. Some slugs are elusive soil-dwellers.	Soft parts of plants most susceptible; some slugs eat tubers. Very destructive, especially on seedlings.	▶ Hand-pick at dusk and on damp days; check under leaves and plant debris. ▶ Set beer traps; arrange barriers of grit, soot or copper bands (see also *page 178*). ▶ Encourage thrushes, toads and other amphibians.
Red spider mites	Minute sap-sucking insects that revel in warm, dry conditions like greenhouses.	Leaves are spotted yellow with a bronze sheen. Fine webs.	▶ Deter by keeping plants moist. ▶ Forcefully mist foliage; damp down regularly under glass. ▶ Spray with insecticidal soap. ▶ Introduce predatory mite under glass.

Blackfly feasting on broad beans.

FRIENDS & FOES

'If it moves, shoot it' is not sound gardening policy. Most of the pests you are likely to meet are part of a natural food chain and are consumed by birds and carnivorous or parasitic insects or their larvae. Learn to distinguish pest from predator: slow or static insects tend to be plant-feeders, whereas agile creatures are often hunters. The fast-moving centipede, for example, preys upon and can often control sluggish vegetarian millipedes.

Welcome these garden allies by creating their favourite habitats. Black beetles and newts, which feed on soil pests, shelter under stones, prostrate plants and mulches; ladybirds, lacewings and hoverflies, whose larvae devour huge numbers of aphids, browse flowers such as asters, chrysanthemums, marigolds and sedums, and will overwinter in artificial nesting boxes; a pond can attract frogs, toads and newts as part of your war on slugs. Specialized predators can be bought at the appropriate time for greenhouse pests. Above all, avoid using pesticides, which do not discriminate between friend and foe.

Well-spaced wigwams of runner beans ensure that the plants are not overcrowded and are therefore less prone to disease.

and check new plants for symptoms. Inspect them regularly for early signs, and cull, isolate or treat affected plants without delay.

TREATMENTS Survival of the fittest is often the wisest policy, and removing a diseased plant and destroying it can reduce the risk to the rest of your crop and to neighbouring plotholders. Fungicides will rarely save an ailing plant and are effective as protectants only before a disease appears or spreads. Even then success is unpredictable, and it is better to take cultural precautions than to rely on chemical treatments.

Many diseases are specific and can often be prevented by attention to cultural details. For example, maintaining the right pH level in the soil helps guard against clubroot disease of brassicas; covering plant foliage when the risk is high protects against peach leaf curl; controlling the pests that spread infection helps prevent reversion disease of blackcurrants. Other conditions are relatively common and affect a range of plants, especially if weather conditions are favourable or alternative hosts such as weeds grow nearby.

Note that symptoms can be common to more than one disease, and that apparent signs of disease are very often caused by a nutrient deficiency or prolonged bad weather, so do not automatically assume the worst. First make sure your diagnosis is accurate, and then act promptly and firmly.

AVOIDING DISEASES Plant diseases often seem more sinister than pests because the organisms that cause them are usually invisible and arrive without warning. They are also more difficult to treat, and by the time symptoms appear a plant can be infected beyond control. Many pathogens have developed resistance to common fungicides (largely due to their excessive use) and can survive for many years in soil or plant tissues, waiting dormant for a new host. Since most diseases are also easily transmissable, there is a good case

for the traditional practice of culling and destroying a diseased plant before the infection can spread.

Prevention is easier and more dependable than treatment. As with pests, good cultivation to encourage strong, vigorous growth is essential, together with attention to basic garden hygiene. Avoid overcrowding, drought stress, under- and over-feeding and poor drainage, clear away dead plants and decaying leaves, and never propagate cuttings or divisions from diseased plants. Choose resistant or tolerant varieties wherever possible,

SEE ALSO ▶ Coping with clubroot *page 185*

DISEASE	DESCRIPTION & DAMAGE	TREATMENT
Cankers	Lesions often girdle and kill complete shoots. Causes bark and tissue death on fruit trees and other woody plants.	▶ Prune affected shoots back to clean unstained wood. ▶ Avoid susceptible varieties, especially in damp or humid areas.
Mildews	These are two kinds of parasitic fungi: powdery mildew and downy mildew. Powdery mildew leaves grey dusty deposits on distorted foliage, while downy mildew produces yellow areas on upper leaf surfaces and grey fuzzy patches beneath.	▶ Powdery mildew: avoid overcrowding and prolonged dry conditions; water and mulch during drought. ▶ Downy mildew: occurs in prolonged damp or humid conditions, often late season; avoid overcrowding and evening watering. ▶ Pinch off infected shoots. ▶ Grow resistant varieties.
Rots	These fungi and bacteria cause decay of plant tissues. Rots include vegetable disorders like parsnip canker and damping off disease. Usually occur in damp or waterlogged conditions, often after injury.	▶ Maintain air circulation above and below ground. ▶ Ensure good drainage. ▶ Avoid overwatering, overcrowding and damage while using tools. ▶ Destroy infected plants promptly.
Rusts	Fungal diseases causing tiny dark spots on leaves and stems, with bright yellow, red or brown spore-bearing pustules. Disfiguring rather than disabling.	▶ Clear away fallen affected leaves to prevent transmission. ▶ A serious ailment on mint: clear and burn plants, sterilize tools, and plant new stock elsewhere.
Scabs	Fungal and bacterial diseases causing rough crusty patches on leaves, twigs, fruits and root crops. Often superficial but may admit other diseases.	▶ Prevent soil forms by watering and manuring regularly, avoid over-liming. ▶ Clear scabby leaves and prune off infected shoots in autumn. ▶ Use affected fruit and roots first, and do not store. ▶ Grow resistant kinds.
Viruses	Common and widespread on a range of plants. Symptoms include yellow, spotted, crinkled or unusually small leaves, and stunted growth or poor yields. Generally spread by pests and contact with infected hands and tools.	▶ No reliable treatment. ▶ Buy plants certified virus-free. ▶ Practise good garden hygiene. ▶ Destroy affected plants. ▶ Control insect pests. ▶ Some fruits are tolerant but can infect others; restock if yields decline. ▶ Destroy, never compost, infected plants.
Wilts	Soil diseases affecting some herbs, cane fruits and vegetables, especially cucumbers and tomatoes, often causing total collapse. Usually the result of poor drainage, overwatering or cold, wet weather.	▶ Make sure soil or compost is never waterlogged. ▶ Avoid planting susceptible crops too early. ▶ Collapsed plants are usually beyond recovery.

keeping your plants healthy

allotment story
A TASTE OF HONEY

Bees are a gardener's allies, essential for ensuring our plant and tree flowers are fertilized – without them many crops would be meagre or fail altogether – so it's not surprising that there are many working hives kept on allotments by plot-holders and dedicated beekeepers. Beekeeping, or apiculture, is concerned with the practical management of honey bees, which live in large colonies of up to 100,000 individuals. Hives are often prudently placed at the remote outer edges of a plot, well away from paths or busy areas of the allotment, as some people are allergic to bee stings or are scared of bees at close quarters. Being marginalized is no handicap to the bees, which happily fly to collect pollen and nectar from miles away yet return home to the allotment to fertilize plants, fruit trees and flowers.

It is possible for bees to have a happy, symbiotic relationship with the allotment keeper and his crops and, with the right equipment, knowledge and a sense of respect for these useful little insects, a gardener could reap the rewards of the honey-comb as well as an abundant fruit yield. Any person wishing to keep bees on allotments must first seek the agreement of their Allotment Manager as in a few cases allotment associations may class bees as 'Livestock' and there may be restrictions on keeping them. However, bees are great propagators and can really improve plot productivity so why not suggest it to other plot holders and see if they approve? Local Beekeeping Associations will gladly offer advice to anybody thinking of adding this hobby to their allotment.

harvesting & storing

The fruits of your labour

Harvesting is the all-important (and extremely satisfying) climax to all your hopes, hard work and good husbandry on the allotment. Crops in peak condition always look and taste better when fresh than after storage, but there is often more ready than can be consumed immediately, and many crops are grown purposely for keeping and using long after they are ripe. Timing the harvest and careful handling are critical to avoid damage or premature deterioration, so an eye for detail can be important. But don't let this need for care spoil the sheer joy of gathering in your own produce. Harvest is festival time!

WHEN TO HARVEST & STORE

With very few exceptions (such as pears and late apples), crops should be just fully mature when picked because both under- and over-ripeness can impair flavour. Judging when a crop is ready is not always easy. Condition and appearance may vary between varieties or from one season to the next; early colouring can indicate pest attack rather than ripeness, while some crops, such as pears or marrows, change colour only after storage or when they are over-ripe. Sampling is the surest test, together with more specific signs (see crop profiles, *pages 66–109*), such as cracking at the base of melon stalks or whether fruit parts easily from the plant.

Once you have approved flavour and quality, harvest as much as possible for immediate use or storage, but remember to distinguish between crops that ripen together and deteriorate quickly, like radishes and raspberries, and those that mature or stay good over a long period: carrots, leeks and redcurrants, for example. If you need to clear a crop wholesale, be prepared to store or preserve it soon afterwards, because quality can deteriorate quickly (within hours in the case of sweetcorn). Where this proves to be a problem, you might want to make a note to try another, more lasting variety next time or possibly stagger sowings to extend picking.

Leaf crops Soft leafy crops like lettuces, spinach and sprouting broccoli deteriorate quickly. Gather just before use, ideally in the morning or evening while they are cool. Keep in a cold place such as a fridge cool box. Firm vegetables like cabbages and Brussels sprouts will keep for several days in a cool, frost-free place. Leave winter greens to harvest as required, or pull up whole cabbage and sprout plants, and hang them upside down in a cool, airy shed until needed.

Root crops Most summer roots, like early carrots and beetroot, can stay in the ground to pull or fork up for fresh use. Maincrops are usually left for as long as possible and then lifted en masse for storing when the soil is fairly dry and falls off easily – roots store better when dry and clean. Keep potatoes in paper or woven sacks, frost-free and in darkness. Carrots, beetroot, turnips, swedes and winter radishes can be stored, with their foliage twisted off, in layers of moist sand in boxes in a cool dry shed. They can also be clamped (see *pages 210–12*).

Legumes Pick peas and beans before they become large and tough, checking plants every 2–3 days as more ripen. Most will keep for a few days in unsealed polythene bags in a cool place, or can be frozen. Peas and beans for shelling should be left until ripe. Then cut complete plants at ground level, hang in a cool, well-ventilated place to dry, and shell out the seeds for storing in tins or jars.

Bulbs Crops like onions, garlic and shallots are very versatile, and can be used before or when they are fully ripe, and they also store successfully. To store, lift the crops carefully to avoid damage and dry thoroughly, then spread them out on newspaper or hang in bunches in a warm, airy spot outdoors or in a coldframe or greenhouse. Once the skins feel dry and papery, store in shallow trays, in nets or suspended in plaits. Keep dry and frost-free at all times.

COLD-TOLERANT CROPS

The following crops will normally withstand temperatures as low as 5°C (11°F) without protection, so can be left in the ground during cold weather.
- Broad beans (autumn-sown)
- Brussels sprouts • cabbages (savoy, spring and winter varieties) • celeriac
- chard • chicory (hardy red forms)
- corn salad • garlic • Jerusalem artichokes • kale • land cress • leeks
- onions (autumn-sown) • parsnips
- peas (autumn-sown) • perpetual spinach • rocket • salsify • scorzonera
- sprouting broccoli • winter radish

Flowering & fruiting crops There is no single rule for harvesting and storing these crops. Tender vegetables like tomatoes, aubergines, sweetcorn and summer cauliflowers are used as needed when completely ripe, while any surplus can usually be frozen, dried or turned into preserves. Squashes need curing by leaving them in the sun for 1–2 weeks until the skins are dry and hard (see *page 204*), before they are stored in a cool, frost-free place.

Herbs Many herbs are cut-and-come-again plants, and the leaves or shoots are picked as needed, a process that keeps them bushy and rejuvenated. Culinary herbs develop their best flavour during or just before flowering, when large quantities can be harvested for drying, freezing or infusing. Gather the material on a dry morning, combining the harvest with overall pruning to reshape plants.

Keep different varieties separate to avoid their flavours mingling, and process them before the foliage starts to wilt. Trim off old or damaged leaves and thicker portions of stems, and then tie shoots in bundles and hang up to dry in an airy place out of full sun, or freeze in polythene bags or chopped up in ice-cube trays.

Fruit Most kinds of fruit are harvested when fully ripe and eaten soon afterwards, but few crops mature all at once and you will need to check several times to test and pick fruits that are ready. Gooseberries can be gathered for cooking while still small and immature, thinning the crop and leaving spaced berries to reach dessert quality. Many pear varieties are picked while still hard to continue ripening for several weeks in store.

Always pick fruit carefully as many kinds bruise easily. This is vital for surplus fruits because only perfect specimens store successfully. All soft-fleshed fruits can be frozen, bottled or turned into cooked preserves. Hard

Squashes will keep for several months if they are first cured then nestled in straw on shelves in a dry, frost-free and well-ventilated shed.

fruits like apples and pears (especially early kinds) can be treated in the same way, but long-keeping varieties are more often spread out on shelves or in boxes, or packed in perforated plastic bags, and then stored in a cool, dark airy place.

BLANCHING & FORCING Some vegetables need additional treatment before or after harvest to improve their eating qualities (see crop profiles, *pages 66–109*). Blanching involves excluding light from green crops to give them a tender texture or sweeter flavour: trench celery and sweet fennel, for example, are earthed up to blanch their stems crisp and white, while covering dandelion leaves and the hearts of some endive and cos lettuce varieties

TRY THIS

► For best results, look out for varieties that are recommended specifically for freezing, drying or long-keeping.

► Grow maincrop or late-maturing varieties for the longest storage life. Leave them growing as late as possible, but gather them in before the first frosts.

► Leave the stalks or a small tuft of foliage on stored fruit and vegetables, and make sure they are roughly clean; never wash them.

► Always use up small or damaged roots and thick-necked onions first, as they quickly spoil in store.

► Separate fruit, vegetables and strong-tasting crops when in store to avoid cross-flavours.

► Check stored produce regularly for signs of attack by mice and other rival consumers.

► Darkness and good ventilation are essential to keep most stored crops from spoiling; watch temperatures to prevent freezing or overheating.

► Lift early potatoes when they start flowering, clean and pack them in a biscuit tin of dry sand or compost, and bury in the ground for use in winter.

► Cut off exhausted pea and bean plants at ground level after harvest, leaving their nitrogen-rich roots to rot in the soil.

removes unpalatable bitterness. Forcing also takes place in partial or total darkness, and is intended to coax a crop into growing out of season. Witloof chicory roots, for example, are stored and then grown in pots during winter to produce their fat, crisp leaf buds, while rhubarb is forced into early growth under boxes or upturned pots, a technique that also blanches the stems, making them sweet and tender.

SALVAGING STORED PRODUCE

As time passes, the quality and nutritional value of unused produce in store deteriorate until the crop is either inedible or starts to rot. Inspect supplies regularly, and before they are well past their best choose another way to preserve what is left. Most fruits and vegetables can be cut up and frozen in bags, either raw or cooked, although they may need using before other produce frozen in peak condition. Fruit can also be bottled and turned into

Autumn crab apples are too tart to eat straight off the tree but make delicious wines and preserves.

preserves such as jam and wine, even after quite long storage. Vegetables can be puréed or made into soups, pickles and sauces.

HEDGEROW HARVEST As well as gathering in your own crops, explore the hedges that enclose and divide many allotment sites. They often contain wild produce that can be safely harvested, especially if you are any distance from busy roads and other sources of pollution. Elderflowers add sweetness, flavour and fragrance to gooseberry and rhubarb dishes, and can be turned into a range of summer drinks. Autumn fruits like blackberries, crab apples, elderberries, sloes, haws and rosehips all make delicious (and nutritious) preserves, or can be combined in a hedgerow jelly or wine.

SEE ALSO ► Elderflower champagne recipe *page 187* Storing potatoes *page 206* **Forcing chicory page 208** Ways with rhubarb *page 208* **Sloe gin recipe *page 209***

harvesting & storing

the allotment year

Every crop has its season. Knowing the best times to carry out the various tasks around the allotment will help you to organize the most suitable cropping programme for your produce, and to coordinate all those other seasonal demands on time and space.

an overview

Getting the timing right

'Everything in its proper season' is a sound resolution. Many jobs on the allotment need to be done at the right moment for best results. They, in turn, can depend on earlier preparations or must not be delayed too long lest plants suffer or have insufficient time to grow to maturity. But timing gardening tasks is not an exact science, despite traditional advice to sow onions or plant potatoes on particular days of the year, and there are many shortcuts or compromises to compensate for the fact that you were unable to get near your plot during a long wet spell. More important, and certainly more reliable than following the calendar, is an appreciation of the seasons and the key changes they bring, together with the natural gardening cues that can help you to work with them.

WATCHING THE WEATHER

Successful gardeners keep at least one eye on the weather. Plants under glass might revel in a protected environment that you can manipulate for their welfare (see *pages 170–5*), but the majority of crops are exposed to outdoor elements, which are changeable and often unpredictable, especially with the impact of climate change.

Learn to anticipate the effects of particular weather conditions. Warm winter sunshine, often followed by sharply cold nights, distresses standing crops more than (to us) gloomy cloud cover. A coating of snow can insulate

A light covering of frost indicates that winter is on its way.

plants from winter cold, provided the ground was not frozen when it fell, whereas alternate freezing and thawing may be lethal. Persistent winds dry bare soils and leafy foliage, quickly causing drought stress, even in winter when frozen ground can deny the roots water – shelter from wind is often more critical than shelter from cold.

LOCAL VARIATIONS Every allotment plot has its own microclimate, affected locally by shade, shelter and terrain, as in frost hollows, for example (see *page 25*), and in the wider context is influenced by its regional location. Inland districts are often colder than coastal sites just a few kilometres away, temperatures fall with increased altitude, and urban areas can be warmer and more sheltered than the country. Latitude affects the timing of seasons. In the south of the UK, for example, soils may be warm enough for sowing 3–4 weeks earlier than in the north. Together with a later start to autumn, this can lengthen the average growing season by 50 days or more.

RELIABLE CUES Older gardeners may claim that they simply 'feel it in their bones', but judging the right time for critical allotment jobs like sowing and planting takes a blend of experience, wariness and observation. Keep a diary of activities and results to gradually build a record of success and failure to guide your decisions, but always temper confidence by caution. Be ready to rescue or protect crops if the weather changes, keep some seeds or plants in reserve as replacements, and never be in a hurry to take risks. Someone will always gamble and have first pickings, but not every year, and later crops often catch up: parsnips sown in late winter can take 4–5 weeks to appear, but only 10–14 days if sown in spring.

WEATHER INFLUENCES

- ▶ Most plants start growing in spring when the average temperature in the day is around 6°C (43°F), and become dormant below this in autumn.
- ▶ In late summer, soils can be as warm as 24°C (75°F), which causes stress to many crops and inhibits the seed germination of plants like onions and lettuces.
- ▶ A leafy vegetable crop can lose more than 5.4 litres/sq.m (1 gal/sq.yd) of water *per day* in hot sun.
- ▶ Cabbage root flies start to lay eggs when cow parsley begins flowering, which can vary by more than 3 weeks, depending on spring weather.
- ▶ Warm, dry summers favour the growth of powdery mildew, while wet summer weather encourages downy mildew and grey mould. Late summer thunderstorms and fogs help the spread of potato and tomato blight.

The blossom on fruit trees, while a welcome sign of spring, is still vulnerable to late frosts.

Watch out for natural signals around you. Nature does not always get it right: some years young beech leaves are blasted by late frosts and early birds lose their first broods, but evidence from hedgerows and wildlife is often more reliable than calendar dates. Hawthorn breaking into leaf is a traditional cue to start spring crops, for example, but you should still beware the odd late frost.

Even weather lore can be useful: winds and temperatures are usually wildly unpredictable around the spring and autumn equinoxes, and honey bees tend to return to their hives when a storm is likely. Finally, note when other, more seasoned plot-holders act and be prepared to ask advice. But remember the proverb 'all gardeners know better than other gardeners'.

growing under glass

The greenhouse year

How much you can do in the greenhouse depends on the kind of structure you have (see *pages 46–7*) and whether it is meant to be primarily a growing house, or a place for you to work in bad weather, or to store materials. When used intensively for protecting plants, it is a valuable asset that extends the range and growing season of crops, as well as allowing an earlier start outdoors.

PLANNING THE SPACE The most economical way to arrange your greenhouse is to grow plants at ground level as well as on removable staging. With a soil border running either side of the path (and perhaps at one end of the greenhouse), you can grow tall crops like tomatoes, cucumbers or fruit.

Even in this limited space, crop rotation is feasible to prevent soil sickness and a build-up of problems, or you could renew a section by exchanging the soil for a fresh supply from outdoors. On a solid floor, a collection of growing bags and containers will support similar crops. Use the staging as a potting bench and somewhere to grow young plants; in summer, make room for ground-level plants by moving the staging outside, where it will still be a useful work area.

In winter, soil borders will be less susceptible to frost than containers, and they can be fully planted up with hardy vegetables, herbs out of season, and plants that will benefit from indoor protection. Keep the fertility levels high with dressings of compost, and top up the soil levels with discarded potting compost; blended with a little fertilizer, this makes a good mixture for filling large containers or empty growing bags.

Managing the greenhouse

Looking after plants under glass is quite different from open ground cultivation. While the greenhouse environment is more stable than outdoors and you can create or adjust conditions to suit, it is also more demanding because plants depend for their welfare entirely on you. You also need to appreciate each crop's

---

THE GREENHOUSE YEAR

SPRING
- ▶ Gradually increase ventilation, but watch out for night frosts.
- ▶ Sow, prick out and harden off early crops in sequence.
- ▶ Protect seedlings from scorching, and lightly shade glass.
- ▶ Plant tender crops early in a heated house, in late spring in a cool house.
- ▶ Pollinate early fruit.

SUMMER
- ▶ Ventilate freely day and night, and fully shade the glass.
- ▶ Grow and train summer crops.
- ▶ Water, feed and damp down regularly.
- ▶ Guard against pests and diseases, and treat any symptoms promptly.
- ▶ Sow winter vegetables for transplanting in the autumn.

Aubergines in the greenhouse border, almost ready for training.

AUTUMN
- ▶ Gradually reduce watering, feeding and damping down.
- ▶ Close vents at night but keep air circulating; remove shading.
- ▶ Have insulation handy for early frosts.
- ▶ Clear summer crops, dry onions and ripen fruit.
- ▶ Sow winter vegetables and pot up herbs for forcing.

WINTER
- ▶ Fully insulate and protect from frost.
- ▶ Ventilate for short periods in mild weather, and keep the air dry.
- ▶ Clean and sterilize the greenhouse and equipment ready for the new season.
- ▶ Force early crops such as strawberries and rhubarb.
- ▶ Start early sowings towards the end of winter.

GOOD GREENHOUSE CROPS

As well as being a comfortable propagator for sowing, pricking out and potting, a greenhouse is ideal for growing a varied range of crops. These include:

► Early and late sowings of carrots, radishes, dwarf beans and leafy salads.
► Cold-sensitive plants like aubergines, cucumbers, peppers, tomatoes, basil and lemon verbena.
► Hardy crops such as endive, chard, spinach, perpetual spinach, parsley (for improved quality).
► Climbers such as grapevines, figs, kiwi fruits and yard-long beans.

Young greenhouse cucumbers trained along a string.

requirements, especially if you plan to grow several together: for example, tomatoes and cucumbers cohabit uneasily because they prefer different levels of heat, light and humidity.

All greenhouse plants benefit from attention being paid to the four key essentials for trouble-free growth under glass: air, light, water and health

Ventilate the greenhouse for short periods in winter.

Cleaning off greenhouse paint.

AIR Even in the depths of winter, plants appreciate a daily change of air, so try to open a vent just a crack for an hour or so to prevent a stale atmosphere. During the growing season ventilate whenever possible to stabilize temperatures and discourage disease. Fitting an automatic vent to at least one window can prevent extreme changes in temperature.

LIGHT Plants grow towards the light, and where levels are inadequate they become weak, spindly and unhealthy. Clean the glass thoroughly in spring as the season starts, and again in autumn when you remove any shading. Active plants do best close to the glass during the winter months, but seedlings should be lightly shaded from bright sunlight with newspaper until they are growing strongly. Shade the greenhouse with paint or netting as the days lengthen – a light covering in spring, a full coat all summer – and remove in early autumn.

WATER Watering can be time-consuming in hot weather unless you set up an automatic watering system with capillary matting or drip pipes and a reservoir, plus a mulch for ground-level plants. Small pots and trays may need checking daily, although shading the glass and covering seedlings with a sheet of newspaper will reduce water loss and stress. Cool and moisten the air by 'damping down': watering or spraying the floor, paths and staging.

Use a can with a sprinkler rose to damp down the floors regularly.

GREENHOUSE TOMATOES

Cordon tomatoes are one of the most popular crops for allotment greenhouses. They often fruit earlier and more predictably than outdoor plants, especially if you choose an indoor variety, which will be shorter jointed and more prolific.

1 Sow indoors at 21°C (70°F), in late winter for a heated house or in early spring if unheated. Prick out the seedlings into 8cm (3in) pots when they have two true leaves.

2 Transplant the seedlings into borders, growing bags or 25cm (10in) pots when the roots have filled their pots and before the first flower truss.

3 Tie the main stem at intervals to a cane or a length of taut vertical string.

4 Remove all sideshoots.

5 Water regularly, tap flowering plants to disperse the pollen, and feed from the time the first fruits develop.

6 Pinch out the growing tips in late summer to encourage the remaining fruit to ripen.

Reduce watering when growth is less vigorous, and keep conditions on the dry side in winter, when overwatering can cause rot.

HEALTH In a protected environment, plants become soft and susceptible to disorders. Fortify them by watering and feeding according to their rate of growth – too much is as harmful as too little – and maintain the correct temperature range by insulating or ventilating the greenhouse. You could confine tender plants to a separate insulated area in winter, rather than protect the whole structure. Take precautions like suspending sticky yellow cards to trap flying insects, or planting marigolds (*Tagetes*) to deter whitefly.

HELPFUL HINTS

▶ Sow a bush variety with the maincrop and grow at the foot of the taller plants to crop earlier and save space.

▶ Water at regular intervals to prevent blossom end rot, but avoid giving more water than is needed, which spoils the flavour.

▼ Sow basil at the same time as a companion plant for deterring pests, and harvest it along with the tomatoes.

GREENHOUSE CUCUMBERS

Together with tomatoes, cucumbers are the favourite allotment crop for growing under glass, provided the long, straight greenhouse varieties are given the warmth, shelter and humidity they need. For best results, keep plants at 15°C (60°F), but give all-female varieties a few degrees more.

▶ Sow and transplant like tomatoes (see left), into 30cm (12in) pots when plants are 15cm (6in) high.

▶ Pinch out the growing tips of bush varieties after transplanting; pinch out tall kinds when they reach the top of their canes or strings.

▶ Train the sideshoots of tall varieties sideways and stop them 2 leaves after a female flower; remove male flowers.

▶ Water regularly and carefully around, but not over, plants, and damp down to keep the air moist.

▶ Feed every 10–14 days, starting 6 weeks after transplanting.

Harvest full-size fruits before they turn yellow and bitter or start to fatten at one end. Cucumber 'Petita' is being harvested in this picture.

HELPFUL HINTS

▶ Extra warmth and humidity are essential in the early stages to keep growth vigorous until natural heat levels rise.

▲ Female flowers have a tiny cucumber behind their petals; all-female varieties produce male flowers when stressed.

▶ Spray the foliage occasionally to control red spider mite, but reduce in late summer when the risk of mildew increases.

Fruit under glass

Several kinds of fruit can be grown in a greenhouse without necessarily taking up much room, and compact kinds thrive in a cold frame. The extra warmth can protect blossom early in the year and help late-maturing fruit to ripen in autumn. Some disorders, such as peach leaf curl, will be avoided, but pests like scale, whitefly, mealy bug and red spider mite can be a problem without due precautions, and you may have to fertilize early blooms by hand.

Tree fruits like apricots, peaches, nectarines and figs grow well in the ground or large containers. Training them flat against the sunny side of the greenhouse will save space, and plants will receive the most warmth and sunlight, at the same time shading the rest of the greenhouse in summer.

Grapes can be grown up to the roof provided they are pruned and trained carefully (see *page 212*).

Apples and pears on dwarfing rootstocks, genetically dwarf peaches and citrus fruits in containers can pass the winter safely under glass.

Melons are ideal for small greenhouses if they are grown like cucumbers in a soil border, large pots or growing bags, and trained on netting or strings suspended from the roof. Grow them in cold frames by planting centrally, pinching out the growing tip and training a sideshoot to each of the four corners of the frame.

Strawberries potted in late summer and brought indoors in late winter will crop very early on greenhouse shelves close to the glass. Cropping will be a little later in a cold frame.

Rhubarb crowns, dug up in autumn and exposed to frost for a month, can be forced in darkness under the staging or in a frame for extra-early sticks.

A well-trained grapevine.

THE COLD FRAME YEAR

Although often used only to harden off plants in the spring and as a store for canes and other materials for the rest of the time, a cold frame is a valuable accessory for the long-term protection of plants. Portable frames can be used in the same way as large cloches, while a soil-based model is an extra bed for crops wherever space is at a premium. (See also *pages 48–9*.)

Use a cold frame to harden off tender plants.

EARLY SPRING
- ▶ Sow early dwarf beans.
- ▶ Plant early potatoes.
- ▶ Harden off sowings.
- ▶ Grow early salads.
- ▶ Strike chrysanthemum cuttings.

LATE SPRING
- ▶ Sow summer crops.
- ▶ Harden off tender plants.
- ▶ Plant melons, cucumbers, self-blanching celery.
- ▶ Start dahlias.

EARLY SUMMER
- ▶ Take soft cuttings.
- ▶ Grow and train summer crops.
- ▶ Use as a nursery bed.

LATE SUMMER
- ▶ Sow parsley, oriental brassicas.
- ▶ Root strawberry runners.
- ▶ Dry garlic and shallots.
- ▶ Sow salads for winter use.

EARLY AUTUMN
- ▶ Dry onions.
- ▶ Sow salads.
- ▶ Plant lettuces.
- ▶ Sow hardy annuals for early blooms.
- ▶ Plunge bulbs for forcing.

LATE AUTUMN
- ▶ Overwinter spare brassicas, such as spring cabbages, and chrysanthemum stools.
- ▶ Root hardwood cuttings.

EARLY WINTER
- ▶ Protect winter herb supplies and sweet peas.
- ▶ Force rhubarb, seakale and chicory.

LATE WINTER
- ▶ Continue forcing.
- ▶ Sow early salads and crops for transplanting.
- ▶ Make a hot bed (see *page 53*).

seasonal guide
early spring

SOW NOW

IN SITU beetroot, broad beans, bulbing onions, carrots, chard, early peas, kohlrabi, land cress, perpetual spinach, radishes, rocket, salsify, scorzonera, spring onions, summer spinach, turnips

IN A NURSERY BED early Brussels sprouts, globe artichokes, leeks, lettuce, rhubarb, summer and autumn cabbage

UNDER GLASS aubergines, calabrese, celeriac, celery, indoor tomatoes, parsley, peppers, summer cauliflowers

PLANT NOW

OUTDOORS asparagus, bulbing onions (seedlings and sets), early potatoes, garlic, globe artichokes, horseradish, Jerusalem artichokes, mint, perennial herbs, shallots, spring cabbage, strawberries, summer cabbage, summer cauliflowers

UNDER GLASS early salads, tomatoes

IN SEASON NOW

Brussels sprouts, celeriac, celery (trench), chard, chicory (forced), corn salad, good king henry, kale, land cress, leeks, lettuces, parsnips, perpetual spinach, radishes, rhubarb (forced), salsify, scorzonera, seakale (forced), spring cabbages, spring onions, sprouting broccoli, swedes, turnip tops, winter cabbages and cauliflowers, winter spinach

KEY JOBS

Have all your seeds and supplies like canes and potting compost ready for the new season. Use cloches and fleece to protect seeds, seedlings and crops from frost.

Prepare seedbeds and nursery beds; cover with cloches or plastic film to warm the soil. Plant first early potatoes in a sheltered position, plus second earlies and maincrops in milder districts and light soils.

Feed overwintered crops with a general fertilizer or compost mulch to refresh growth. Finish planting and pruning fruit trees and bushes; feed soft fruit with high-potash fertilizer or mulch with compost.

Watch out for early signs of pests; continue feeding birds to encourage nesting and foraging.

SOW CUT-AND-COME-AGAIN CROPS

These seedling crops can give a high yield from a small space, and will be ready to use well before their cousins sown to mature outdoors or in a frame. Sow in the open ground under cloches, in trays on the greenhouse staging or a window sill, or in a soil-based cold frame. This method works for lettuces, chicories, spinach, rocket, endive and oriental greens, or you can buy special blends variously listed as salad leaves, saladini, mesclun or miscuglio.

Sow in rows 10cm (4in) apart or broadcast seeds at about 12g/sq.m (½oz/sq.yd); either sow sparingly or thin seedlings to 2.5cm (1in) apart. When seedlings are 8–10cm (3–4in) high, you can start harvesting from one end, using scissors to cut them down to leave 2.5cm (1in) stumps. These will sprout again, often several times over a period of many weeks.

Pick cut-and-come-again varieties when young.

SLUG & SNAIL PROTECTION

Evidence of slugs and snails may appear early in the season, especially on seedlings and young leafy transplants, so it is important to take precautions from the start. (See also *pages 154–5*.)

▶ Encircling plants with a barrier of ash, grit, sharp sand or fresh soot, sprinkled down the sides of an upturned pot as a guide, will often deter slugs and snails, as will a serrated collar cut from a plastic bottle with pinking shears (see right).

▶ Maincrop potatoes are often tunnelled by small keel slugs (see far right). These elusive species live almost entirely underground and can reach alarming numbers by late summer. Tackle this problem by growing less susceptible varieties of potato such as 'Charlotte', 'Estima', 'Sante', 'Romano' and 'Wilja'. When crops start flowering, water with the parasitic nematode *Phasmarhabditis hermaphrodita*. This is widely available as a dehydrated preparation for use in moist soils when they reach a temperature of 5°C (40°F).

▶ Beer traps are effective, and you can buy several types or make your own. Cut around a plastic bottle to remove the neck and shoulders. Invert this piece inside the open end of the bottle and staple in position – this forms the entrance to the beer trap. Pour a little stale beer or fruit cordial into the bottle before resting it on its side next to vulnerable plants (see right).

▶ Trap slugs and snails under grapefruit skins or with pieces of turnip.

EARLY PEAS

If the ground is too cold for sowing peas, use plastic guttering instead. Fill the guttering with seed compost and sow the seeds in two staggered rows. Keep in a warm place until the weather improves. Then, slide out the growing contents into a channel in the ground. The crop should be strong enough to survive the vagaries of spring weather.

PLANNING FOR PEAS Depending on the variety, peas mature from about 70 days after sowing (early kinds) to 100 days (tall maincrops). A fast, first early variety can be sown regularly from now to midsummer for continuous pickings – as seedlings of one batch fully emerge, sow the next – but make sure your variety does not produce all its crop in a single flush. Alternatively, you can use two to three varieties that mature in sequence: sow simultaneously in separate rows or mixed together, and repeat every four weeks. For the earliest crops, sow a hardy, usually round-seeded pea in late autumn and keep cloched throughout the winter; many mangetout varieties are also hardy enough to overwinter, and some newer kinds can be successfully left to mature like podding peas. In cold areas, sow peas indoors in plastic guttering (see above) or degradable pots. (See also *page 70*.)

CATCHING UP ON STRAWBERRIES

Although strawberries are normally planted in late summer to ensure a crop the following year, in early spring there is still time to plant up a new bed with a summer-fruiting variety and, with care, plants will flower and fruit later in the year, especially if you buy expensive cold-stored runners. Alternatively, plant now and remove any flowers that appear this year, to build up strong crowns for the following year. Alpine and autumn-fruiting varieties can be planted now to crop at their normal time. If you have an established bed of summer strawberries, cover one or two rows with cloches to advance picking by about 2 weeks. (See also *page 109*.)

MAKING POTATOES GO A LONG WAY

Potatoes will grow almost anywhere, even in a compost heap, and often from just a fragment of tuber: in times of shortage, such as during World War II, many gardeners successfully used potato peelings where these included the eyes.

You can multiply a few seed tubers and increase your crop by chitting them in the usual way (see *page 135*) then cutting them into pieces, each with an eye or young shoot. Dig a trench 10–15cm (4–6in) deep and line out the pieces about 30cm (12in) apart. Backfill with the excavated soil, and water. (See also *page 66*.)

Volunteer potato plants from tubers left in the previous season often appear well before spring-planted crops, and some gardeners like to plant a few saved earlies in autumn to gain a head start. If volunteers emerge in the way of other crops, try carefully forking them out (with the tuber) for transplanting elsewhere; bury them at their original depth, water well, and they will usually resume growth unchecked.

Seasonal flowers such as these spring irises bring colour to the allotment.

early spring

Sweet potato shoots ready for planting.

BERRY PARTNERS

Underplant highbush blueberry varieties (which are the normal form) with dwarf relatives such as cranberries (see below) and also bilberries. These berries will coexist well, as they enjoy the same growing conditions.

ALTERNATIVE ROOT CROPS A number of less familiar root vegetables, which were once very popular, are often overlooked today, although they are easily grown from seed. Crops worth sowing in early and late spring include:

▶ **Hamburg parsley** A distinct form of parsley, with uncurled leaves and a swollen turnip-like root. Grow plants like ordinary parsley, about 20cm (8in) apart each way, and use in winter from the ground or store like beetroot.

▶ **Jicama** The Mexican potato needs warm conditions in a greenhouse or polytunnel, planted in the ground or large containers. Sow and grow like runner beans, and leave well into autumn for the tubers to finish swelling.

▶ **Salsify** White roots like small, slim parsnips, with a mild flavour. Sow direct and thin to 15cm (6in) apart each way. Dig as needed from mid-autumn onwards.

▶ **Scorzonera** Like a thinner, black-skinned version of salsify, and grown in the same way. Leave thin roots a second year to fatten up. It has attractive yellow blooms. Surplus roots can be transplanted to flower beds.

▶ **Skirret** An ancient plant with bundles of slim, sweet roots. Very hardy, and can be sown outdoors now for thinning to 15–20cm (6–8in) apart. Dig and store like maincrop carrots (old roots develop hard cores).

▶ **Sweet potato** A crop for greenhouses and polytunnels, needing about 140 warm days' growth. Keep a tuber in heat to sprout, and pull off young rooted shoots for planting 10cm (4in) deep and 30cm (12in) apart. Train vines up strings or nets, and dig tubers when growth dies back or before hard frosts.

PRUNING BLUEBERRIES Young bushes seldom need pruning unless they refuse to bush out, in which case shorten long stems by one-third now. When 3–4 years old, prune annually by thinning spindly growth and any crossing shoots; cut out a quarter of the oldest and weakest growth from mature bushes. Top-dress with compost or an acidic mulch of pine needles, grass clippings or composted bark, together with a general fertilizer on poorer soils. (See also *page 108*.)

PLAN AHEAD
Check that there is plenty of space in the cold frame for hardening off young plants for the open ground. Install stakes and wires for cane and bush fruits so their new stems can be tied in before they get damaged. **Collect twiggy sticks from under trees and hedgerows (or your own prunings) ready to support peas and early strawberry trusses.** Plan successional sowings to avoid any break in the supply of carrots, salads and other fast crops. **Send for young plants, seedlings and chitted seeds before the cut-off date for orders.** Keep up to date with pricking out and potting on: you may need space soon for planting greenhouse crops. **Inspect stored fruit and vegetables, as they deteriorate quickly when temperatures rise.**

seasonal recipe

CARROT CAKE

This is a very moist, scrumptious cake that will help use up any carrots left over from your stores. You could substitute parsnips for the carrots, although the cake will be less colourful.

1 Grease and line the base of an 18cm (7in) cake tin.

2 Grate the carrots finely. Whisk the eggs and sugar together until they form a thick and creamy mixture. Whisk in the oil slowly.

3 Add the carrots and remaining ingredients, and combine together evenly. Spoon the mixture into the prepared cake tin. Level the surface and bake in the oven at 190°C/375°F/ gas mark 5 for 20–25 minutes, until firm to the touch and golden brown. Cool on a wire tray.

4 To make the icing, beat the butter or margarine until soft. Beat in the sugar and orange rind. Spread the icing over the cake when the cake has cooled completely.

MAKES AN 18CM (7IN) CAKE

CAKE

- 175g (6oz) carrots
- 2 free-range eggs
- 100g (4oz) raw brown sugar
- 75ml (3fl.oz) sunflower oil
- 100g (4oz) wholemeal self-raising flour
- 1 tsp ground cinnamon
- ½ tsp ground nutmeg
- 50g (2oz) desiccated coconut
- 50g (2oz) raisins

ORANGE ICING

- 40g (1½oz) butter or margarine
- 75g (3oz) raw pale brown sugar
- grated rind of ½ an orange

seasonal guide

late spring

SOW NOW

IN SITU annual herbs, beetroot, broad beans, cabbages (summer and autumn), calabrese, carrots, chard, chicory (heading and forcing), endive, kohlrabi, land cress, lettuce, onions (salad and pickling), parsley, parsnips, peas, perpetual spinach, radishes, rocket, salsify, scorzonera, spinach, swedes, sweet fennel, turnips

IN A NURSERY BED Brussels sprouts, cabbages (winter), cauliflowers (autumn and winter), kale, leeks, sprouting broccoli

UNDER GLASS aubergines, courgettes and other squashes, cucumbers (outdoor), French and runner beans, melons, sweetcorn, tomatoes (outdoor)

PLANT NOW

OUTDOORS asparagus, artichokes (globe and Jerusalem), cardoons, early brassicas, onions (seedlings and sets), potatoes. If frosts are over: aubergines, celeriac, celery, French and runner beans, peppers, sweetcorn, outdoor tomatoes

UNDER GLASS all tender crops such as aubergines, cucumbers, and tomatoes

IN SEASON NOW

asparagus, broad beans, Brussels sprouts, carrots, cauliflowers, chard, good king henry, gooseberries (thinnings), kale, land cress, leeks, lettuce, parsley, perpetual spinach, radishes, rhubarb, salad onions, seakale, spinach, spring cabbages, sprouting broccoli, turnip tops, turnips

KEY JOBS

Finish planting all potatoes; earth up earlies when frost threatens or when foliage is about 20cm (8in) high. Thin or transplant brassica seedlings in the nursery bed to grow on and make 3–4 true leaves before planting out.

Change from early to late and maincrop roots, leeks and brassicas, unless repeat-sowing an early kind all season. Hoe, mulch or pull weeds by hand before crops need rescuing from them.

Tuck straw or mats around strawberry plants, and have nets ready to protect all maturing soft fruits. Check in dry seasons whether to start watering; mulch when soils are moist and warm.

Sow annual herbs like coriander at monthly intervals for continuity.

THE HUNGRY GAP As traditional winter supplies like Brussels sprouts and parsnips come to an end, there can be a significant break in continuity unless you deliberately plan crops for this hungry gap. Vegetables you could be harvesting in late spring include:

- ▶ kale, sprouting broccoli (sown late last spring), winter cauliflowers
- ▶ leeks (sown in early summer)
- ▶ spring cabbages, spring onions (sown in late summer)
- ▶ broad beans (sown under cloches in late autumn), peas
- ▶ lettuce (sown direct in late autumn or started in pots in late winter)
- ▶ potatoes (planted in late winter and grown in pots indoors)
- ▶ turnips (sown in a frame in late winter)
- ▶ radishes (sown under cloches in early spring)

Mixed salad leaves sown in late autumn.

TIDYING TIPS

▶ Clear and compost overwintered vegetables as they finish cropping. Brassica stumps are slow to rot unless chopped into small pieces, crushed with a hammer or run over with a loaded wheelbarrow.

▶ Dig up any surviving parsnips and leeks, replant them packed close together in a spare corner, and use them up quickly.

▶ Cull stored apples – only the very latest varieties will be of any use now. Any remaining cooking apples are best cut up and frozen, either raw or cooked.

CLIMBERS FOR COLOUR It is always useful to have a few annual climbers handy for training into fruit trees or up posts and arches – they supply colour and fragrance, and attract pollinating insects to your plot. The kinds to sow now in modules for potting about 4 weeks later include climbing nasturtiums (*Tropaeolum majus*), black-eyed Susan (*Thunbergia alata*), *Cobaea scandens* and morning glories (*Ipomoea*). Plant tall sweet peas to complement runner beans, ramble happily over boundary hedges and supply armfuls of cut blooms.

REJUVENATING PERENNIAL HERBS

The quality and vigour of established herbs can decline as they age unless you propagate them every few years. Clumps of hyssop, fennel and lemon balm are easily dug up and chopped into 3–4 pieces, using a spade, for replanting in a fresh spot. Lovage and tarragon produce young offsets that can be dug and separated for transplanting. Thyme and sage are best multiplied by cuttings taken now, but you could also bury the stems of low shoots to root as layers by autumn. Leave some of last year's parsley to flower and self-seed: a carpet of seedlings will appear in late summer for transplanting elsewhere.

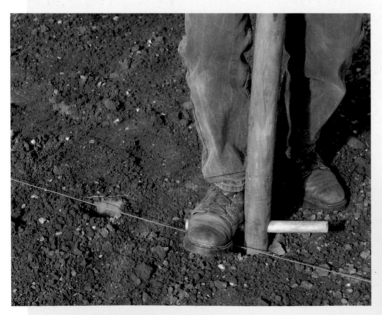

POGO STICK POTATO PLANTER

Cut a round 8cm (3in) garden stake to a length that suits your height. Trim one end to a stubby point. Drill through the stake 20cm (8in) from the point and insert a piece of broomstick to serve as a foot rest. Drill through the other end of the stake and insert another piece of broomstick to protrude on both sides as a handle. Tread holes into the ground at measured spacings (left) and drop a seed potato in each (below).

STRIP CROPPING Cloches and mini-tunnels are invaluable while there is a risk of frost, but many crops will need protection at different times of year. Put covers to maximum use (and conserve your time and effort) by planning crops so that the cloches only need moving between adjacent rows. For example, carrots and lettuces sown in late winter can be covered until late spring, when the cloches are moved over sweetcorn sown nearby. Once the corn is safe from frost, transfer the cloches over melons or peppers planted in early summer, and leave them in place throughout the summer. When the summer crops finish, move the cloches to salad onions, radishes and early carrots that you have sown nearby in late summer for autumn and winter use. (See also *pages 48-9*.)

COPING WITH CLUBROOT If you confirm or suspect that clubroot disease is in your soil, especially where brassicas have been grown for several years in the same spot, there are several practical steps you can take.

▶ Clubroot loves acid soils, so always add lime to planting sites – liming as high as pH7.5 has been shown to suppress the disease.

▶ Strictly rotate crops to treat the whole plot gradually, and grow all brassicas together, including turnips, swedes and flowers such as wallflowers (*Erysimum cheiri*).

▶ Rigorously control weeds, especially crucifers like bitter cress and shepherd's purse, which are alternative hosts.

▶ Grow fast-maturing varieties like early calabrese and mini-cauliflowers, rather than long-term crops such as Brussels sprouts.

▶ Raise seedlings in pots of sterilized compost, and plant out when they have 2–3 true leaves.

▶ Earth up stems to delay the consequences of infection by encouraging new roots.

▶ Scrub or disinfect boots and tools after working on infected land.

▶ Burn or otherwise dispose of exhausted roots when clearing plants.

▶ Don't become complacent: clubroot can survive for 20 years in the soil.

ABOVE A rustic trellis supports a white-flowering clematis and a morning glory (*Ipomoea*), which will bloom in late summer. The perennial sunflower (*Helianthus*) helps screen the shed.

ABOVE RIGHT Hazel twigs provide good support for sweet peas (*Lathyrus odoratus*).

SOWING FOR SUCCESSION Although a glut of produce can usually be frozen or preserved in some other way, many gardeners prefer to gather their vegetables and fruits when the crops are young and eat them fresh. Successively sowing fast-growing varieties little and often is the best way to ensure a steady supply of produce, and also makes the most economic use of relatively small patches of ground.

You need to find out from seed catalogues how long a particular variety takes to mature, and perhaps its anticipated yield from a given space or number of plants. Use this information to judge how little seed you need to sow every 3–4 weeks to meet your requirements.

Vegetables that respond well to successional sowing include carrots, beetroot, radishes, turnips, peas, salad onions and small lettuces (see *pages 67–70, 85 and 90–1*).

TIMING TENDER CROPS The most important anniversary to remember on the allotment (other than rent day) is the average date of the last spring frost, because you can use this to calculate roughly when to sow tender crops like courgettes and runner beans. Most vegetables take 4–6 weeks from sowing to transplanting stage, so allow for this if sowing under glass; harden plants off during the last 2 weeks of that period, and keep protection handy in case of late frost after planting out. If indoor sowing is delayed, don't panic: younger transplants often establish faster, so you can still plant out on time. Sow tender crops outdoors about 10–14 days before the last frosts, 2 weeks earlier if under cloches.

ALTERNATIVE SPINACH Summer (and, to a lesser extent, winter) spinach varieties are notorious for uneconomical yields and premature bolting in hot dry weather. The leaf beets – Swiss chard (seakale beet) and perpetual spinach (spinach beet) – are often much easier to grow and remain in good condition over a long period (see *page 93*). Sowing now, and again just after midsummer, will ensure pickings all year round: gather individual leaves or cut whole plants to leave 2.5–5cm (1–2in) stumps to resprout.

PLAN AHEAD
Towards the end of late spring, start sowing tender crops such as runner beans, squashes and sweetcorn in the ground outdoors. Plan successional sowings of salad crops and fast-growing vegetables. **Prepare leek beds ready for transplanting main- and late crops.** Press on with hardening off all tender crops for planting out. **Most brassicas will be planted out soon, so test the acidity of the soil where they are to grow.**

NEW ZEALAND SPINACH

The best spinach alternative for dry seasons and soils is New Zealand spinach (*Tetragonia expansa*), a tender annual that can spread 1.2m (4ft) each way and makes good groundcover under other crops. Sow now at 90cm (3ft) stations outdoors, or in early spring under glass for planting out when frosts cease. Pinch out the growing tips when they are 15cm (6in) high. Harvest complete trailing stems, stripping the leaves and tips just before cooking. Plants last until the autumn frosts, and often self-seed.

Swiss chard 'Bright Lights'.

seasonal recipe

ELDERFLOWER CHAMPAGNE

Elderflowers are prolific in late spring when the shrubs are covered with intoxicating, sweet-smelling blooms. And they are free! They have myriad uses, from drinks and preserves to eye lotions. Their flavour is akin to muscat grapes. Elderflower champagne is a wonderful sparkling non-alcoholic wine, which is very quick and simple to make.

MAKES 14 LITRES (3 GALS)
- 10–12 heads of elderflowers
- 900g (2lbs) white sugar
- juice and rind of 2 lemons
- 2 tbsp white wine vinegar

1 Pick the elderflower heads in full bloom. Don't wash the flowers but check for insects.

2 Dissolve the sugar in a bowl of hot water. Add the lemon juice, grated rind and vinegar and stir.

3 Pour the contents into a sterilized bucket. Make the liquid up to approximately 14 litres (3 gals) with cold water. Leave for 3 days, stirring occasionally.

4 Strain the liquid into glass bottles, cork firmly and lay them on their sides. After 2 weeks the liquid will be sparkling and ready to drink.

seasonal guide
early summer

SOW NOW

IN SITU annual herbs, beans (French and runner), beetroot, carrots, chard, chicory (forcing and heading), endive, kale, kohlrabi, land cress, lettuces, parsley, peas, perpetual spinach, radishes, salad onions, squashes, swedes, sweetcorn, sweet fennel, turnips
IN A NURSERY BED biennial and perennial flowers, perennial herbs, winter brassicas

PLANT NOW

OUTDOORS autumn and winter brassicas, celery, claytonia, cucumbers, globe artichokes, leeks, lettuces, melons, peppers, summer and winter squash, sweetcorn, tomatoes
UNDER GLASS melons, sweet potatoes

IN SEASON NOW

asparagus, broad beans, cabbage (spring and summer), calabrese, carrots, cauliflowers, chard, cherries, corn salad, endive, gooseberries, kohlrabi, land cress, lettuce, onions (salad and overwintered bulbs), peas, perpetual spinach, potatoes, radishes, raspberries, rhubarb, spinach, strawberries, turnips

KEY JOBS
Complete sowings of winter brassicas as early as possible, or buy young plants for transplanting. Earth up later potato crops; start digging early varieties when a trial scrape reveals tubers or as they come into flower. **Stake, tie in, train and sideshoot crops like cucumbers, melons, tomatoes.** Stop cutting asparagus on the longest day; weed, and give a general fertilizer 2–3 times at 14-day intervals. **Harvest herbs for preserving as they come into flower; trim woody perennials to shape as the flowers fade.** Pinch out the tips of broad beans when 2–3 clusters of flowers have set to speed up podding and deter blackfly. Cook clean tips as greens. **Tidy the plot, cut and edge grass paths (use the clippings as mulch) and trim hedges.**

TRAINING TOMATOES Cordon tomatoes need regular attention from now onwards to keep them supported and confine growth to a single stem. Give each outdoor plant a sturdy cane or stake, and tie the stem to this at intervals. For greenhouse plants, the easiest method is to suspend a string from the roof, bury the other end under the rootball at planting time, and twine the stem round the string as it grows. Remove sideshoots while small, or leave them until 5–8cm (2–3in) long and then root them in water to supply more plants for continuity. Long, overlooked sideshoots can be cut off or left as extra stems to train at an angle and produce a fan or multi-stemmed cordon. (See also *page 97*.)

A well-ordered row of cordon tomatoes trained to canes.

Covering carrots with fleece is an effective defence against carrot fly.

Sliced radish 'Mantanghong', revealing its brightly coloured flesh.

FLY-FREE CARROTS Carrot fly larvae spoil crops by tunnelling galleries through the roots. The flies are usually on the wing in late spring and again in early autumn, and a fast variety sown now often escapes damage. For earlier and later sowings, use a partially resistant variety like 'Sytan'. (See also *page 67*.)

▶ Sow seed sparingly to reduce the need to thin seedlings.

▶ Hide rows among a strong-smelling crop like onions.

▶ Cover with fleece throughout the life of the crop. Alternatively, build a defence barrier. Use fine mesh or clear plastic film 38–45cm (15–18in) wide, attached like a fence to canes or sticks, and completely surround the bed: the flies cruise at ground level and will be deterred.

WINTER RADISHES Growing radishes for winter use normally means choosing a special variety tolerant of low temperatures and short days, and sowing in autumn in a cold frame or greenhouse. (See also *page 68*.) An easier method is to sow a true winter radish now, and again in late summer. Older kinds are often variable and misshaped, but varieties like 'Mantanghong' (greenish-white skin and bright red flesh) are consistent and attractive, and may be cooked as well as sliced or diced for salads.

Thin seedlings 15–20cm (6–8in) apart, and lift from early autumn when they are the size of tennis balls. Store for winter use like maincrop carrots (see *page 160*).

TRANSPLANTING BRASSICAS Most of the brassica seedlings in the nursery bed will need planting out soon. (See also *pages 74–9*.)

▶ Make sure you water seedlings beforehand, 'puddling' them (see *pages 140–1*) into their new positions in dry weather and firming well.

▶ For plants that are removed completely when harvested (cabbages, for example), you can transplant them to grow closer together and use alternate plants while young. Otherwise use full distances and sow a catch crop in between to economize on space.

▶ To extend the harvest move out a quarter of the plants each week, from about 6–9 weeks after sowing. Batches will mature in sequence.

PROPAGATING STRAWBERRIES Summer-fruiting varieties start developing their runners now, and these carry the plantlets used to replace 3–4 year old crowns when yields decline. If left alone, the plantlets will root themselves and the strongest can be transferred in late summer to a new bed. You can improve their vigour and quality by choosing the best healthy and disease-free parent crowns. Allow these to make 3–4 plantlets each, and remove any other runners. Arrange the plantlets to give them space, and let them root where they lie. Alternatively, peg them down into small pots of compost plunged in the ground: this is ideal if they will be potted on for forcing, but remember to water them in dry weather. (See also *page 109*.)

HAND FERTILIZING In a cool summer, the flowers of squashes and melons may need hand-pollination, especially if they are under glass. Plants have both male and female flowers, and you need to identify the females: these bear miniature fruits behind the petals, whereas males have just a plain stalk. First test a male to see if any pollen sticks to your fingertip. If it does, pick the bloom and strip off its petals before gently pushing it into the centre of a fully open female flower. Use a fresh bloom each time, or fertilize up to 4 females with each male. This should be sufficient, but if no fruit starts to develop, repeat after 3–4 days.

PLANTING SQUASHES Marrows, pumpkins and other squashes (together with similarly greedy crops like melons and outdoor cucumbers) need good food supplies at their

Wild flowers, including cornflowers (*Centaurea cyanus*) and poppies (*Papaver*), sown in spring will start to bloom in early summer.

WEED-FREE LEEKS
Leeks are usually transplanted into 10cm (4in) deep holes, with a seedling dropped and watered into each (right). This ensures a good thickness of blanched stem but makes cultivation difficult because hoeing or handweeding can fill in the hole. To keep the leeks weed-free, spread several layers of newspaper over the moist soil (far right) and make holes through this mulch. Cover the paper with grass clippings for a neat finish and to delay drying out.

early summer

roots to fuel vigorous growth. Either plant on hills, made by digging a large hole, emptying in a bucketful of compost or rotted manure, and replacing the soil to leave a gentle mound. Or grow them in rows: dig a trench about 15cm (6in) deep, fill with organic material, and replace the soil to make a low broad ridge. With this method you can arrange wire or tubular hoops along the row for temporary cover on cold nights. Leave a shallow depression at the base of each plant for watering. (See also *pages 86–8*.)

LAST CHANCE TO...

▶ Sow early carrots to mature in the open at the same time as maincrops. Later sowings may need protection before they are ready.

▶ Sow runner and French beans in situ for a late crop. Sow extra dwarf beans to transplant to a frame or greenhouse to prolong the harvest.

▶ Sow parsnips for small sweet roots in autumn, and leeks to grow as mini-veg 8cm (3in) apart.

▶ Feed and build up onions for show: maximum top growth before the longest day boosts bulb development afterwards.

THINNING FRUIT Reducing a heavy crop improves fruit size and quality, relieves the weight on overladen branches and helps ensure an equally good yield next year. Start with gooseberries from late spring onwards, thinning the green fruits in stages wherever they are overcrowded, until you are left with berries 5–8cm (2–3in) apart to continue maturing. Cook the thinnings for desserts, jams and jellies.

Thin plums to the same distance now, and prop up heavily laden branches. Wait until apples and pears shed their excess (the 'June drop') and then thin for quality by removing any damaged or misshapen fruit; reduce clusters to the best one or two specimens so that fruits are about 10cm (4in) apart. When you have finished, suspend pheromone traps among the branches to protect the fruits from moth pests.

SUPPORTING CLIMBING CROPS
Climbing beans and cucumbers, trailing squashes and other sprawling plants should be trained on supports to maximize space and ensure clean, healthy growth. Bamboo canes, coppiced poles and collapsible metal or plastic frames are all suitable, and should be erected before plants are sown or transplanted into position. Depending on the layout of your allotment, you can arrange the structures as wigwams or in continuous rows, or tailor them to fit as arches over a path or as a screen against a shed. They must be robust and firmly fixed, and plants should be tied in where necessary unless self-supporting.

Runner beans trained on an inverted V-shape framework are easier to pick.

PLAN AHEAD
Feed young plants in pots and trays if bad weather delays planting out. Cut some mint almost to the ground to stimulate fresh young growth for late use.

Dig and manure a sunny area to make a new bed for strawberries. Prepare for the main soft fruit harvest: you might need jars and rings for bottling, or bags, containers and freezer space.

Check you have seeds of the right varieties for late and last sowings; supplementary seed catalogues are sometimes issued at this time. Plan a feast soon to enjoy all the early vegetables and fruits that are now becoming available.

seasonal recipe

COURGETTE BREAD

This recipe is very quick and simple to make, as it is based on low-fat soda bread, which means there is no need for yeast and no waiting for the bread to rise. The courgettes give moisture and texture to the bread, and the recipe is a novel way of using up any gluts of the vegetable and also any oversized ones. They can also be used to make delicious cakes. Courgette bread is best eaten freshly baked but can be kept for up to 2 days.

1 Preheat the oven to 200°C/400°F/gas mark 6. Coarsely grate the courgette (including the skin) and press in between several sheets of kitchen paper to absorb the excess moisture.

2 Sift the flour, bicarbonate of soda and salt into a large bowl. Add the sugar and garlic, then stir in the grated courgette. Drizzle in the oil and gently stir in with the buttermilk. Stir until the mixture is combined into a soft dough (overmixing will make the bread tough). Gather the dough together and turn it out onto a lightly floured work surface. Knead very briefly until smooth. With floured hands, very gently make a round ball. Lift the loaf onto a greased baking sheet and sprinkle over a little extra flour. Make a deep cross with a sharp knife.

3 Bake for 25–30 minutes or until risen and brown. Transfer to a wire rack and leave to cool slightly before slicing.

MAKES 1 LOAF

- 1 small, firm courgette, about 115g (4oz)
- 400g (14oz) plain flour, plus extra to sprinkle
- 2 tsp bicarbonate of soda
- 1 tsp salt
- 1 tbsp light muscovado sugar
- 1 plump garlic clove, finely chopped
- 1 tbsp sunflower oil
- 400ml (14fl oz) buttermilk, or as needed

seasonal guide

late summer

SOW NOW

IN SITU carrots, chard, chicory (heading), claytonia, corn salad, endive, land cress, kohlrabi, lettuces, onions (bulbing and salad), oriental greens, perpetual spinach, radishes (summer and winter), sweet fennel, turnips
IN A NURSERY BED cabbage (spring and red varieties), kale
UNDER GLASS dwarf beans in pots

PLANT NOW

OUTDOORS cabbages (winter and spring), cauliflowers (winter and spring), kale, leeks, sprouting broccoli
UNDER GLASS potatoes in pots

IN SEASON NOW

apples, aubergines, beetroot, blackberries, blueberries, broad beans, bulbing onions, calabrese, carrots, cauliflowers, celery, chard, cherries, claytonia, corn salad, cucumbers, currants, endive, French beans, garlic, globe artichokes, gooseberries, hybrid berries, kohlrabi, land cress, leeks, lettuce, melons, perpetual spinach, plums, potatoes, radishes, raspberries, redcurrants, runner beans, salad onions, shallots, spinach, squashes, strawberries, summer cabbages, sweetcorn, tomatoes, turnips

KEY JOBS

Harvest, ripen and store onion crops; prepare a bed for sowing or planting bulbing onions for overwintering.
Summer-prune trained forms of tree and bush fruits, and start harvesting early tree fruit for immediate use.
Finish transplanting winter brassicas and leeks, and make 2–3 sowings of spring cabbages.
Earth up potatoes; watch out for signs of blight on maincrops, especially after prolonged wet, humid weather.
Harvest and preserve produce as it ripens; ask someone to harvest and water crops if you go away.
Hoe, weed, mulch and water crops, especially transplants and those in flower or fruiting.
Stay alert for pests and diseases, as attacks can spread rapidly if plants are stressed by drought or heat.

MANAGING THE HARVEST You need to keep up with an increasing yield of ripe produce at this time of year, especially from plants like beans, peas, cucumbers, courgettes and peppers, all of which can stop flowering and fruiting if crops are left unpicked. Check every 2–3 days in warm weather, and freeze or otherwise preserve any produce that cannot be used fresh. Soft fruits will be ripening rapidly, too, while the earliest apples could be ready soon. Test regularly for ripeness as they colour up, and eat them straight from the tree – most early apples keep for only a few weeks. Herbs grown for their seeds, such as dill and coriander, need harvesting before they are fully ripe and shedding: dry the heads in the sun on newspaper or hang up in paper bags. Leave one or two flowering plants of parsley and chervil to self-seed and produce next year's seedlings for transplanting in the autumn.

Keep harvesting blueberries as they ripen.

HOLIDAY PREPARATIONS

With so many crops maturing at this time, leaving the allotment while you go away on holiday needs some forethought. Before you leave, make sure that you:

▶ Water thirsty plants thoroughly if the weather is dry.

▶ Mulch growing plants, especially leafy crops at wider spacings.

▶ Harvest anything that is ready, and store or preserve.

▶ Remove flowers that could set in your absence, if the plot is untended.

▶ Ask a friend or plot-holder to harvest the produce in return for watering.

RIPENING ONIONS As bulbing onions mature, start using up any that have split or flowered, or have thick necks. Sound bulbs, together with garlic and shallots, can be stored but need ripening first. Lift them carefully with a fork to avoid damaging the root plates, and spread out to dry in the sun, off the ground on netting or sacks, or under glass in a wet year. When skins are dry and papery, rub off any soil and loose tissue, and store in nets and boxes or plaited on strings. (See also *page 82*.)

Leave onions to dry and ripen in the sun before storing them indoors.

SUMMER PRUNING Cordons, espaliers, fans and other forms of trained fruit need pruning in summer to control growth and aid ripening; the process is completed by winter pruning when plants are dormant (see *page 212*). Spread the work over 3–4 weeks. Start around the longest day with gooseberries and redcurrants, shortening all new sideshoots and unwanted main shoots to 8–10cm (3–4in) long. Move on to plums and sweet cherries, and shorten their new sideshoots to about half-way. Apples and pears are done last, with new sideshoots cut back to 5 leaves from their base.

Prune the new sideshoots of cherries to about half their length in late summer.

FORCING STRAWBERRIES Strawberries are easy to grow in the greenhouse or cold frame, cropping in late spring, but this can be 2–3 weeks sooner if you can give them 7°C (45°F).

▶ Pot up strongly rooted runners in 15cm (6in) pots, and stand them in a sunny place or a greenhouse. Water regularly and liquid feed every week until mid-autumn.

▶ Bring a few pots indoors in batches from early winter onwards. Grow the plants in cool, fairly moist conditions and in good light, and give a high-potash feed weekly until flowers open.

▶ Keep the air dry during flowering, and fertilize blooms by gently stroking their centres with a soft brush.

seasonal recipe

ALLOTMENT PICKLE

This recipe takes care of many glut vegetables when all your best ideas for using them up have been exhausted. You can use a mixture of green and red tomatoes or just red. The pickle will be ready to eat in 6 weeks and will keep for 6 months or more.

MAKES ABOUT 2KG (4LBS)

- 500g (18oz) tomatoes, roughly chopped
- 3 tbsp salt
- 250g (9oz) onions, finely chopped
- ½ small white cabbage, shredded
- 1 small marrow, skin removed, deseeded and cut into 2cm (¾in) chunks
- 500g (18oz) cucumbers, skin removed and roughly chopped
- 1 cauliflower, broken into very small florets
- 250g (9oz) runner beans, roughly chopped
- 60g (2oz) plain flour
- 125g (4½oz) granulated sugar
- 30g (1oz) dry English mustard
- 1½ tbsp mild curry powder
- 750ml (1¼ pints) organic cider vinegar

1 Put the tomatoes in a colander and sprinkle with 1 tbsp salt. Leave to drain over a bowl for a few hours. Rinse the tomatoes briefly in cold water, then drain.

2 Put all the other vegetables in a preserving pan, sprinkle with 1 tbsp salt and pour over enough boiling water to just cover. Bring to the boil, lower the heat and simmer until the vegetables are tender. Drain the vegetables and put back in the pan. Add the tomatoes.

3 Put the flour, sugar, mustard, curry powder and remaining tbsp salt in a bowl. Add a little vinegar and mix to a smooth paste. Heat the remaining vinegar in a pan and bring to the boil. Pour a little at a time onto the flour paste and whisk to loosen the mixture. Pour back into the pan and simmer for 5 minutes. Pour over the vegetables in the preserving pan and bring back to the boil. Lower the heat and simmer together for 5 minutes.

4 Put the vegetables into hot sterilized jars (heat the jars in a warm oven 150°C/300°F/gas mark 2 for 5 minutes), adding enough of the liquid to cover the contents. Seal the jars and label.

▶ Support trusses with small sticks, ventilate in mild weather, and watch out for red spider mite.

▶ After harvest, transplant outdoors, where plants will crop for 2–3 years more.

MAKING A STRAWBERRY BED Although strawberries do well as an edging or cover crop under taller fruit, they are easiest to manage and protect if grown together in a bed. Maincrop varieties are planted in late summer and early autumn, so prepare a sunny, sheltered position for them, where strawberries have not been grown for at least 4 years. (See also *page 109*.)

Dig or fork the soil, working in compost or rotted manure at 6.5kg/sq.m (14lb, or a large bucketful, per sq.yd) well below the surface. On poor soils add a top-dressing of general fertilizer at 105g/sq.m (3oz/sq.yd), and rake level.

GROWING TRENCH CELERY
Self-blanching celery is the easiest kind to grow, especially if it is planted close together in a cold frame to ensure tender white sticks. However, many gardeners still prefer to grow traditional trench celery, which is earthed up regularly from now onwards to blanch the stems. (See also *page 94*.)

▶ Sow early under glass and transplant 30cm (12in) apart in the trench prepared in late winter (see *page 214*).

▶ When plants are 30cm (12in) high, loop the stems together with string and earth them up to half their height. Repeat the earthing up every 3–4 weeks until late autumn, when the stems are finally covered to leave just the green tops showing.

▶ Start lifting heads about 6 weeks later, after the first frosts.

HELPING BEAN FLOWERS SET Around midsummer, when conditions can be hot and dry, flowers on early batches of beans often fall without producing pods. There are many ways to help them set:

▶ Space plants widely in a sheltered position.

Planting maincrop strawberries in a bed makes them easier to manage and protect.

- ▶ Introduce some tall sweet peas to attract pollinating insects.
- ▶ Water generously twice weekly if the weather is dry when buds first open.
- ▶ Keep plants well mulched with organic matter.
- ▶ Spray flowering plants with water when the evenings are warm.
- ▶ Later flowers usually set unaided as conditions become more humid.
- ▶ Include a few white-flowered varieties, which are more reliable in dry weather.

LATE-CROP POTATOES An early potato variety planted now, indoors in pots and buckets or outdoors in a sheltered spot, will yield fresh 'new' potatoes from late autumn well into winter. Use sound tubers from this year's early harvest or tubers that you have kept in reserve in a very cool place; some seedsmen sell specially prepared tubers of varieties such as 'Carlingford', 'Nicola' and 'Maris Peer'. Plant in the usual way, in fresh ground or to double-crop after earlier potatoes are cleared (but revive the soil with compost and a general fertilizer). Keep evenly moist, and harvest in late autumn or leave under a covering of straw until needed. (See also *page 66*.)

Flowering runner bean 'White Lady'.

GROWING POTATOES IN SACKS

1 Use a plastic rubble sack and perforate the bottom. Half-fill with potting compost, space out 3–4 tubers and cover with another 5cm (2in) of compost.

2 Keep the compost moist and outdoors until the first frosts are forecast. Earth up stems with more compost as they grow, by gradually rolling up the bag. Test the crop from late autumn by scraping away some of the compost; if the tubers are ready, either empty the whole bagful or just take those you need, re-covering the rest for later.

EARLIEST BRUSSELS SPROUTS

To have Brussels sprouts ready from late next summer, sow 'Evesham Special' or 'Fillbasket', or early F1 hybrids like 'Cromwell' and 'Oliver', in the nursery bed now. Thin seedlings to 8cm (3in) apart and wait until next spring before transplanting them to their final positions, interplanted with summer cabbages. Protect from slugs and birds over winter. (See also *page 78*.)

WINTER CARROTS

Sow an early carrot variety now in the greenhouse border or soil-based cold frame, and thin the seedlings to about 8cm (3in) apart. Protect from cold weather during autumn, but otherwise grow normally until the roots are ready for use. Then stop watering and allow the soil to dry: the roots will remain sound all winter, and can be dug as needed. (See also *page 67*.)

PLAN AHEAD

Finish or turn summer compost heaps, and make space for material from autumn clearance. Build an extra bin if necessary. Plan and prepare sites for new fruit; order plants in good time, particularly unusual or newly introduced varieties. **Make room in the greenhouse or frame for winter salad and herb supplies, and plants that need frost protection.** Collect boxes, bags, nets and straw for storing and protecting long-keeping crops.

Giant sunflowers (*Helianthus annuus*) brighten up any allotment, as well as attracting masses of pollinating insects.

seasonal recipe

VICTORIA PLUM JAM

Victoria plums make the most delicious golden jam, but you can also use other plum varieties. If you find the jam a little too sweet, add some lemon juice. The jam takes only 20 minutes to make and is ready to eat a day later. It will keep for more than a year.

1   Cut the plums into 2cm (¾in) chunks and put into a preserving pan.

2   Add the warm sugar and, when it dissolves, lower the heat and cook until the plums have softened. Raise the heat and bring the jam to the boil. Keep at a rolling boil for at least 6 minutes, stirring occasionally.

3   To test that the jam has set, spoon a little onto a cold plate and leave to cool - it should become jelly-like. If not, boil for another 5 minutes and repeat the test.

4   Pour into hot, dry sterilized jars (heat the jars in a warm oven 150°C/ 300°F/gas mark 2 for 5 minutes), cover with waxed discs and cellophane tops and label.

MAKES ABOUT 2KG (4LBS)
- 1kg (2¼lbs) Victoria plums
- 1kg (2¼lbs) preserving sugar, warmed in a bowl in a low oven

seasonal guide
early autumn

SOW NOW

IN SITU broad beans, peas, winter spinach

IN A NURSERY BED hardy lettuces, spring cabbages, summer cauliflowers

UNDER GLASS carrots, lettuces, radishes

PLANT NOW

OUTDOORS autumn onions (seedlings and sets), garlic, spring cabbages

UNDER GLASS lettuces

IN SEASON NOW

apples, aubergines, autumn cabbages, beetroot, Brussels sprouts, bulbing onions, calabrese, cardoons, carrots, cauliflowers, celeriac, celery, chard, claytonia, cucumbers, endive, French beans, grapes, sprouting broccoli (green), heading chicory, Jerusalem artichokes, kale, kohlrabi, land cress, leeks, lettuces, melons, oriental greens, parsnips, pears, peas, peppers, perpetual spinach, plums, potatoes, radishes, raspberries, runner beans, salsify, scorzonera, spinach, squashes, strawberries, swedes, sweetcorn, sweet fennel, tomatoes, turnips

KEY JOBS

Harvest and store squashes and root crops; cut down outdoor tomatoes and finish ripening inside; continue harvesting fruit. Protect late and overwintering crops with fleece, cloches or mini-tunnels in an early cold snap. **Dismantle exhausted crops and supports; clear ground scheduled for liming and autumn digging.** Move spring cabbages to final positions and plant *firmly*: a tugged leaf should tear before it is uprooted. Sow more for succession. **Plant autumn onion sets and transplant seedlings in a sunny, well-drained bed.** Pot up winter supplies of herbs and leave out until frost threatens; cut back parsley, chives, sage and savory, and cloche for late use. **Plant hardy garlic.**

FINISHING TOMATO CROPS Ideally, tomatoes should be allowed to mature on the plants; under glass you can often leave fruits to ripen naturally as late as early winter, if diseases do not intervene. Outdoor crops need help before they are damaged by deteriorating weather. Cover bushes with cloches or mini-tunnels; cordon varieties can be treated similarly by releasing stems from their supports and laying them down on a bed of straw. Alternatively, and particularly if low temperatures loom, cut down whole plants and suspend them, leafless and upside down, in gentle warmth under glass or indoors. You can also pick off trusses and individual fruits, even

To hasten the ripening of cordon tomatoes growing in the greenhouse, cut the plants down and suspend them from a pole.

Fitting a grease band to an apple tree trunk.

DRYING PULSES

Pea and bean varieties for drying produce better-quality pulses than any you can buy and also make a useful green manure crop. Sow broad bands of lima, or butter, beans (pictured), 'Dutch Brown' (tastiest haricot bean variety for Boston Baked Beans) or 'Progreta' (a modern alternative to the classic 'Lincoln' pea), and grow as normal until flowering finishes and all pods are swollen and turning colour.

In a fine autumn, pods can be left until dry before picking; afterwards, cut down the foliage, chop with a rotary mower and dig in with the nitrogen-rich roots. Otherwise, cut plants at ground level and hang in a dry, airy place until brittle; remove pods, compost the vines and dig in the roots. Save shelling the pods for a cold night round the fireside at home, then store the seeds in airtight jars or tins.

fully green ones, and spread them in boxes or a drawer lined and covered over with newspaper. Include an orange or banana to hasten ripening.

PROTECTING FRUIT TREES Wrapping fruit tree trunks with sticky grease bands or anointing them with a girdle of special grease is a simple and effective way to trap various fruit pests that migrate down to the soil in autumn to hibernate and return aloft in spring to lay eggs. Apply the bands 60–90cm (2–3ft) above ground level, and treat stakes in the same way to prevent pests bypassing the main traps. Remove bands in late spring for burning – grease applied direct breaks down naturally.

CURING & STORING SQUASHES Surplus courgettes are easily preserved if sliced or diced, and blanched before freezing. Most other squashes, such as marrows and pumpkins, will keep for several months if suspended in nets or nestled in straw on shelves, in a dry, frost-free and well-ventilated shed. Cut fully ripened specimens before the frosts and then ripen their skins in full sun for 2 weeks, under glass if necessary, until they sound hard when tapped. (See also *pages 86–7*.)

OUT-OF-SEASON PARSLEY For pickings throughout the winter, lift self-sown seedlings or thinnings from a late summer sowing, and plant 15cm (6in) each way in a soil-based cold frame. Water in and feed once or twice before winter; cover during frost but ventilate the rest of the time. Pot up a few seedlings at the same time to keep on the window sill for use in really hard weather. (See also *page 102*.)

Cure squashes in the sun before storing them.

PLAN AHEAD
Assess fruit plants for condition and age to identify those that deserve or need propagating from hardwood cuttings after leaf fall.
Where there are plenty of trees nearby, construct a wire mesh enclosure for making leafmould as a soil conditioner and mulch material. **Remove shading on greenhouses and frames, and organize insulating materials like bubble polythene in time for the first frosts.** Gradually gather up used pots, boxes, canes, labels and watering equipment, which all need drying, cleaning and storing before winter arrives.

seasonal recipe

PUMPKIN CHUTNEY

This is a sweet and spicy chutney that makes good use of pumpkin, which keeps its shape during cooking. The chutney will be ready to eat in 4 weeks and will keep for about 9 months.

1 Put all the ingredients, except the sugar and salt, in a preserving pan. Bring slowly to the boil over a medium heat and let simmer for about 20 minutes until the pumpkin is tender.

2 Add the sugar and salt and on a low heat let the sugar dissolve. Increase the heat and simmer for about 45 minutes until the mixture has thickened. Stir from time to time to prevent the mixture from sticking.

3 Put the mixture directly into hot, sterilized jars (heat the jars in a warm oven 150°C/300°F/gas mark 2 for 5 minutes). Seal the jars and label.

MAKES ABOUT 2KG (4LBS)

- 1.25kg (2¾lbs) pumpkin, peeled, deseeded and cut into 2.5cm (1in) chunks
- 2 onions, chopped
- 750g (1lb 10oz) apples, peeled, cored and chopped
- 85g (3oz) fresh ginger, peeled and finely shredded
- 4 red chillies, deseeded and shredded
- 2 tbsp white mustard seed
- 2 tbsp black mustard seed
- 750ml (1¼ pints) organic cider vinegar
- 500g (18oz) soft brown sugar
- 1 tbsp salt

seasonal guide

late autumn

SOW NOW

IN SITU broad beans, peas
UNDER GLASS lettuces, radishes

PLANT NOW

OUTDOORS autumn onion sets, fruit, garlic, spring cabbages

IN SEASON NOW

apples, Brussels sprouts, carrots, cauliflowers, celeriac, celery, chard, chicory (forced), claytonia, corn salad, endive, grapes, heading chicory, kohlrabi, Jerusalem artichokes, kale, land cress, leeks, lettuces, oriental greens, parsnips, pears, perpetual spinach, potatoes, salsify, scorzonera, spinach, swedes, sweet fennel, turnips, winter cabbages, winter radishes

KEY JOBS

Harvest early leeks before severe frost, as they are less hardy than darker-leaved late varieties. Use up any summer and autumn brassicas. Protect plants in containers by moving them under cover or insulating pots with bubble polythene to keep roots frost-free. **Clear all non-hardy crops; cut down asparagus and Jerusalem artichoke stems.** Dig over heavy ground and leave rough or in ridges to crumble gradually over winter. Lime if necessary. **Insulate all or part of the greenhouse or cold frame if it contains vulnerable plants.** Start winter pruning fruit as soon as leaves begin to fall; heel in new fruit if unable to plant immediately; take hardwood cuttings.

STORING POTATOES

Main crops are dug up and stored in autumn, but if time presses, you can lift alternate rows and cover those that are left with the loosened soil for use later. If blight appears, cut off any foliage for burning and wait 2–3 weeks before harvesting. Always use a fork to minimize damage, and spread tubers on the surface to dry for a few hours before roughly cleaning and sorting them. Store the best in boxes, paper or hessian sacks, or in a clamp (see *pages 210–12*), and keep dry and frost-free.

PROPAGATING NEW FRUIT

Gooseberries and currants can be propagated by hardwood cuttings. Since virus diseases eventually affect most fruit stocks, causing

Leave potatoes to dry on the ground before storing them for winter.

yields to decline, it is worth doing this every 5–6 years, provided your plants are still healthy and vigorous.

▶ Cut off strong, straight shoots produced this year, and trim off the thin tips to leave sturdy 30cm (12in) cuttings – identify the top by leaving a sloping cut at this end.

▶ Push the shoots half way into clean soil, about 15cm (6in) apart, and tread firm. On heavy ground, make a slit trench with a spade and part-fill with sharp sand for extra drainage before inserting the cuttings.

▶ Leave undisturbed for 12 months before moving to final positions.

MAKING LEAFMOULD You are fortunate if you have access to fallen tree leaves, as these are a free and renewable source of organic material. Although containing few nutrients, they are rich in fibre that can be turned into a valuable soil conditioner or ingredient for potting compost. Add small amounts to the compost heap or pack them in black plastic

A simple, loosely built compost bin made of woven willow wands for producing leafmould.

bags, tied up and perforated here and there, and leave to rot down for a year. Gather large quantities in a simple compound of wire netting wrapped around 4 stakes, and tread to compress: they sink dramatically as they decompose. Dig in or use as a mulch after a year, or leave for a further year and sieve out the finer particles for potting compost or to improve the soil in cold frames and greenhouse borders. Coarser remains can be composted or dug in.

FORCING CHICORY Witloof, or Belgian, chicory is too bitter to eat fresh, but the roots can be forced in darkness to produce fat, blanched leaf buds, or 'chicons', that are an important winter salad ingredient.

▶ Start digging up the largest roots from mid-autumn onwards.

▶ Trim the topgrowth to 2.5cm (1in) stumps and remove the tapering root tips.

▶ Pack several roots upright in a large pot of moist compost, and invert another over the top to exclude light; keep at around 10°C (50°F).

▶ Cut the chicons when they are 8–10cm (3–4in) long and then discard the roots.

You can also force plants where they grow by heaping soil over them in a ridge 15cm (6in) high; this is the best way with older varieties that need a soil covering. Transplant thinner roots to wild corners where their handsome blue flowers will attract beneficial insects.

WAYS WITH RHUBARB

▶ Smother plants with plenty of rotted manure for juicy, heavy crops.

▶ Cover strong crowns with upturned boxes or flower pots to force early sticks.

▶ Dig up large crowns and split them with a spade to rejuvenate them or increase stocks.

▶ Leave surplus pieces on the ground and bring indoors after frost for forcing.

▶ Transplant unwanted pieces to use as a barrier against rabbits, which detest rhubarb plants.

▶ Sow the variety 'Glaskin's Perpetual' next spring if you want sticks throughout summer.

PLAN AHEAD
Check over onion crops in storage; select healthy, medium-size shallots for replanting during early winter. Earth up the stems of cabbages, cauliflowers and Brussels sprouts, especially if growing in exposed positions, to prevent wind rock. **Mow any grass and trim edges and hedges for the last time while the weather remains dry.** Assess the results of your allotment year, then plan any changes and improvements. Send off for seed and plant catalogues, and decide which crops to grow.

seasonal recipe

SLOE GIN

Sloe gin is a potent and refreshing liqueur, ideal to make in late autumn so that it will be ready for drinking at Christmas. The best time to pick the sloes is immediately after the first frost, which makes the skins softer and more permeable. Wear gloves when picking the marble-sized berries because the spines are sharp. The gin will keep for about a year.

- Sloe berries
- Granulated sugar
- Gin

1 Pierce the skins of each berry with the head of a pin to help the gin and juice combine more easily.

2 Fill a kilner jar up to a third with berries and top up to the halfway mark with sugar.

3 Pour in the gin to fill the jar and then close it.

4 Leave the liqueur for at least 2 months, shaking daily to help dissolve and disperse the sugar. The liqueur will gradually take on a deep pink colour.

5 Before drinking, strain the liqueur through a coffee filter and decant into smaller bottles.

seasonal guide

winter

SOW NOW

UNDER GLASS asparagus, broad beans, carrots, celeriac, celery, chives, cucumbers, leeks, lettuces, onions, parsley, radishes, salad onions, spinach, strawberries (including alpine varieties), summer cabbages, summer cauliflowers, sweet peas

PLANT NOW

OUTDOORS fruit, globe artichokes, garlic, rhubarb, shallots

UNDER GLASS fruit, garlic (in pots)

IN SEASON NOW

Brussels sprouts, carrots, celeriac, celery, chicory (forced and heading), claytonia, corn salad, endive, Jerusalem artichokes, kale, kohlrabi, land cress, leaf beet, leeks, lettuces, oriental greens, parsnips, rhubarb (forced), salsify, scorzonera, seakale, spinach, sprouting broccoli, swedes, sweet fennel, winter cabbages, winter cauliflowers, winter radishes

KEY JOBS
EARLY WINTER

Press on with winter digging if your soil warrants it – the heavier the ground, the earlier it should be cultivated. Order seeds and seed potatoes. **Check stored crops for signs of mould, rot or vermin attacks; if roots start sprouting, the store could be too warm.** Clear and compost as much as possible, particularly exhausted brassicas to avoid pest and disease persistence. **Note where water lies after heavy rain and explore possible drainage problems if it disperses slowly.** Turn compost heaps to revive activity. **Ventilate occupied cold frames on mild days, but keep insulation handy in case of severe weather.**

CARING FOR TOOLS Good tools make for light work. With regular care they will last and perform well, but very often winter is the only opportunity to give them the attention they deserve. Clean off soil residues with a scraper and wire brush, remembering the handles for your own comfort. Use a file to resharpen edge tools like spades, hoes and secateurs. Treat wooden handles with linseed oil, and coat metal parts with lubricating oil. Suspend or store them under cover, and make sure they are securely locked up. (See also *page 54*.)

Oiling blades Roll up a strip of carpet underfelt and pack this in an empty tin. Soak the felt in old mower sump oil or discarded vegetable oil, and use to wipe a protective film on metal blades after every use.

CLAMPING ROOT CROPS A traditional way to store large quantities of root crops is to make a clamp, or heap, of roots either outdoors in a sheltered spot on well-drained soil or in a

Most tools will not be needed during winter, so clean them and store somewhere secure.

corner of the allotment shed floor. The roots must be sound and undamaged, with any loose soil rubbed off.

- Spread out a 15–20cm (6–8in) deep bed of dry straw in a circle or square, and arrange the roots in a neat tapering heap on top.
- Cover the heap all round with the same thickness of straw.
- Finish indoor clamps with a layer of old sacks to keep the straw in place. Dig a shallow drainage ditch around outdoor clamps, and pile the excavated soil over the straw-covered heap about 15cm (6in) thick.
- Use roots from one end or side of the clamp, and protect those left by replacing the covering in the same order.

LOOKING AFTER BIRDS Winter is a challenge for allotment birds but you can help by offering them shelter as well as food. Hanging up nesting boxes now supplies them with valuable winter roosts and gives them time to identify potential nest sites. Hang up nuts and seeds where squirrels cannot reach them. A nutritious bird cake is easily made by softening lard and left-over fats in the oven or microwave and mixing in a variety of foods: finely chopped nuts, sunflower and pumpkin seeds, porridge oats, flour past its use-by date, old vegetable seeds. Mix in as much as the fat will bind together, and mould into cakes or balls. Pack in holes drilled in a log or smear on branches.

A tit feeding from a squirrel-proof feeder.

GROW YOUR OWN SUGAR

Sweet cicely is a hardy herb with ferny sweet foliage traditionally used to halve the amount of sugar needed when cooking sour fruit. As the large seeds need frost to break their dormancy, sow now, 2–3 seeds in a 13cm (5in) pot, and stand outdoors where they can freeze. Cover with wire mesh against mice, birds and squirrels. Plant next autumn near your rhubarb or gooseberries so that the leaves can be gathered with the fruit.

WINTER PRUNING: THE BASICS

- Always cut out dead, damaged and diseased wood first.
- Then remove crossing or rubbing branches, and thin overcrowded growth.
- Prune out a few complete branches from neglected specimens to admit air and light.
- Shorten summer-pruned sideshoots on trained plants to one or two buds.
- Cut autumn-fruiting raspberry canes to the ground.
- Remove fruited stems from summer raspberries and brambles, and tie in new stems.
- Thin crowded spurs on older apples and pears, and shorten very long spurs.
- Remove one-third of older stems from blackcurrants; check for big bud mite.
- Cut out cankered shoots on apples and pears; pick and destroy mummified fruits.
- Do not prune plums, cherries and other stone fruits until growth resumes (see *page 196*).

PRUNING INDOOR GRAPEVINES

Prune greenhouse grapevines when the fruit is picked and all the leaves have fallen. Shorten main rods to fit the available space, and cut back all sideshoots to one or two buds. Rub off loose bark from the rods to reduce hiding places for pests. Lightly fork over and manure the soil, and replace the top 5cm (2in) of compost in pots with a fresh supply. In late winter, untie the rods and lower them to below horizontal, to encourage the buds to break uniformly. Retie the rods when the buds are all in growth.

PLAN AHEAD
EARLY WINTER

Clean any spare cloches ready for the new season; clear, wash and insulate part of the greenhouse for early sowings. Order a load of manure, stack it neatly to decay or warm it up for a hotbed (see *page 53*). Alternatively, barrow heaps of manure onto bare beds when the ground is frozen. **Plan new crops and rotations, and resolve to keep a diary next season: jot down sowing reminders, weather records and performance of varieties.** Lift a few parsnips, leeks and other winter supplies when freezing weather is expected.

allotment story
EGGS FOR BREAKFAST

Not every allotment association will allow livestock, but on many allotments there are increasing signs of plot-holders keeping chickens and rabbits. For many people this is an essential part of the whole organic and self-sufficient lifestyle, and one that is relatively easy to do well. Half-a-dozen rehabilitated battery hens or traditional layers like Rhode Island Reds or Light Sussex, even a few busy bantams to clear weeds and pests, will soon settle down to give you fresh eggs with your fresh vegetables. Come the winter, though, hens like to snug down as much as gardeners – with the shorter days, all but the youngest hens produce very few eggs, and tend to rest until spring when laying starts again with renewed energy.

Terry has kept chickens since he was a boy, when he was first put in charge of his family's backyard coop, and when he had his allotment, keeping hens was one of the first things he wanted to do. Like any livestock, they are a responsibility. They need daily attention, not only to let them in and out of the coop, but also feeding, moving the coop, collecting the eggs and, above all, making sure they are safely tucked up at night: foxes really love chickens, so you must have a secure lock-up.

As a rule, Terry doesn't name his hens because there are so many of them. But when a fox ran amok recently and slaughtered his flock, other allotment-holders chipped in to pay for replacements and named them all. Now there is a new flock of birds on Terry's allotment with some very fancy names.

KEY JOBS
LATE WINTER

Contemplate early sowings under glass.

Finish digging heavy soils, and break down to a tilth areas needed for seed- and nursery beds. Start cultivating light ground.

Plant garlic and shallots now, rather than in autumn, in cold areas – start them in pots if the soil is wet or heavy.

Stand seed potatoes in a well-lit, frost-free place to chit for at least 6 weeks before planting.

Test new brassica beds for soil acidity, as well as light or organic soils which soon become acid after heavy winter rains.

Warm the ground for first sowings by covering a bed with cloches or plastic sheeting; protect prepared ground in the same way.

Finish winter pruning fruit, and feed with a mulch of compost or top-dressing of general fertilizer; revive overwintered vegetables in the same way.

RECYCLING GROWING BAGS The contents of last year's bags are useful for topping up greenhouse borders, covering seeds after sowing or adding to the compost heap, but you may be able to second-crop the bags first. Clear away any crop residues, including root networks, and stir up the contents with a hand fork, adding a light dressing of general fertilizer. Then use them for one of the following:

► to grow salad leaves and cut-and-come-again crops during early spring.
► for starting chrysanthemum stools and dahlia tubers into growth.
► to root and grow soft cuttings until ready for potting up.
► to grow an early crop of radishes, short carrots, lettuces, salad onions, baby beet.
► to provide extra root space under pots or another layer of bags for tomatoes and cucumbers.
► as a seedbed for early sowings to transplant to a cold frame.

EXTRA SPRING GREENS Spring cabbage is not the only source of fresh greens in late winter and spring. The tops of Brussels sprout plants can be as large as cabbages, and are harvested after the sprouts are finished or may be cut from F1 varieties just before picking begins, to help fatten the sprouts. Unused turnips surviving after the winter will produce useful tops, or you can deliberately sow a leafy variety such as 'Green Top Stone' for greens – bring plants on with cloches, or earth them up for sweeter, blanched leaves. Grow good king henry in a corner for the earliest spinach-like leaves, but remove its flowers otherwise self-set seedlings could be widespread and unwelcome.

MAKING YOUR OWN POTS Instead of cleaning and storing plastic pots each year, make your own biodegradable versions that will decompose in the soil after planting. The card tubes of toilet rolls are ideal for deeper rooted seedlings, like peas and beans. Pages from old telephone directories – folded in half, rolled round a piece of dowel and securely glued or taped – can be used for general sowing or

These pots made from the card tubes of toilet rolls will disintegrate in the soil when the broad bean seedlings are planted out.

pricking out under glass. Stand the containers on absorbent paper in seed trays, use a funnel to fill them with compost, and then treat like conventional pots. Make sure they are moist at planting time, and handle carefully.

CELERY TRENCHES Traditional celery is grown in a deep trench, which can also improve the quality of self-blanching varieties by shading the stems.

► Dig out a straight channel 45cm (18in) wide and 30cm (12in) deep, and fork compost or manure into the bottom.
► Replace some of the soil to leave the surface of the trench about 10–15cm (4–6in) below ground level.
► Tidy the left-over soil into a ridge on each side of the trench, and plant these up with early lettuces.
► Transplant celery in the trench after the frosts; leave self-blanching kinds to grow unearthed, but start covering trench varieties in late summer (see *page 198*).
► Use the trench site for climbing beans the following year.

GRAIN CROPS An allotment novelty perhaps, but a cereal or grain can serve as a break crop during rotation to rest the ground, and will supply masses of compost material as well as a useful seed harvest. Fill a whole bed with a crop, underplanted with clover for extra fertility, or arrange rows as a temporary windbreak or shelter belt. Seeds are available from specialist suppliers (see Resources, *pages 216–18*).

Wheat Grow your own straw! A productive crop, yielding about 450g/sq.m (1lb/sq.yd) of grain. Ancient emmer and einkorn wheats are heritage kinds. Sow in early spring; they may also be autumn-sown, which helps protect the soil over winter.

Maize Try North American parching corn for popping. Shorter and bushier than sweetcorn, it needs 3 months to reach maturity. Sow under glass to plant in late spring.

Teff One-metre (3ft-) high grasses from Ethiopia with nutritious seeds used to make a flat bread. Attractive plants for flower arranging. Sow in late spring.

Grain amaranth A prolific annual, related to love-lies-bleeding but over 2m (6ft) tall, with fine oily seeds for flour and bread. Drought-tolerant but tender – plant out after frost.

Quinoa South American grain annuals, with seeds like millet and young leaves to use like spinach. Plant out after frost.

Sunflowers Decorative as well as productive. Sow under glass to plant after frosts, and multi-crop as supports for climbing beans: use the dry stems for next year's bean poles. 'Tarahumara' is an old US variety with pure white seeds.

PLAN AHEAD
LATE WINTER
Assess structures and surroundings before you focus on crops: lay or repair paths, test that supports and ties are sound, clean water tanks and cans. Stock-check seeds and buy fresh compost; service your mower or rotavator. **Keep a bag of compost and a can filled with water in the greenhouse to warm up to indoor temperatures for early sowing and potting.** Restrain yourself: warm, sunny days in late winter are seductive, but not a cue to launch into spring work.

By late winter, scarecrows will be losing their looks! Now is the time to mend their clothes and embark on any other repairs in preparation for spring sowing.

winter

215

resources

SEED SUPPLIERS

Abundant Life Seed Foundation
PO Box 157, Saginaw, OR 97472, USA
Web: www.abundantlifeseeds.com
US organic source of heritage and
gourmet varieties

Anioleka Vegetable Seeds
Web: www.vegetableseed.net
**Roguelands Heirloom Vegetable
Seeds Co**
Web: www.seedfest.co.uk
1475 SunGlo Drive, Grants Pass,
OR 97527, USA
Hundreds of classic UK and US varieties
lost from mainstream catalogues

J W Boyce
Bush Pasture, Fordham, Ely,
Cambs CB7 5JU
Tel: 01638 721158
Long-established growers' list, with
seeds in a range of quantities

D T Brown and Co
Bury Road, Kentford,
Newmarket, Suffolk CB8 7PR
Tel: 0845 166 2275
Web: www.dtbrownseeds.co.uk
Another plot-holders' favourite,
blending new and heritage varieties

Chiltern Seeds
Bortree Stile, Ulverston,
Cumbria LA12 7PB
Tel: 01229 581137
Web: www.chilternseeds.co.uk
Botanical paradise, offering
thousands of species including
unexpected edibles

Dobies Seeds
Long Road, Paignton, Devon TQ4 7SX
Tel: 0870 112 3625
Web: www.dobies.co.uk
Mainstream seed supplier

Mr Fothergill's Seeds Ltd
Gazeley Road, Kentford,
Newmarket, Suffolk CB8 7QB
Tel: 01638 751161
Web: www.fothergills.co.uk
Nicely balanced list, plus large tempting
potato, tomato and squash selections

**Garden Organic (Henry Doubleday
Research Association)**
Ryton Organic Gardens,
Coventry, Warwickshire CV8 3LG
Tel: 024 7630 3517
Web: www.hdra.org.uk
Heritage seedbank for members;
see also under Organizations

S E Marshalls & Co
Alconbury Hill, Huntingdon,
Cambs PE28 4HY
Tel: 01480 443390
Web: www.marshalls-seeds.co.uk
Classic fruit and vegetable catalogue,
with special rates for allotment societies.
Also do fruit bushes and plug plants

The Organic Gardening Catalogue
Riverdene Business Park, Molesey Road,
Hersham, Surrey KT12 4RG
Tel: 0845 130 1304
Web: www.organiccatalog.com
Comprehensive organic list, plus
green manures and approved
pest treatments

Seeds of Italy
Phoenix Industrial Estate,
Rosslyn Crescent, Harrow,
Middx HA1 2SP
Tel: 020 8427 5020
Web: www.seedsofitaly.co.uk
Mouth-watering revelation
of Mediterranean and Slow Food
ingredients

Suffolk Herbs
Monks Farm, Kelvedon,
Colchester, Essex CO5 9PG
Tel: 01376 572456
Web: www.suffolkherbs.com
The widest range of vegetable,
herb and wildflower seeds in a
single list

Suttons Seeds
Woodview Road, Paignton,
Devon TQ4 7NG
Tel: 0800 783 8074
Web: www.suttons.co.uk
Mainstream seed supplier

Tamar Organics
Woodlands Estate, Gulworthy,
Tavistock, Devon PL19 8JE
Tel: 01822 834 887
Web: www.netgardeners.co.uk/
g_centres/devon.html
Seed and garden supplies

Terre de Semences
Ripple Farm, Crundale,
Canterbury, Kent CT4 7EB
Tel: 0966 448379
Web: www.terredesemences.com
Supplier of organic seeds

Thompson & Morgan Ltd
Poplar Lane, Ipswich, Suffolk IP8 3BU
Tel: 01473 688821
Web: www.thompson-morgan.com
Adventurous collection, with many
new, unusual or exclusive varieties of
seeds and plug plants

Unwins Seeds
Freepost ANG 1015, Wisbech,
Cambs PE13 2BR
Tel: 01945 588522
Web: www.unwins-seeds.co.uk
Mainstream seed supplier

Vida Verde Seed Collection
14 Southdown Avenue, Lewes,
East Sussex BN7 1EL
Tel: 01239 821107
Web: www.vidaverde.co.uk
Heirloom and rare vegetable seeds

PLANT SUPPLIERS
British Field Products Ltd
Corkway Drove, Hockwold, Thetford,
Norfolk IP26 4JR
Tel: 01842 828266
Web: www.enviromat.co.uk
Suppliers of Enviromat Sedum Matting
for landscaping and simple green roofs

The Fruit & Vegetable Company
Staion Road, Terrington St. Clement,
King's Lynn, Norfolk PE34 4BR
Tel: 0870 9505911
Tree and soft fruit, potatoes, onions,
seeds and plants

Jekka's Herb Farm
Rose Cottage, Shellards Lane,
Alveston, Bristol BS35 3SY
Tel: 01454 418878
Web: www.jekkasherbfarm.com
Wide and expanding range of organic
herb plants and seeds

Keepers Nursery
Gallants Court, East Farleigh,
Maidstone, Kent ME15 0LE
Tel: 01622 726465
Web: www.fruittree.co.uk
Far-ranging tree fruit list; will propagate
other varieties to order

Ken Muir Ltd
Rectory Rd, Weeley Heath,
Clacton-on-Sea,
Essex CO16 9BJ
Tel: 0870 74 79 111
Web: www.kenmuir.co.uk
Reliable source of soft fruit (plus
some others) and sound cultural
information

Reads Nursery
Hales Hall, Loddon, Norfolk
NR14 6QW
Tel: 01508 548395
Web: www.readsnursery.co.uk
Large, discriminating collection
of grape, peach, citrus varieties,
amongst others

ORGANIZATIONS
Agroforestry Research Trust
46 Hunters Moon, Dartington,
Totnes, Devon TQ9 6JT
Tel: 01803 840776
Web: www.agroforestry.co.uk
Masses of absorbing information
on edible and useful trees, plus
forest gardening

Allotments Regeneration Initiative
The Greenhouse, Hereford Street,
Bedminster, Bristol BS3 4NA
Tel: 0117 9631 551
Web: www.farmgarden.org.uk
Lively campaign partnership, with
a range of events and essential
newsletters

**Federation of City Farms and
Community Gardens**
The Green House, Hereford Street,
Bedminster, Bristol BS3 4NA
Tel: 0117 923 1800
Web: www.farmgarden.org.uk
Provides information and advice on
a wide range of community projects
throughout the UK

The Garden Gate
Northdown Park Road,
Margate, Kent CT9 3IP
Tel: 01843 570992
Email: thegardengate@thanetmind.
fsnet.co.uk
Organic community garden run by
the charity Thanet Mind, established
to help adults experiencing mental
health issues

**Garden Organic (Henry Doubleday
Research Association)**
Ryton Organic Gardens, Coventry,
Warwickshire CV8 3LG
Tel: 024 7630 3517
Web: www.hdra.org.uk
The chief UK society for organic
gardeners; *see also* under Seed suppliers

**National Society of Allotment &
Leisure Gardeners**
O'Dell House, Hunters Road, Corby,
Northants NN17 5JE
Tel: 01536 266576
Web: www.nsalg.org.uk
Umbrella organization; good source of
info about finding and starting a plot

National Vegetable Society
5 Whitelow Road, Heaton Moor,
Stockport SK4 4BY
Tel: 0161 442 7190
Web: www.nvsuk.org.uk
Advice and information on growing
and showing produce

Natural Growth Project
Medical Foundation, 111 Iseldon Road,
London N7 7JW
(co-ordinator: Mary Raphaely)
Tel: 020 7697 7777
Web: www.torturecare.org.uk
London-based allotment project
helping victims of torture and
persecution

Number One Allotment Project
Chiswick Horticultural Society in
partnership with the London Borough
of Hounslow, Learning Disability
Service
Tel: 0845 4562 972
Scheme for people with learning
disabilities to develop their
horticultural skills and interact
with other gardeners

Royal Horticultural Society
80 Vincent Square, London
SW1P 2PE
Tel: 020 7834 4333
Web: www.rhs.org.uk
Huge databases to explore online,
superb journal and numerous
useful events

Soil Association
Bristol House, 40–56 Victoria Street,
Bristol BS1 6BY
Tel: 0117 314 5000
Web: www.soilassociation.org.uk
Organization at the heart of the
campaign for organic food and farming

Thrive
The Geoffrey Udall Centre, Beech Hill,
Reading, Berks RG7 2AT
Tel: 0118 988 5688
Web: www.thrive.org.uk
Unrivalled advice, support and tuition
for disabled and disadvantaged
gardeners

REFERENCE LIBRARY
The Allotment
DVD set produced by Wild Fire
Productions, based on TV series,
from Permanent Publications
Tel: 01730 823311
Email: info@permaculture.co.uk

**The Allotment Handbook: A Guide to
Protecting and Promoting your Site**
Sophie Andrews; Eco-Logic Books, 2001

**The Allotment: Its Landscape
and Culture**
David Crouch & Colin Ward; Five
Leaves, 2003

Collins Kitchen Garden
Andi Clevely; Collins, 1999

**Collins Practical Gardener:
Kitchen Garden**
Lucy Peel; Collins, 2003

**The Complete Book of Vegetables,
Herbs and Fruit**
Matthew Biggs, Jekka McVicar and Bob
Flowerdew; Kyle Cathie, 2004

Growing Fruit
Harry Baker; RHS/Mitchell Beazley, 1999

The Integrated Garden
Andi Clevely; Barrie & Jenkins, 1988
(in the USA entitled **The Total Garden**;
Sterling, 1989)

Jekka McVicar New Book of Herbs
Dorling Kindersley, 2004

Jekka's Complete Herb Book
Jekka McVicar; Kyle Cathie, 1997

**Jekka's Culinary Herbs: A Guide to
Growing Herbs for the Kitchen**
Jekka McVicar; Kyle Cathie, 1995

The Kitchen Garden
Andi Clevely; RHS/Conran Octopus,
1995

The Kitchen Garden Month-by-Month
Andi Clevely; David & Charles, 1996

Plants for a Future
Ken Fern; Permanent Publications, 1997

**Seeds: The Ultimate Guide to
Growing Successfully from Seed**
Jekka McVicar; Kyle Cathie, 2001

**Seed to Seed: Seed-saving Techniques
for the Vegetable Gardener**
Suzanne Ashworth; Seed Saver
Publications/Chelsea Green, 1991

The Vegetable Garden Displayed
Joy Larkcom; RHS, 1992

WEBSITES TO EXPLORE
Allotment forestry
www.allotmentforestry.com

**Allotment & Vegetable Gardening
Ring**
q.webring.com/hub?ring=allotmentring

**American Community Garden
Association**
www.communitygarden.org

BBC
www.bbc.co.uk/gardening/advice/
weather

Biodynamic Agricultural Association
www.biodynamic.org.uk

City Farmer
www.cityfarmer.org

Gardenweb
www.uk.gardenweb.com

Permaculture Association
www.permaculture.org.uk

QED virtual potting shed
www.btinternet.com/~richard.
wiltshire/potshed1.htm

index

acknowledgments

AUTHOR'S: It is a huge pleasure for me to acknowledge the contributions of many people to this book. Gardeners absorb skills and experience from a multitude of sources, and any aptitude I have for growing good food is due to the influence of countless tutors, foremen, colleagues and plot-holders, and to my family, whose usually constructive opinions helped raise standards. Love and thanks go to my wife Meg, willing and resourceful gardener's mate on more veg plots than we can recall and brilliant cook of all they produced. And very special thanks, mixed equally with wonder and admiration, go to the incomparable design and editorial team at Airedale Publishing.

FOR AIREDALE PUBLISHING: A big thank you to Andi, who not only provided marvellous copy but also composed the wittiest emails ever! To Mike Newton, the inspiration for this book, for letting us use his superlative pictures of people on his local allotment. To the in-house team: Amanda, Helen, Elly, Max, Tony, Lucy, Mandy, Olivia, David and Sarah. To Hilary for persuading us to go ahead. To Geoff at Chiswick Horticultural Society for all his help all of the time. To Linda Tubby for writing the recipes and Norma MacMillan for checking them. To Rhiann at Windsor Allotments for giving us so much of her time and introducing us to some wonderful allotmenteers. To Alastair for his peas and support! To Gil and Patsy and everyone at Alexandra Palace Allotments for letting us photograph there. To Thanet Mind and the Natural Growth Project for permission to show how horticulture can heal. To Terry for his chickens and Mel for his bees. To Niels Jensen for his Danish allotment pictures.

   We would also like to thank the following companies for providing seeds, plants and tools: Colin Hambridge at Mr Fothergills for seeds and plants; Rowena Hall at Thompson & Morgan for seeds; Jeff Taylor at Marshalls/Unwins for seeds and plants; The Fruit and Vegetable Company for the vegetable starter plants and fruit bushes; Stuart Elsom at Bulldog Tools for the lovely forks, spades and rakes; Gemma at Bryant Nurseries, Hemel Hempstead, for starter plants; Angela Lambert at British Field Products for the sedum roof mat.